BRITISH PARLIAMENTARY LISTS,

1660 - 1800

BRITISH PARLIAMENTARY LISTS, 1660 - 1800

A REGISTER

EDITED BY G.M. DITCHFIELD,
DAVID HAYTON AND CLYVE JONES

THE HAMBLEDON PRESS

LONDON   AND   RIO GRANDE

Published by The Hambledon Press 1995

102 Gloucester Avenue, London NW1 8HX (U.K.)
P.O. Box 162, Rio Grande, Ohio 45674 (U.S.A.)

ISBN 1 85285 131 7

A description of this book is available from
the British Library and from the Library of Congress

Typeset by The Midlands Book Typesetting Company
Printed on acid-free paper and bound in
Great Britain by Cambridge University Press.

Contents

Figures   vii

Acknowledgments   ix

Contributors   xi

Abbreviations   xiii

Explanatory Note   xvii

General Introduction   xix
   David Hayton and Clyve Jones

I. THE HOUSE OF LORDS, 1660–1800

Introduction   3
   Clyve Jones, G.M. Ditchfield and Richard Davis

List of Lists   29

Appendix A: Lost Lists   91

Appendix B: Undated and Unidentified Lists   92

Appendix C: Proxy Lists   93

II. THE HOUSE OF COMMONS, 1660–1761

Introduction   99
   David Hayton and Eveline Cruickshanks

List of Lists   109

III. THE PARLIAMENT OF SCOTLAND, 1660–1707

Introduction   139
    Patrick Riley

List of Lists   144

Figures

Fig. 1   The Parliamentary Buildings in the Eighteenth Century   7

Fig. 2   The Interior of the House of Lords in the
         Eighteenth Century   11

Fig. 3   St Stephen's Chapel (House of Commons) in the
         Eighteenth Century   103

Fig. 4   The Parliament of Scotland, 1641–1707   143

Acknowledgements

As with *A Register of Parliamentary Lists, 1660–1761*, this register is a collaborative work, not only of the editors and named contributors, but also of many scholars who have brought lists and other information to the notice of those responsible for the present work. We wish to thank those who have given of their time and expert knowledge: James Alsop, Peter Barber, Robert Bergh, Jeremy Black, J.C.D. Clark, J.M. Collinge, Andrew Federer, Elizabeth Read Foster, J.P. Ferris, Sarah Gray, Stephen Green, Edward Gregg, Andrew Hanham, Frances Harris, the late Basil Henning, D.R. Hirschberg, the late Geoffrey Holmes, J.R. Jones, Paul Kelly, Newton Key, Robert Latham, A.P.W. Malcomson, Aubrey Newman, Sir John Sainty, David Shaw, J.M. Simpson, the late Dame Lucy Sutherland, Stephen Taylor, P.D.G. Thomas, H.C. Tomlinson, Patrick Woodland, and Christopher Wright.

We thank also, for their help, the owners of manuscripts whose private collections have been cited and the staffs of the various public institutions, libraries, and record offices in which research has been carried out, in particular the staffs of the British Library, the History of Parliament Trust, the Institute of Historical Research, the Henry E. Huntington Library, the Leicestershire Record Office, the National Maritime Museum, the National Register of Archives (Scotland), and the Public Record Office. Dr G.M. Ditchfield would like to thank the Scouloudi Foundation which financed some of the research for this project, and the Trustees of the National Maritime Museum for allowing him to use and quote from the papers of the 4th Earl of Sandwich.

Contributors

Eveline Cruickshanks	The Institute of Historical Research, University of London
Richard W. Davis	Washington University, St Louis
G.M. Ditchfield	University of Kent at Canterbury
Stephen Farrell	The History of Parliament Trust
David Hayton	The Queen's University of Belfast
Clyve Jones	The Institute of Historical Research, University of London
Michael W. McCahill	Brooks School, North Andover, Massachusetts
Patrick Riley	Late of the University of Manchester

Abbreviations

Please note the place of publication is London unless otherwise stated.

Almon, *Parl. Reg.*	J. Almon, *The Parliamentary Register; or History of the Proceedings and Debates of the House of Commons [and Lords] during the . . . Fourteenth Parliament of Great Britain* (17 vols., 1775–80)
Annual Reg.	*The Annual Register, or a View of the History, Politics and Literature for the Year*
A.P.S.	*Acts of the Parliament of Scotland*
Aspinall, *Later Correspondence*	*The Later Correspondence of George III*, ed. A. Aspinall (5 vols., Cambridge, 1966–70)
B.I.H.R.	*Bulletin of the Institute of Historical Research*
B.L.	British Library, London
Bodl. Lib.	Bodleian Library, Oxford
Burton *et al.*, 'Political Parties'	I.F. Burton, P.W.J. Riley and E. Rowlands, 'Political Parties in the Reigns of William III and Anne: The Evidence of Divisions Lists', *B.I.H.R.*, special supplement VII (1968)
Chandler	R. Chandler, *The History and Proceedings of the House of Commons from the Restoration to the Present Time* (14 vols., 1742–4)
C.J.	*Commons' Journals*
C.K.S.	Centre for Kentish Studies (formerly Kent Archives Office)
Cobbett, *Parl. Hist.*	W. Cobbett, *The Parliamentary History of England from the Norman Conquest . . . to the Year 1803* (36 vols., 1806–20)

Cruickshanks *et al.*, 'Ten New Lists'	E. Cruickshanks, D. Hayton and C. Jones, 'Divisions in the House of Lords on the Transfer of the Crown and Other Issues, 1689–94: Ten New Lists', *B.I.H.R.*, LIII (1980)
C.W.H.	Committee of the whole House
Danby	A. Browning, *Thomas Osborne, Earl of Danby and Duke of Leeds, 1632–1712* (3 vols., Glasgow, 1944–51)
Debrett, *History, Debates and Proceedings*	J. Debrett, *History, Debates and Proceedings of Both Houses of Parliament, 1743–1774* (7 vols., 1792)
Debrett, *Parl. Reg.*	J. Debrett, *The Parliamentary Register: or the History of the Proceedings and Debates of the House of Commons [and Lords], 1780–96* (45 vols., 1781–96)
E.H.R.	*English Historical Review*
Farrell, thesis	S.M. Farrell, 'Divisions, Debates and "Dis-Ease": The Rockingham Whig Party and the House of Lords, 1760–1785' (University of Cambridge Ph.D thesis, 1993)
Fortescue, *Correspondence*	*The Correspondence of King George III from 1760 to December 1783*, ed. Sir J. Fortescue (6 vols., 1927–8)
Hanham, thesis	A. Hanham, 'Whig Opposition to Sir Robert Walpole in the House of Commons, 1727–34' (University of Leicester Ph.D. thesis, 1993)
Hardy, thesis	A. Hardy, 'The Duke of Newcastle and his Friends in Opposition, 1762–1765' (University of Manchester M.A. thesis, 1956)
Hist. Jnl.	*Historical Journal*
H.L.R.O.	House of Lords Record Office, London
H.M.C.	Historical Manuscripts Commision
Holmes, *British Politics*	G. Holmes, *British Politics in the Age of Anne* (1967; 2nd edn., 1987)
Horwitz, *Parliament*	H. Horwitz, *Parliament, Policy and Politics in the Reign of William III* (Manchester, 1977)
J.R.U.L.M.	John Rylands University Library of Manchester

L.J.	*Lords' Journals*
Lowe, 'Archbishop Secker'	W.C. Lowe, 'Archbishop Secker, the Bench of Bishops and the Repeal of the Stamp Act', *Historical Magazine of the Protestant Episcopal Church*, XLIV (1977)
Lowe, 'Bishops and Representative Peers'	W.C. Lowe, 'Bishops and Scottish Representative Peers in the House of Lords, 1760–1775', *Journal of British Studies*, XVIII (1978)
Lowe, thesis	W.C. Lowe, 'Politics in the House of Lords, 1760–1775' (Emory University Ph.D., 1975)
Namier, *Age of American Revolution*	Sir L. Namier, *England in the Age of the American Revolution* (2nd edn., 1961)
New Annual Reg.	*The New Annual Register, or General Repository of History, Politics and Literature for the Year*
Nicolson's London Diaries	*The London Diaries of William Nicolson, Bishop of Carlisle, 1702–1718*, eds. C. Jones and G. Holmes (Oxford, 1985)
N.M.M.	National Maritime Museum
N.Y.R.O.	North Yorkshire Record Office, Northallerton
O'Gorman, *Rise of Party*	F. O'Gorman, *The Rise of Party in England: The Rockingham Whigs, 1760–82* (1975)
Pillar of Constitution	*A Pillar of the Constitution: The House of Lords in British Politics, 1640–1784*, ed. C. Jones (1989)
Proceedings North America	*Proceedings and Debates of the British Parliaments Respecting North America, 1754–1783*, eds. R.C. Simmons and P.D.G. Thomas (6 vols. to date, Millwood, New York, 1982–6)
P.R.O.	Public Record Office, London
Ransome, 'Division-Lists'	M. Ransome, 'Division-Lists of the House of Commons, 1715–1760', *B.I.H.R.*, XIX (1942–3)
R.O.	Record Office
Sainty and Dewar	*Divisions in the House of Lords: An Analytical List, 1685–1857*, comp. J.C. Sainty and D. Dewar (House of Lords Record Office Occasional Publication, II, 1976)

Sedgwick	R. Sedgwick, *The House of Commons, 1715–1754* (2 vols, 1970)
The Senator	*The Senator, or Clarendon's Parliamentary Chronicle. Containing a Weekly Register, Recording . . . the Proceedings and Debates of the Houses of Lords and Commons*, ser. 1, 1790–1800 (27 vols., 1791–1800)
Snyder, 'Occasional Conformity'	H.L. Snyder, 'The Defeat of the Occasional Conformity Bill and the Tack: A Study in the Techniques of Parliamentary Management in the Reign of Anne', *B.I.H.R.*, XLI (1968)
s.o.	*Standing orders*
S.P.	Public Record Office, State Papers (Domestic)
Speck, thesis	W.A. Speck, 'The House of Commons, 1702–14: A Study in Political Organisation' (University of Oxford D.Phil. thesis, 1965)
Stockdale, *Debates and Proceedings*	J. Stockdale, *The Debates and Proceedings of the House of Commons [and Lords] during the Sixteenth Parliament of Great Britain* (19 vols., 1785–90)
Thomas, *Stamp Act Crisis*	P.D.G. Thomas, *British Politics and the Stamp Act Crisis: The First Phase of the American Revolution, 1763–1767* (Oxford, 1975)
Turner, thesis	D.J. Turner, 'George III and the Whig Opposition (1760–1784): A Study of the Organization, Principles, Policy and Conduct of the Rockingham-Portland Whigs' (University of Nottingham Ph.D thesis, 1953)
Walcott, 'Division-Lists'	R.R. Walcott, 'Division-Lists of the House of Commons, 1689–1715', *B.I.H.R.*, XIV (1936–7)
Wentworth Papers	*The Wentworth Papers, 1705–1739*, ed. J.J. Cartwright (1883)
Woodfall, *Debates*	W. Woodfall, *An Impartial Report of the Debates that Occur in Two Houses of Parliament, with some Account of the Respective Speakers, and Notes and Illustrations* (12 vols., 1794–6)
W.R.O.	Warwickshire Record Office, Warwick
W.W.M.	Sheffield City Library, Wentworth Woodhouse Muniments (Rockingham Papers)

Explanatory Note

An explanatory note on four collections in the British Library, and on the Eighteenth-Century Short Title Catalogue (E.S.T.C.)

1. The Blenheim Papers

All the Blenheim papers were originally at Blenheim Palace, Woodstock, Oxfordshire. The greater part, comprising most of the Marlborough and Sunderland papers, were transferred to the British Library in the 1970s. A catalogue of this collection was published in 1985 by the British Library. The papers now have Additional MS. numbers and these are given in the lists below, followed by the original Blenheim Palace number in brackets: e.g., B.L., Add. MS. 61496, ff. 188–9 (formerly Blenheim papers D.II.9, D.II.10). Those lists which remain with the papers left at Blenheim are described as Blenheim Palace papers together with their original reference. In 1992 the Royal Commission on Historical Manuscripts produced a report on the papers remaining at Blenheim Palace.

Five of the lists described in the 1979 edition of the *Register* as being part of the Blenheim papers transferred to the British Library cannot now be found. These are Lords list no. 65, and Commons lists 76, 79, 87 and 133. We now believe that these may never have been transferred to the British Library and are probably still at Blenheim Palace. If so, it is likely that they are to be found in the Treasury Box VIII, Bundle 23, which is described in the H.M.C. report as 'Lists indicating ministerial strength in the House of Lords and the House of Commons early 18th cent'. But Bundle 20 in this box contains 'papers relating to parliamentary proceedings 1711–21', while Box IX, Bundle 28 contains 'Papers relating to parliamentary proceedings 1710–46', and Box XIII, Bundle 46 contains 'Lists, mainly printed, of members of Parliament *c.* 1719–22'.

2. Portland Loan 29

This collection has now been incorporated into the Additional MS. sequence, but the volumes have not yet been foliated. Below we give the new Additional numbers, followed in brackets by the original Loan 29 reference to aid identification: e.g., B.L., Add. MS. 70331 (formerly Loan 29/10/4).

3. Spencer Papers from Althorp

This collection has temporary call numbers; eventually items will be given Additional MS. numbers (see Lords list no. 34).

4. Trumbull Papers

Formerly at the Berkshire Record Office, this collection was acquired by the B.L. in 1989. The collection will shortly be given Additional MS. numbers. The original references are given here: e.g., B.L., Trumbull Add. 136.

The E.S.T.C.

In the original *Register* and *Supplement*, before the *E.S.T.C.* was widely available, we usually gave one or two locations for the printed lists. Now that the *E.S.T.C.* is available on CD-Rom it is possible to search for other locations. However we have kept the original locations in this revised *Register* as they are still useful as a first option in finding the lists. It should be noted that the present CD-Rom is not a complete listing of all publications in the eighteenth century. The data base at the British Library is being continually updated. This should be consulted if the CD-Rom fails to produce a bibliographic record or a location. A revised edition of the CD-Rom will be issued in 1997.

General Introduction

David Hayton and Clyve Jones

This register has been designed as a revised and expanded version of *A Register of Parliamentary Lists, 1660–1761*, edited by David Hayton and Clyve Jones, and publised by the University of Leicester, History Department, in 1979.[1] There followed three years later a *Supplement*, which added to the numbers and made corrections to some of the lists in the register.[2] In the 15 years since publication of the original *Register* many more lists have been found: for the House of Lords the number of lists for the period 1660 to 1761 has risen from 144 to 212, but with the two deletions from the original *Register* (see pp. 9–10 of the *Supplement*) this is an actual increase of 70 lists; for the Commons in the same period the figures are 194 to 241. In 1991 the journal *Parliamentary History* published 'A Register of House of Lords Lists, 1761–1800', edited by G.M. Ditchfield and Michael W. McCahill[3], in which there appeared 231 lists. Even in the short time since this register's publication, 20 new lists have been found. Thus it was felt by the editors of this volume that the time had come for a revision and an amalgamation of the two registers. Opportunity for publication arose with the announcement by The Hambledon Press of the publication of Donald Ginter's six-volume edition of *Voting Record of the British House of Commons, 1761–1819*.[4] The present revised register forms an ideal bibliographical adjunct to that work, covering lists for the House of Commons from 1660 to the start of Ginter's volumes in 1761, and those of the House of Lords from 1660 to the Act of Union with Ireland in 1800. It was also decided to include in the present volume the lists for the Parliament of Scotland from 1678 to 1707, as a considerable number have been found since the original listing in 1979. The Parliament of Ireland, which was covered in the original register, has not been included in this

---

[1] *A Register of Parliamentary Lists, 1660–1761*, edited by D. Hayton and C. Jones (University of Leicester, History Department, Occasional Publication No. 1, 1979). The general editor of this series was Aubrey Newman.

[2] *A Register of Parliamentary Lists, 1660–1761: A Supplement*, edited D. Hayton and C. Jones (University of Leicester, History Department, Occasional Publication No. 3, 1982).

[3] G.M. Ditchfield and M. McCahill, 'A Register of House of Lords Lists, 1761–1800', *Parliamentary History*, X (1991), 194–220.

[4] D. Ginter, *Voting Records of the British House of Commons, 1761–1819* (6 vols., 1995).

revision, as the forthcoming history of the Irish Parliament is expected to include such a listing.

As in the original register, each section of this present volume – Lords, Commons and the Parliament of Scotland – is prefaced by an introduction discussing the lists, commenting on their utility, and explaining procedural matters and other technical problems. These introductions contain new material which has come to light since 1979. Plans of the various Parliaments have been supplied to clarify the procedural questions discussed.

As for the lists themselves, the entries in each listing have been arranged as in the original register, that is chronologically by Parliament, with each list dated and briefly described and further information given under the following headings: (a) the original manuscript or printed source; (b) the most accessible published version; and (c) where a modern commentary on the list can be found. New or revised interpretations and attributions, principally the work of the compilers, have been inserted without acknowledgment or explanation, but we have been careful not to over-indulge in speculation and not to mask conjecture.

Our definition of parliamentary lists has remained as strict as in the original register. Only included are those lists in which every person named was a Member of the Parliament at the time of the drawing up of the list. Lists of commoners or peers, some of whom were in Parliament and some not, have been omitted, as for example lists of electoral candidates or electoral interests, or lists of the Scots peerage as a whole after 1707 in connexion with the voting for the representative peers. Also excluded are lists which simply enumerate the members of a Parliament and contain no information about their politics; thus contemporary printed lists of the Parliaments, which were printed in considerable numbers and were popular with the public,[5] have not been recorded unless bearing some possibly useful contemporary markings or endorsements. The official group protests published in the *Journals* have been left out of the section on the British House of Lords, largely for reasons of space, but those appearing in the *Acts of the Parliament of Scotland* have been included in the section on the Scottish Parliament, since their number is smaller and more manageable.[6] Similarly for reasons of space, we have omitted lists of speakers in particular debates, of which there is a vast number in the parliamentary reports and political correspondence of the period. The

[5] In 1722 at the time of the general election it was reported that 'our Pamphlet Shops begin to be Crowded with Black Lists and other Curiositys, which will be plentifully Dispersed, the Country it seems being Eager to See them that they May Distinguish who and who is together': B.L., Add. MS. 47076 (Egmont newsletters), f. 336, 8 March 1722. By the 1760s (and earlier) such lists were regularly published in such periodicals as the *Royal Kalendar*.

[6] See below, pp. 147–50.

items remaining after this panning-out process consist mainly of four types of lists: division lists themselves; forecasts of divisions; canvassing lists and other aides-memoires of parliamentary managers; and analyses of entire Parliaments.[7] Even so, not all of these lists have been included. We have left out modern reconstructions, usually of division lists,[8] and also contemporary lists for which there is evidence but which appear not to have survived.[9]

Finally, it must be said that all the various lists of lists, as distinct from the sectional introductions, which are the work of separate hands, are in differing degrees co-operative enterprises in which the compilers have shared, though the collective responsibility for any errors extends no further than the editors.

[7] An important body of lists coming into none of these categories is the lists of the proxies registered by peers and bishops in the House of Lords. These are principally recorded in the surviving Proxy Books in the H.L.R.O. Because of their very broad chronological span, which makes it difficult to fit them into the main House of Lords listing, they have been catalogued separately (see below, Appendix C pp. 93–5).

[8] For example, the Lords' division list on the 'No preferment' vote on Dr Sacheverell of 21 March 1710, reconstructed by G. Holmes and printed in his *The Trial of Doctor Sacheverell* (1973), pp. 285–7.

[9] See, for example, the list on the 1712 Grants Bill sent to Sir William Trumbull (B.L., Trumbull Add. MS. 134, T. Bateman to Trumbull, 28 May 1712; see below, pp. 22–3), and the 1727 list on the disputed patent of Earl Graham sent to Mungo Graham (Scottish R.O., GD 220/5/858/4, 5 [Montrose papers], [Montrose to Mungo Graham], 20, 26 Jan. 1727; and GD 220/5/1054/5 [John to Mungo Graham], 24 Jan. 1727). We have, however, included three 'fugitive' or 'lost' division lists recorded in a modern calendar of some family papers but not now to be found (see below, Appendix A p. 91).

I

THE HOUSE OF LORDS, 1660–1800

Introduction

Clyve Jones, G.M. Ditchfield and Richard Davis

The House of Lords lists calendared below fall into four basic types: general analyses of the political complexion of the House, usually classifying the peers and bishops by group or party; more specific analyses, for particular purposes, often differentiating between those 'for' and those 'against' a certain measure or proposal, which were produced by or for parliamentary managers and were intended to assist in their work; forecasts of divisions, probably also constructed in many cases by or for the managers; and, of course, division lists themselves. The distinction between the different types was not always clear to contemporaries; sometimes a division list might be employed as the basis for a forecast or for some other kind of working management list, as in the Earl of Ailesbury's forecast for the Duke of Norfolk's Divorce Bill in 1693 (no. 48 below); or a forecast might be annotated subsequently as a means of recording a division, as happened with the forecast for the Pension Bill in 1731 (no. 144).

The type of list which has most frequently survived is the division list. About 40 per cent of the lists in the 1660 to 1761 section of the Lords' register are division lists and the figure rises to 53 per cent for the period 1761–1800. This is not surprising, as division lists were the most 'public' of the four main types of list, generated frequently by contentious issues of great public interest and therefore likely to have had both a wider circulation and a higher survival rate than, say, management lists, which were compiled for the private use of one individual or a small group. What is surprising, perhaps, is that of the 1,085 divisions recorded in the manuscript minutes of the House between 1685 (when the clerks began systematically to record divisions) and 1761, only 34 are known to have division lists associated with them, a mere three per cent. The comparable figure for the years 1761 to the Act of Union with Ireland on 1 Janaury 1801 is 33 lists (of which no fewer than 31 are minority lists only) from the 573 recorded divisions, only 5.76 per cent. These low figures might mean no more than that many further surviving division lists await discovery. However, many of the recorded divisions were on non-controversial issues which aroused little public interest and are therefore unlikely to have given rise to lists.[1] A comparison between the frequency of recorded divisions

---

[1] Private legal cases, which usually aroused no general public interest, occasionally produced a division list, see e.g. below list no. 129 (and C. Jones, 'Jacobites under the
continued

and of the known survival of division lists throughout this period shows a distinct correlation between the two. Both increased in numbers at times of heightened political tension, and reached peaks during political crises, in 1689–96, 1701–3, 1710, 1714, 1718–19, 1733–4, 1739–41, 1765–6, 1767–8, 1778–9 and 1782–3. Rockingham told Portland in February 1768 that the opposition should attack the Chatham-Grafton administration 'with frequent debates and as frequent *divisions*'.[2]

Management lists, on the other hand, probably with a lower survival rate, produced only for private consumption, and not necessarily more numerous during periods of intense political activity, do not seem to correspond in their numbers to the frequency of divisions. They do, however, survive in clusters, a reflection of the changing responsibilities and interests, as well as the fluctuating diligence, of their compilers. Among the parliamentary managers well represented by Lords' lists are Philip, Lord Wharton, a leading opponent of the Court under Charles II; the Earl of Danby, later Marquess of Carmarthen and Duke of Leeds, a minister of Charles II and William III; Robert Harley, 1st Earl of Oxford, who headed Queen Anne's ministry from 1710 to 1714; Charles, 3rd Earl of Sunderland, who had the responsibility of managing the House for George I;[3] and the Duke of Newcastle, 'leader' of the Lords for a time under George II and briefly at the start of George III's reign.[4] The numerous management lists found in Harley's papers testify to his interest and skill in the techniques of managing the upper House (nos. 88, 90, 92–96, 100–5, below). This skill did not desert him even when he was imprisoned in the Tower between 1715 and 1717, for in May 1717 he was able to forecast with a high degree of accuracy how the Lords would vote on the revived impeachment proceedings against him (nos. 116–7, below), this after being out of active politics for two years and imprisoned in the Tower.[5] The use to which management lists in general were put may be illustrated succinctly by the following quotation from a letter from Viscount Bolingbroke to Queen Anne in January 1714, before the meeting of the new Parliament:

continued

Beds: Bishop Francis Atterbury of Rochester, the Earl of Sunderland and the Case of the Westminster School Dormitory of 1721', *British Library Journal*, [forthcoming]); and list 130 (and F. Harris, 'Parliament and Blenheim Palace: The House of Lords' Appeal of 1721', *Parliamentary History*, VIII [1989], 43–62).

[2] Nottingham University Lib., Portland papers, PwF 9011, Rockingham to Portland, 15 Feb. 1768.

[3] J.C. Sainty, 'The Origin of the Leadership of the House of Lords', *B.I.H.R.*, XLVII (1974), 67.

[4] *Ibid.*, 68–9.

[5] C. Jones, 'The Impeachment of the Earl of Oxford and the Whig Schism of 1717: Four New Lists', *B.I.H.R.*, LV (1982), 66–87.

I was yesterday with my lord chancellor [Harcourt], and my lord treasurer [Oxford]. We went exactly over the list of lords, and, I believe, I may venture to say, that, notwithstanding the opposition of those who are cloathed with the markes of your Majesty's favour, we shall be able to form a very considerable majority.[6]

From the 1770s, however, management lists compiled for private use (and derived almost always from manuscript sources) form a much smaller proportion of the total of surviving Lords lists. This is partly explained by the absence of anything to compare with the Newcastle papers after the death of the first duke in November 1768. From *c.* 1770, ministerial control of the House of Lords became somewhat easier and more predictable than had been the case in the 1760s and earlier; North and the Younger Pitt experienced far fewer difficulties with the House of Lords than did the brief ministries of Rockingham (1765–66) and Chatham (1766–68). It is true that ministerial management lists survive from the 1770s, with such leaders of the Lords under North's ministry as the 4th Earl of Rochford (nos. 306–7, 310 and 320, below) and Viscount Stormont (nos. 339, 342 and 344) quite well represented among the lists in this register. But although there was a short-lived crisis in 1782–3 and a flurry over the Regency in 1788–9, opposition in the Lords had become so attenuated by the 1790s that it seems that ministerial organization apparently no longer required the detailed surveys and lists of peers and bishops which had been necessary when the balance of forces was much closer. 'The minority gets less and less', proclaimed *The Times* in May 1791, while the Earl of Kinnoull, explaining to Portland why he would give priority to his Scottish estates at the start of the 1795 session wrote

Not having heard [from] Your Grace I did not think my Attendance in Parliament particularly wanted and understanding Ministers would meet with the same substantial support at the Meeting of Parliament as they had at the Close of the last Session, I thought the Absence of an Individual or two of no matter.[7]

The minority vote of 21 for a motion on the state of Ireland on 21 March 1797 was so unusually high that the *Oracle* felt it necessary to assure its readers that it was a special case, 'and not caused by a junction of party or any coalition of general sentiment'.[8] There were occasions when peers with particular campaigns to pursue, such as the 3rd Earl Stanhope over electoral reform compiled management-style lists (no. 375, below), but

---

[6] *Letters and Correspondence . . . of . . . Lord Viscount Bolingbroke . . .*, ed. G Parke (4 vols., 1798), IV, 437. This list appears not to have survived.

[7] *The Times*, 14 May 1791; Nottingham Univ. Lib., Portland papers, PwF 4958, Kinnoull to Portland, 1 Nov. 1795.

[8] *The Oracle*, 25 Mar. 1797.

these had nothing to do with the maintenance of ministerial control in the upper chamber.

Voting in the Lords

The House of Lords began in 1857 to record officially the names of lords who voted in divisions. All division lists before that date are by this definition unofficial, although they might have been drawn up by members of the House or by its officials, such as the clerks. The official published record of proceedings in the House, the *Journals*, do not usually register the fact that a division had occurred.[9] The only notes of divisions kept by the clerks in the manuscript minutes were of the numbers (but not the names) on each side of the question,[10] the number of proxy votes cast on each side, and the names of the tellers, and even this information was not systematically recorded until 1685.[11] The first known division list for the Lords dates from 24 April 1640. It names only one side, those voting in opposition to the King.[12] An earlier printed list of the entire Parliament in 1626, on which Archbishop Laud made some kind of analysis into groups, may be the earliest surviving forecast or management list.[13]

For most of the period covered by this *Register* there were three methods of voting in the Lords. There was the formal procedure, first noted in the sixteenth century, of voting by 'individual voice', whereby each peer stood in turn, in reverse order of precedence, and declared Content or Not Content for himself and his proxies. This cumbersome method continued to be used for certain formal votes until the twentieth century.[14] Perhaps the most famous instance of it being used in our period was at the impeachment of Dr Sacheverell in 1710.[15] The breakdown of the seating

[9] Except in the Convention Parliament, 1689–90: see Sainty and Dewar, p. 3, n.6. Much of the following description of procedure is based on this work. Divisions are also sometimes noted in *L.J.* for 1661 and 1666–7.

[10] Two exceptions are the votes to acquit Lord Somers, 17 June 1701 (no. 61, below), and Lord Orford, 23 June 1701 (no. 62).

[11] Fifty-six divisions have been found between 1660 and 1685: Sainty and Dewar, p. 4; R.W. Davis, 'Recorded Divisions in the House of Lords, 1661–1680', *Parliamentary History*, I (1982), 167–71; A. Swatland, 'Further Recorded Divisions in the House of Lords, 1660–1681', *Parliamentary History*, III (1984), 179–82.

[12] P.R.O., S.P. 16/451/93. We are grateful to Elizabeth Read Foster for this reference.

[13] P.R.O., S.P. 16/20/36, ff. 109–10. See E.S. Cope, 'Groups in the House of Lords, May 1626', *Parliamentary History*, XII (1993), 164–70; C. Russell, *Parliaments and English Politics, 1621–1629* (Oxford, 1979), p. 311 note 3.

[14] It was used in the trial of peers until 1935. For a discussion of voting practices in the eighteenth century see A.J. Rees, 'The Practice and Procedure of the House of Lords, 1714–1784' (Wales [Aberystwyth] Ph.D., 1987), pp. 426–59.

[15] For a description see G. Holmes, *The Trial of Doctor Sacheverell* (1973), pp. 223–4. This method was also used at the end of the impeachment of Warren Hastings on 23 Apr. 1795.

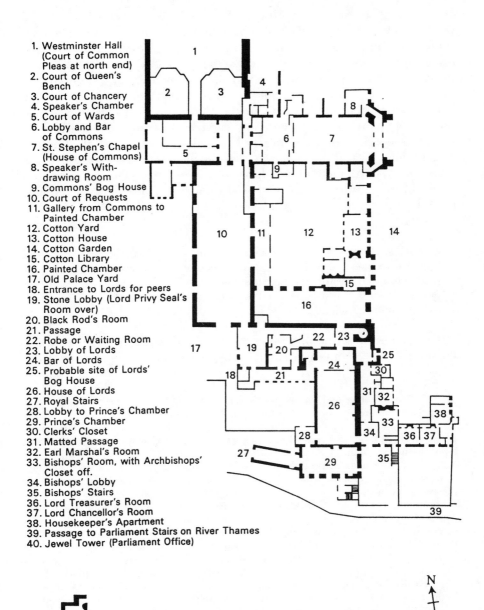

1. Westminster Hall (Court of Common Pleas at north end)
2. Court of Queen's Bench
3. Court of Chancery
4. Speaker's Chamber
5. Court of Wards
6. Lobby and Bar of Commons
7. St. Stephen's Chapel (House of Commons)
8. Speaker's Withdrawing Room
9. Commons' Bog House
10. Court of Requests
11. Gallery from Commons to Painted Chamber
12. Cotton Yard
13. Cotton House
14. Cotton Garden
15. Cotton Library
16. Painted Chamber
17. Old Palace Yard
18. Entrance to Lords for peers
19. Stone Lobby (Lord Privy Seal's Room over)
20. Black Rod's Room
21. Passage
22. Robe or Waiting Room
23. Lobby of Lords
24. Bar of Lords
25. Probable site of Lords' Bog House
26. House of Lords
27. Royal Stairs
28. Lobby to Prince's Chamber
29. Prince's Chamber
30. Clerks' Closet
31. Matted Passage
32. Earl Marshal's Room
33. Bishops' Room, with Archbishops' Closet off.
34. Bishops' Lobby
35. Bishops' Stairs
36. Lord Treasurer's Room
37. Lord Chancellor's Room
38. Housekeeper's Apartment
39. Passage to Parliament Stairs on River Thames
40. Jewel Tower (Parliament Office)

N

Fig. 1. The Parliament Buildings in the Eighteenth Century

Source: Plan of the Palace of Westminster by William Benson, c. 1719, from a copy dated 1793 (Sir John Soane Museum: 35.5.25).

arrangements in the House stipulated by the Act of 1539, whereby each peer was allocated a special place, a provision which increased membership rendered impracticable in a small chamber,[16] led gradually to the method of individual voice being replaced by that of 'collective voice', whereby the House shouted 'Aye' or 'No' and the volume of sound on each side (judged by the Lord Chancellor or Speaker) determined the question. This was probably imported from the Commons.[17] It continued to be used throughout the seventeenth and eighteenth centuries, and it is clear, from a comparison of the number of recorded divisions with the number of questions decided, that it was the one most commonly used in the House.[18] A third method developed, however, to determine questions when the collective voice did not produce a clear-cut majority acceptable to both sides, as happened, for example, in a Scottish legal case in 1733 when Ilay

> moved for Reversing. The question was put when all Cry'd reverse Except L[or]d Marchmont who Insisting for a Division the whole Lords got to their feet and moved towards the Bar, the Duke of Argyle at their head, Except his grace of Montrose who ... moved towards to [sic] the throne as not intending to vote on either side ... [19]

The earliest description of this third method dates from 1610, when the Lords were counted in two groups, the Contents standing and the

[16] C. Jones, 'Seating Problems in the House of Lords in the Early Eighteenth Century: The Evidence of the Manuscript Minutes', *B.I.H.R.*, LI (1978), 132–9.

[17] For the Lord Chancellor and the collective voice see Rees, 'Practice and Procedure', p. 428. The collective voice method was used less often in the Commons than in the Lords, especially in the turbulent Parliaments of William III and Anne: see an account of the debate in the Commons in December 1697 on the standing army reports when the motion was carried by a 'great cry', which another observer interpreted as a difference between the two sides in the ratio of three to one (Bodl. Lib., MS. Carte 130, f. 385, R. Price to the Duke of Beaufort, 11 Dec. 1697; *Calendar of State Papers Domestic*, 1697, p. 506). An example of its use in the Lords when there was no question of which side won is described in 1713: 'On Tuesday when the bill for Commissioners of accounts came before them [the Lords] 3 or 4 Tory Lords, Lord North and Grey, Lord Carteret and D[uke] of Bucks [Buckingham] cryed no at the passing of it, but that was all' (B.L., Trumbull Add. MS. 136, R. Bridges to Sir W. Trumbull, 8 May 1713, printed in C. Jones, '"Party Rage and Faction" - The View from Fulham, Scotland Yard and the Temple: Parliament in the Letters of Thomas Bateman and John and Ralph Bridges to Sir William Trumbull, 1710–1714', *British Library Journal*, XIX [1993], 166).

[18] Even a contentious issue might not lead to a vote: 'There was also yesterday a Great Question Debated in the House of Lords and Resolved at last without a Division tho' a strong party had been made in it' (*The Correspondence of John Locke*, ed. E.S. de Beer [8 vols., 1976–89], VI, 755, J. Freke and E. Clarke (?) to Locke, 7 Dec. 1699).

[19] National Library of Scotland, MS. 16553 (Fletcher of Saltoun papers), f. 213, J. Johnston to Lord Milton, 29 May 1733. See also *ibid.*, 16571, ff. 40–1, Provost Lindesay to Milton, 19 Mar. 1736/7, where the collective voice failed and was followed, after a debate, by a division.

Not Contents seated. A later refinement, to facilitate counting, was for the Contents to withdraw below the bar of the House. They were then counted by a teller as they passed back through the bar, the other side having been counted where they sat in the chamber. This refinement originated in 1675, when, in connection with a division on the Test Bill:

> Some of the Lords being unsatisfied whither the question were resolved in the affirmative or in the negative the Lords (it being candlelight and therefore difficult to tell the House) who gave their Contents withdrew below the Bar for easier counting of the House.[20]

In 1691 it was made official procedure, being enshrined as a standing order (*s.o.* 77), and continued so until 1859, when separate lobbies were introduced. At first the only way to abstain was to withdraw from the Chamber before the question was put, but in the eighteenth century the practice seems to have been developed of lords abstaining by withdrawing to the woolsacks or the throne, which for this purpose were not considered part of the House.[21] For example, in a Scottish legal case in 1733, all the 'Scots Lords withdrew behind the Chancellour, thereby signifying they were not to vote'.[22]

It was the Lord Chancellor (or Lord Keeper), as *ex officio* Speaker of the House, who decided when the collective voice should be called for; in Committees of the Whole House the chairman of the committee undertook that function in his place. If the collective voice seemed not to have produced a definite majority, or one side was dissatisfied, a lord might call for a division,[23] and provided that the request were seconded a division had to be taken. The procedure is described in the following extract from an account of the debate on the Union Bill in 1707, in

[20] H.L.R.O., Manuscript Minutes, quoted in Sainty and Dewar, pp. 8–9. Occasionally it became clear in a division that one side did not have the support it thought it had and the division was abandoned: B.L., Add. MS. 36293, ff. 195–6, Hardwicke to [Newcastle], 4 Apr. 1740. See also H. Walpole, *Memoirs of King George II*, ed. J. Brooke (3 vols., New Haven, 1985), I, 223 (22 Mar. 1753), and below, list no. 188. For perhaps the most famous case of an abandoned vote see C. Jones, 'The Division That Never Was: New Evidence on the Aborted Vote in the Lords on 8 December 1711 on "No Peace Without Spain"', *Parliamentary History*, II (1983), 191–202.

[21] Sainty and Dewar, p. 11. The following division lists cited below record abstainers : nos. 50 ('went out'), 79 ('went out'), 95 ('went out') and 117 ('went out' and 'withdrew'). For a report of a mass abstention by the Scots representative peers in 1712, who 'to a man went out of the house and would not vote one way or another', see *Wentworth Papers*, p. 261.

[22] Nat. Lib. Scotland, MS. 16553, f. 125, R. Graham to Milton, 15 Mar. 1732/3. For a description of 15 lords abstaining by retiring to the throne see B.L., Add. MS. 39311, ff. 29–30, [Bishop Benson of] Gloucester to [Bishop Berkeley], 13 May 1735. See also Hertfordshire R.O., D/EP, F250 (Panshanger papers), J. Savage to Lord Cowper, 30 Jan. 1741[/42].

[23] See letter quoted above, p. 8.

a Committee of the Whole House, which also reveals a piece of neat parliamentary footwork:

> After having canvas'd the Proposition for some time the Question was put Content or not Content for a federal Union, and the Bishop of Salisbury [Gilbert Burnet, in the Chair] having given the Majority for the Not Contents by a general Survey of the Voters, Lord Stawell demanded a Division, which Lord Nottingham and other of his side would afterwards have waved for fear of showing the Thinnesse of their Party, But Lord Wharton said since it had been demanded he joyn'd in the motion and accordingly the House came to a Division where the Contents ammounted but to Twenty and the Not Contents to Seaventy [sic] one.[24]

The actual counting of the votes in a division was the job of the tellers, except on the rare occasions that the individual voice method was used, when the clerks reckoned the votes. Two tellers, one from each side of the question (usually, and after 1712 invariably, of the same rank in the peerage),[25] were named by the Lord Chancellor or the chairman of the Committee of the Whole House, and the tellers were themselves included in the voting numbers, contrary to the practice of the Commons. When the numbers at a division were equal, the question was decided in the negative. In his diary Bishop William Nicolson of Carlisle describes one such instance, over Prince George's Bill in 1703:

> The House being resumed, a strong debate arose . . . which occasioned a new Question – *Whether this debate should be adjourned till Wednesday? Contents*, 61. *Not Contents*, 61 . . . The latter carried it, according to the Rules or Orders of the House; which preferr the negatives, in all Equal Divisions.[26]

On judicial questions — and the House acted as the final court of appeal for England and Wales, for Scotland after the Union in 1707, and for Ireland from the infamous 'Sixth of George the First' of 1720 until the Renunciation Act of 1783 — all the members could vote.[27] It was

---

[24] C.K.S., U.1590/C.474, f. 24 (Stanhope MSS.), enclosure in Joseph Addison to Horatio Walpole, 18 Feb. 1706–7.

[25] To have tellers of different degrees in the peerage was quite common under William III, less so under Anne, and utterly unknown afterwards; the last occasion on which this occurred was on 16 May 1712: see the division listed in Sainty and Dewar. John Relph, Reading Clerk 1664–1711, certainly regarded it as proper that tellers should be 'of the same quality' (H.L. R.O., Relfe's Book of Orders, p. 683, quoted in Sainty and Dewar, p. 9).

[26] *Nicolson's London Diaries*, p. 166. See also *ibid.*, p. 175, where a tied vote is described as being carried 'Praesumitur pro Negante',

[27] See I. Victory, 'The Making of the Declaratory Act, 1720', in *Parliament, Politics and People: Essays in Eighteenth-Century Irish History*, ed. G. O'Brien (Dublin, 1989), pp. 9–29.

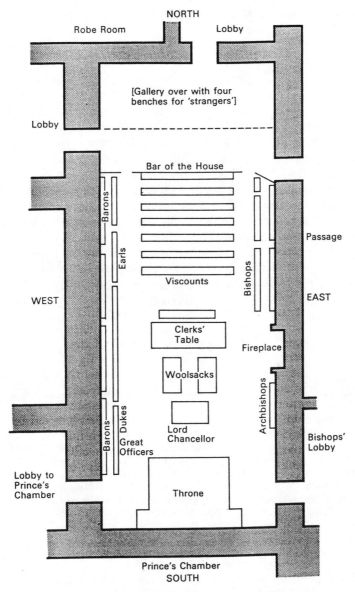

NORTH

Robe Room   Lobby

[Gallery over with four
benches for 'strangers']

Lobby

Bar of the House

Barons

Earls

Viscounts

WEST

Bishops

Passage

EAST

Clerks'
Table

Fireplace

Woolsacks

Archbishops

Barons
Dukes

Bishops'
Lobby

Great
Officers

Lord
Chancellor

Lobby to
Prince's
Chamber

Throne

Prince's Chamber
SOUTH

Fig. 2. The House of Lords in the Eighteenth Century

Sources: Westminster City Library, Extra-illustrated copy of T. Pennant, *Some Account of London*, III (1825), f. 105 (plan by Sir Christopher Wren); *Designs by Sir Christopher Wren*, ed. A.T. Bolton and H.D. Hendry (Wren Society, XI, 1934), plates XXX, XXXII, XXXVII, XXXVIII and XL (plans dated 1704–5); Westminster City Lib., Box 56, no. 22 (plan of Sir John Soane dated 1823); British Museum, Dept. of Prints and Drawings, T. Pennant, *London*, Extra-illustrated by J.C. Crowle (14 vols., 1801), III, illustration no. 200 (engraving by J. Pine, 29 Sept. 1749). Reproduced from C. Jones, 'Seating Problems in the House of Lords in the Early Eighteenth Century: the Evidence of the Manuscript Minutes', *B.I.H.R.*, LI (1978), 133, by kind permission of the Editor.

a convention, however, that the bishops did not do so in cases involving the death penalty.[28]

The lords had one privilege denied to Members of the lower House, that of voting by proxy. An absent lord could, if he wished, leave his proxy with a colleague to cast on his behalf. After 1690 a royal licence to be absent from the House, which had long been a mere formality, was no longer required.[29] Several restrictions had been placed on the use of proxies: (a) they could not be used in select or private committees, nor in the Committee of the Whole House;[30] (b) spiritual proxies could only be held by bishops and temporal proxies by peers (*standing order* no. 45);[31] (c) in 1626 it was resolved that no lord could hold more than two proxies at any one time (*s.o.* 45);[32] (d) in 1689 (*s.o.* 75) the casting of proxies in judicial cases was restricted to 'Preliminaries to private Causes but not in giving Judgement', and in 1698 (*s.o.* 88) their use was forbidden altogether 'in any Judicial Cause in this House although the proceedings be by way of Bill';[33] (e) in 1695 (*s.o.* 81) it was decided that, if proxies were called for, and it was up to the House to decide whether they were to be used, then any lord voting who held a proxy had to cast it; (f) in 1697 (*s.o.* 98) it was resolved that no proxy entered in the Proxy Books after prayers which opened each day's proceedings could be used on that day;[34] (g)

[28] See list no. 20.

[29] It appears that the Lords had in practice controlled its own attendance since at least 1669 (*L.J.*, XII, 256, 263–4).

[30] See *Nicolson's London Diaries*, p. 139.

[31] Bishop Crew of Durham, who was also Baron Crew of Steane in the peerage, invariably left his proxy with a peer rather than a bishop (H.L. R.O., Proxy Books, VI–VIII, *passim*). For the full list of standing orders, see H.M.C., *Lords MSS.*, new ser. X, 1–27.

[32] This was a result of an opposition victory over the Duke of Buckingham, who had held 13 proxies in the 1625 session: K. Sharpe, 'The Earl of Arundel, his Circle and the Opposition to the Duke of Buckingham, 1618–1628', in *Faction and Parliament: Essays on Early Stuart History*, ed. K. Sharpe (Oxford, 1978), p. 231.

[33] Sainty and Dewar, pp. 12–13. On 27 June 1717, the House in effect acquitted Lord Oxford of the charge of high crimes and misdemeanours after a discussion on the propriety of using proxies in what was really a judicial case. The resulting vote was carried for the Not Contents by proxy votes, 79 (including seven proxies) to 76 (including three). See C. Jones, 'The Impeachment of the Earl of Oxford and the Whig Schism of 1717: Four New Lists', *B.I.H.R.*, LV (1982), 66–87. The previous impeachment vote in which proxies had been used had been in 1689 (H.M.C., *12th Report*, appendix IV, p. 204).

[34] The 1697 resolution was not entered as *s.o.* 98 until 16 Jan. 1703. Bishop Nicolson described the occasion (*Nicolson's London Diaries*, p. 175). During a debate on the Occasional Conformity Bill

Lord Haversham acquainted their Lordships that . . . he had cast his eye into the Book of Proxies and had observed there was one entered since Prayers this morning which (he hoped) they would not suffer to be made use of in the Question of this night. 'Twas

continued

it became customary during the seventeenth century that a lord cast a proxy on the same side as his own vote;[35] and finally (h) in 1790 it was determined that no proxies should be used on any question pertaining to the petitions arising from the election of Scottish representative peers, which had been referred to the committee of privileges.[36]

Many questions, of course, never got as far as a division. If matters were uncontroversial; if one side were so greatly outnumbered that it realised a division would be futile and would only serve to 'show the Thinnesse of their party'; if the vote on the main question had been decisive and everything else were let go by default, then the question would be decided *nemine contradicente*. Bishop Nicolson's diaries record many occasions similar to the following, in October 1704:

> Lord Halifax moved that an Order might be made against the Reading of any Private Bill, not first printed and delivered at the Doors of the House. Which was seconded, and agreed to *Nemine Contradicente*.[37]

Who Could Have Compiled Division Lists?

This question can be partly answered by noting the restrictions on entry into the House, and by examining whether it was possible for persons to get in without permission. Besides the 1539 Act which laid down the membership of the House,[38] there were several standing orders aimed at controlling entry into the chamber.[39] Between them the 1539 Act and

continued
> Duke Schomberg's, given to the Prince [George of Denmark]. Whilst this was debated, the Duke himself (being privately sent for) came in person; but what Lord H[aversham] moved being an Order of the House before, was now Ordered to be added to the Roll of Standing Orders.

[35] In the sixteenth century it had not been uncommon for a lord to leave his proxy with another who held opposing views: V.F. Snow, 'Proctorial Representation in the House of Lords during the Reign of Edward VI', *Journal of British Studies*, VIII, no. 2 (1969), 11. Only two examples have so far come to light of this happening after 1660: (1) on 20 May 1712 Loudoun cast Orkney's proxy in opposition to his own vote over the Land Grants Bill; (2) when Bishop Nicolson left his proxy with his friend Bishop Wake in June 1714. This was during the debate on the Schism Bill, which Nicolson supported and Wake opposed. On the bill's third reading, on 15 June, when it passed by a majority of five, Wake cast Nicolson's proxy on the opposite side to his own vote (*Nicolson's London Diaries*, pp. 606–7 ns. 17–18, 681). For a discussion of proxy voting in the eighteenth century see Rees, 'Practice and Procedure of the House of Lords', pp. 433–44.

[36] *L.J.*, XXXIX, 33 (23 Dec. 1790).

[37] *Nicolson's London Diaries*, p. 215.

[38] For a summary of the membership of the House, see H. Elsynge, *The Ancient Method and Manner of Holding Parliaments in England* (1675), pp. 104–8.

[39] Mainly *s.o.* 18, 30, 55, 100, 109 and 111.

these orders granted permission only to the following: peers and bishops; eldest sons of peers (though not the eldest sons of Scottish representative peers), whose place was behind the throne;[40] the clerks of the House;[41] the gentleman Usher of the Black Rod; Masters in Chancery and King's Counsel, who sat on the woolsacks;[42] judges, called in to give their opinions on judicial cases;[43] the monarch;[44] members of the Court, for example Queen Anne's ladies-in-waiting, when the monarch attended; lawyers called before the bar of the House to plead in judicial cases; and Members of the Commons, at official openings and dissolutions of Parliament.

Unlike the Commons, which had a great many more Members and a much higher turnover in membership, there ought to have been little difficulty in preventing the entry of strangers into the Lords, and indeed in 1704 the House ruled that the doorkeepers were not to stay in the House when it was sitting, thus possibly increasing security.[45] There is no equivalent in the Lords of the almost farcical instance of the Frenchman in the Commons in 1694.[46] The nearest we get to such an intruder in the early eighteenth century is the case in 1714 of a Norfolk squire up in town for a holiday, who had

the good luck without any assistance to place himself so well at the dore of the house of lords, that when the Usher of the Black Rod came with Sir Thomas

---

[40] This was the position formally prescribed by the House, but eldest sons frequently strayed from their places: Jones, 'Seating Problems', p. 136 n.23. It was not unknown for M.P.s and other strangers to stand behind the throne, see, e.g. B.L., Trumbull Add. MS. 136, R. Bridges to Sir W. Trumbull, 18 Jan. 1711/12 , where the Bishop of London's chaplain describes meeting Henry St John and Thomas Harley there. See Jones, '"Party Rage and Faction"', pp. 154, 158. Similarly, M.P.s crowded into the House of Lords to hear the debate on the regency, 15 Dec. 1788: J. Ehrman, *The Younger Pitt: The Years of Acclaim* (1969), p. 655.

[41] The Folger Shakespeare Lib. copy of the Fenwick attainder list (no. 55) may be in the hand of a clerk of the House. The 1692 list of 'the Nobility now in Towne' (below, no. 46), was very probably compiled, for the Earl of Nottingham, by a clerk (John Walker, clerk assistant, perhaps) from the daily presence lists of the first few days of the session.

[42] Masters in Chancery acted as official messengers between the Lords and the Commons.

[43] The House ruled in 1694 that at least two judges should be present during term time to assist (*L.J.*, XV, 364). For an instance in which the judges were called to attend for a particular purpose, see *Nicolson's London Diaries*, p. 167.

[44] Apart from formal occasions, when the monarch attended to open or close Parliament, or to assent to bills (in his absence these tasks were undertaken by a commission), he could attend debates 'incognito' (see Holmes, *British Politics*, pp. 390–1). In the period covered by this register, Charles II, James II, William III and Anne are known to have attended incognito. Indeed, Charles's and James's attendance records were probably better than any single lord. George I was assiduous in attending formal occasions (we owe this information to Sir John Sainty), though there is no record of his having attended incognito. The *Journals* note when a monarch attended, whether formally or otherwise.

[45] *S.o.* 100.

[46] See below, pp. 106–7.

Hanmer [Speaker of the Commons and a knight of the shire for Suffolk] to the dore, he clapt in before all the members at Sir Thomas's Back, and with him to the Barr of the House of Lords, and stood behind him whilst he made his speech to the Lord Chancellor . . . [47]

Later in the century the presence of strangers in the House did at times cause embarrassment. In January 1741 Lord Lovel rose in the middle of a debate with a motion to clear the House, which was opposed by Lord Abingdon, who argued that 'Standing orders [are] not necessary to be inforced whilst persons behave with Decency'. Bishop Secker recorded in his diary that 'the occasion of this was that the Archbishop [Potter] who was about to speak was quite hid by persons standing before him. At length with very great difficulty the House was intirely cleared'.[48]

That this kind of circumstance should have arisen is really no surprise, for the Palace of Westminster was in effect open to the public - the Court of Requests (see Fig. 1), which lay between the two Houses, in particular being a great source of news[49]. *Standing order* no. 55 which forbade all but lords and the necessary attendants of the House from entering the lobby or the 'Little Committee Chamber' (probably the Prince's Chamber), the usual meeting-place for Lords' select or private committees (see Fig. 1) was continually being broken. The lobby was a favourite place to approach a lord about a cause that was to come before the House.[50] Indeed, it was not unknown for the environs of the House to be so crowded that business was interrupted. Bishop Nicolson set down in his diary in January 1703 that

The House did not sit till betwixt Twelve and One. A little before Two, a message came from the House of Commons to acquaint their Lordships that their Managers [at a conference with the Commons] had attempted to get to the Bar in the Painted Chamber [the normal venue for such conferences — see Fig. I]; but could not for the Crowd: And therefore they prayed their Lordships to give Directions to clear the way.[51] My Lord great Chamberlain

[47] W.B. Gurdon, 'The Gurdon Papers, No. XI', *The East Anglian*, new ser., V (1893–4), 145.

[48] B.L., Add. MS. 6043, f. 53. For 'strangers' see Rees, 'Practice and Procedure in the House of Lords', pp. 310–38.

[49] *Nicolson's London Diaries*, pp. 73–4; and Jones, '"Party Strife and Faction"', p. 160, R. Bridges to Trumbull, 25 Jan. 1711/12.

[50] This was true of the Commons' lobby which was also open to the public. On one occasion in 1712 Lord William Powlett M.P. 'hapned to see Abel Roper [a publisher] in the Lobby, and . . . pulld of his Peruque, and beat him I suppose for some of his Old faults for I don't hear of any new Offence that Abel gave his Lo[rdshi]p' (Bodl. Lib., MS. Ballard 20, ff. 45–6, G. Clarke to Charlett, 10 Apr. 1712).

[51] The Painted Chamber was under the control of the House of Lords, and the Lords' housekeeper kept the key: Devon R.O., 63/2/11/1/12 (Ley MSS.) John Ley to John Hatsell, 31 Oct. 1769.

[Lindsey][52] [was] to do this: But he returning told their Lordships that the thing was Impracticable, unless the Commons would call off their own Members. A message was sent, by two Masters in Chancery, to this Purpose: Which being obeyed, the Conference began about a Quarter before Three . . . [53]

The ease with which strangers could gain access to the House increased sharply in 1704. In November of that year the Lords decided to build a gallery at the north end of the chamber (see Fig. 2) 'to prevent those Confusions in the House which had been common of late when the Queen appeared in the Throne'. This was intended to accommodate 'Foreign Ministers and other Strangers, on those Solem Occasions', as well as 'the ladies when her Majesty comes thither in her robes'.[54] Designed by Sir Christopher Wren to seat a hundred, it was disliked by many lords even before it was finished, because it obstructed the light, and a motion to pull it down was narrowly defeated on 21 December 1704.[55] A second attempt was, however, successful in March 1711, and the Lord Chamberlain was ordered to start the work of demolition.

The importance of this gallery to the question we have posed is revealed by the occasion for the motion for its demolition in 1711. 'A. Bowyer ordered to attend: Baker taken into Custody of the Black Rod; and Lord Great Chamberlain [Lindsey] ordered to pull down the Gallery.'[56] Behind this brief entry in Nicolson's diary lies the story of Abel Boyer's publication, contrary to the standing orders of the House, of proceedings and debates in the Lords on the war in Spain. These were based on extensive notes of the debate of 9 January 1711 which Boyer had himself taken from the gallery.[57] It was reported by the end of March that Boyer's account 'already had three impressions and has given so much offence to the House of Lords that . . . they have resolved after this session is ended to admitt no more persons into their hous to hear their debates'.[58] Certainly it seems to have been possible for anyone to gain admission to the gallery, though often it was necessary to have some contact inside the House, either a lord or a doorkeeper. In January 1711, when Lords Galway and Tyrawley were to be examined by the House, many lords were of the opinion that these proceedings were of such public concern that any Member of the

---

[52] The Lord Great Chamberlain claimed jurisdiction over the whole of the Palace of Westminster, on the grounds that technically it was a royal residence.

[53] *Nicolson's London Diaries.*, p. 174.

[54] *Nicolson's London Diaries*, p. 221; N. Luttrell, *A Brief Historical Relation of State Affairs* (6 vols., Oxford, 1857), V, 484.

[55] *Nicolson's London Diaries*, pp. 221–2, 257.

[56] *Ibid.*, p. 555.

[57] *Ibid.*, pp. 531 n. 126, 555 n. 287; *L.J.*, XIX, 245–6; H.M.C., *Lords MSS.*, new ser., IX, 106–7. Boyer's publication is reprinted in Cobbett, *Parl. Hist.*, VI, 938–61. John Baker was his printer.

[58] B.L., Trumbull MS. Alph. 54, R. Bridges to Trumbull, 25 Mar. 1711.

Commons 'ought not to be refused going into the Gallery'. On hearing this Peter Wentworth, who was not an M.P., wrote to his brother Lord Raby, that he knew he 'cou'd get in with them without troubling any lord. Accordingly I got a first row in the gallery'.[59] Wentworth's letters to his brother in fact provided some of the best reports of proceedings in the House during the lifetime of the gallery. He was a frequent attender there, and on occasion supplied Raby with parliamentary lists.[60] It is also worth noting in this connexion that a gallery was again erected in 1737, to the 1704 design. Though it was described by Bishop Secker at the time of its erection as 'not a flying but a lasting one', it only survived three years.[61] The reason was that 'such a crowd' came into the Lords on 16 January 1741 that the House had to be cleared and some M.P.s, who refused to go, had to be threatened with custody before they would leave. This commotion incensed the House so much that the gallery was 'ordered to be taken down'.[62]

There is very strong evidence to suggest that after the 1704 gallery had been pulled down strangers could still gain admittance. The fact that at times, during debates on sensitive issues, the House might take action to exclude strangers implies that usually their presence was accepted. When the Succession was being discussed in the Lords in April 1714, Sir John Perceval, a Member of the Irish House of Commons, found himself for once unable to hear the debate. 'I cannot write you the order in which every Lord spoke', he told his brother, 'because they shut everybody out.'[63] Such action was infrequently taken, however, and even on some important occasions it was possible for outsiders to attend. At Lord Oxford's trial in 1717 'some of the great ladies came to the bar of [the] Lords to hear the debates there'.[64] By 1741, as we have seen, it was

[59] *Wentworth Papers*, p. 170.

[60] See *ibid.*, p. 345.

[61] B.L., Add. MS. 39311, f. 34, [Bishop Secker to his wife], 27 Feb. 1737; *The History of the King's Works*, ed. H.M. Colvin (6 vols., 1963–82), V, 392.

[62] Nat. Lib. Scotland, MS. 16585, ff. 238–9 [J. Maule to Milton], 17 Jan. 1741.

[63] B.L., Add. MS. 47087, f. 64v. For Ralph Bridges not being able to get into the Lords in the absence of a friendly doorkeeper on 20 May 1712, see Jones "'Party Faction and Strife'", pp. 154, 160, 162. Bridges could also not gain entry on 7 June 1712 when a Lords' debate was closed to strangers (*ibid.*, p. 163). For a full discussion of how the three correspondents of Trumbull gained their parliamentary news, see *ibid.*, pp. 152–4.

[64] Beaufort MSS. (the Duke of Beaufort, Badminton House, Gloucestershire), drawer 26, R. Price to [Lady Coventry], 27 June 1717. We should like to thank the late Duke of Beaufort for allowing us to consult his family papers. For another example of ladies gaining access to the gallery, see C. Jones and F. Harris "'A Question . . . Carried by Bishops, Pensioners, Place-men, Idiots": Sarah, Duchess of Marlborough and the Lords' Division over the Spanish Convention, 1 March 1739', *Parliamentary History*, XI (1992), 258. In the late eighteenth century proposals for the restoration of the gallery, either for M.P.s or for the public, were strongly resisted; in 1779 Lord Le Despenser predicted that a gallery would 'only become a laughing receptacle for ladies': G.M. Ditchfield, 'The House of Lords in the Age of the American Revolution', *Pillar of the Constitution*, p. 205.

accepted that the strict enforcement of standing orders was unnecessary if intruders behaved themselves, while in 1747 the journalist Edward Cave, examined by the House for publishing its proceedings in the *Gentleman's Magazine*, confessed that the debates he published he 'wrote himself, from Notes which he took' in the House, 'in Black Lead Pencil', with some assistance from 'his Memory'.[65] Admittedly, in the early 1770s the Lords developed a temporary obsession with 'strangers' and insisted on the exclusion from the chamber not only of the public but of M.P.s as well. This was partly a legacy of the controversy over the publication of parliamentary debates, exemplified in the 'printers' case' of 1771. The previous year Lord Gower attempted to bring about the prosecution of the *Middlesex Journal* for publishing an opposition protest and had cleared the House of 'strangers' during the Falklands debate of 10 December 1770 on the rather specious grounds that a public audience might contain foreign spies.[66] But thereafter public access to the House of Lords became easier, even though the numerous proposals for restoration of the gallery were not taken up before 1800. Great spectacles such as the trial of the Duchess of Kingston (1776) and the impeachment of Warren Hastings (1788–95) drew large crowds to Westminster Hall, and so did the debates on American policy in 1775.[67] By the mid 1770s the newspaper press was reporting Lords' debates with comparative freedom and the regular parliamentary reports of Almon, Debrett, Stockdale and Woodfall soon gave full coverage to the upper Chamber.

The case of Cave in 1741 is instructive, for he also admitted that he had been helped by some Members of the House, who had sent him their own speeches and notes on the speeches of others. Such evidence supports the view that, while it was perfectly possible for strangers, including 'professional strangers' like Cave and other journalists, to construct debates and even division lists from their own observations, more reliable material would be gained from the lords themselves. It is likely that the majority of division lists, though by no means all, originated with the lords, especially earlier in the period, and that these were substantially 'leaked' with the collaboration of outsiders. Certainly by the reign of George III the peer who managed the House for the government was able to supply the King with division lists when required.[68] The Earl of Sandwich, who served as first Lord of the Admiralty in North's ministry and was a frequent target of opposition attack, was an active compiler of lists. His assiduity was recognized by the Earl of Chesterfield in 1782:

[65] *L.J.*, XXVII,107–8. See also J. Hawkins, *The Works of Samuel Johnston* (11 vols., 1787), I, 95, for the way in which Cave organized the collection of material in the House.

[66] G.M. Ditchfield, 'The House of Lords in the Age of the American Revolution', in *Pillar of Constitution*, p. 204.

[67] *Ibid.*, pp. 205–6.

[68] Sainty and Dewar, p. 5.

I remember when you was in office, you used to take down the Names of the Peers, and in what manner they voted. If you should still do so, and there be a division on the Address, I shall be most obliged to you to send me a Copy of it.[69]

Though we have as yet no similar direct evidence for the authorship of a division list in the period before 1761, we come very close in 1714 when Lord Oxford writes to his cousin, Thomas Harley M.P., who had just left on a mission to Hanover, that the Hanoverian diplomat Baron Schutz, accredited to London between 1710 and 1714,

had run about to solicite Lords (about things he did not nor could not understand) and made Lists of the Lords and went to returne them thanks; this you know is always exclaimed against if any of the Sovereigns servants at any time attempt this .... [70]

This, at first, does not seem very conclusive. What kind of lists had Schutz compiled? Fortunately a rough draft survives for part of this letter, in which Oxford is much more informative

He [Schutz] has come into the House of Lords (al others excluded[71]) he has pretended to go about and sollicite Lords, and to give them thereby [end of page]. And is suspected to send lists, he made there is certain, how every one voted. This was never borne from the possessor of the throne. This, though it may flatter those Lords in his list he recommends, it make so many men lok upon themselves desperate with that court [Hanover] . . . [72]

Clearly Schutz was compiling lists of lords favourable to Hanover, presumably from the four divisions on the Protestant Successsion on 5, 8 and 13 April 1714, and he was forwarding these lists to the electoral court. This practice, frowned upon by Oxford, might have been a contributory factor in Schutz being forbidden the Court by Queen Anne and his subsequent repudiation by the Elector, over his demand on 12 April for a writ of summons to Parliament for the Electoral Prince (the future George II), as Duke of Cambridge. His lists might not have been the individual division lists, but a conflation of all four divisions.

---

[69] N.M.M., SAN/F/42/60. See nos. 335–8, 343, 346–7, 353, 359, below.

[70] B.L., Add. MS. 40621, f. 209, [Oxford] to [T. Harley], 13/24 Apr. 1714.

[71] That is all other 'strangers' excluded.

[72] B.L., Add. MS. 70295 (formerly Loan 29/12/4), draft of [Oxford] to [T. Harley], 13/24 Apr. 1714.

How Members of the Lords Could Have Constructed Division Lists

The manner of the House dividing, first with the Contents standing while the Not Contents remained seated, and subsequently with the Contents withdrawing below the bar, suggests that it would have been extremely difficult for any lord voting in his own place to have made very extensive or accurate observations of the votes of others. The arrangement of most of the benches in double rows (see Fig. 2) and the fact that they were all on the same level would have made it particularly so. Those sitting down might have had the opportunity of taking notes,[73] but they would not have had the view, while those standing up, or withdrawing, would probably have been too much in view themselves, quite apart from the awkwardness in writing in such a position.[74]

It is likely therefore that most of these lists would have been made after the event.[75] One possible way to have done this would have been for the individual or group compiling the list to have reckoned up in consultation with others of the same side their own vote, and then to have deducted this number from the total attendance.[76] One instance in which this seems to have been done was the list of the division in January 1709 on the Duke of Queensberry's right to vote in the election of the Scottish representative peers (no. 74, below).[77] Another was Lord Wharton's list of 27 May 1679 (no. 20), and this latter list is probably even more revealing of the methods sometimes used. Among Wharton's papers is a list of 36 'Lords that Protested against the Bishops voting in Capital causes'. In fact, as the *Journal* for that day shows, only 28 actually signed the protest. But the whole 36 are identified by symbols in the form of dots on a list of lay peers organised in exact order of precedence, and thus very likely copied from the finished *Journal*. It is therefore suggested that the remaining 72, including the 15 bishops not identified by name, were on the other side;

[73] For the Earl of Ilay taking notes, see Nat. Lib. Scotland, MS. 16553, f. 213, J. Johnston to Milton, 29 May 1733.

[74] This may be the reason why some lists are incomplete for one side of the vote, see, e.g. the Earl of Egmont's original list for the Woollen Bill, 6 May 1731 (no. 146), though he, being an Irish peer, was not a member of the House. See also the Folger Shakespeare Lib. copy of the Fenwick attainder list which was possibly compiled by a clerk (no. 55).

[75] For Lord Hervey reconstructing a debate from notes, see Suffolk R.O., 941/47/4 (Hervey of Ickworth papers), pp. 495–6, Hervey to H. Fox, 7 Apr. 1735: 'In the papers I Have sent by L[or]d Essex you will find your Questions answered . . . for the original of those papers was written the morning after the Debate by the Help of Notes I had taken, and whilst everything I had heard or Say'd was fresh in my memory.'

[76] For a discussion of the possible compilation of example of such lists, see E. Cruickshanks, D. Hayton and C. Jones, 'Divisions in the House of Lords on the Transfer of the Crown and Other issues: Ten New Lists', *B.I.H.R.*, LIII (1980), 76–80.

[77] See C. Jones, 'Godolphin, the Whig Junto and the Scots: A New Lords' Division List from 1709', *Scottish Historical Review*, LVIII (1979), 157–74.

though the figures 35–65 at the end of the list, presumably the totals at the division, indicate an awareness that the calculations are not exact.[78] A basis for the minority's reckoning up of its own strength would thus appear to have been the 28 lords who signed the protest; and, as at the time it was held necessary in order to sign a protest to have been actually present at the vote[79] (later on it was possible on exceptional occasions for a lord to sign who had not been present),[80] this would have provided a solid basis, which could have been fairly easily supplemented by other enquiries. In this case only eight more names were added. A protest after a vote a couple of weeks before, on 10 May, not to have a committee of both Houses to consider ways of proceeding in the trials of Danby and the Catholic lords in the Tower, would have provided an even broader foundation for a list, one which also seems to have been made use of. On that occasion 50 lords had signed a protest. They all appear in a list of the minority in the division which is to be found among Wharton's papers, and to which only two other names were added (no. 19, below). These 52 in turn appear on a full division list in Wharton's papers, giving both sides of the vote, where they are entered separately from the 52 described as Not Content. Where the latter figure was obtained is unclear, and it seems that it ought to have been 54; perhaps a different attendance list from the final official one had been used.[81]

There is a clear example of a marked manuscript attendance list having been used, with the arrangement of names bearing little relation to the order of precedence. This was for the vote on 23 November 1680 for a joint committee with the Commons to consider the state of the kingdom. On this list (no. 25) a dash to the right of a lord's name indicated a vote for the committee, a dash to the left a vote against. At the end appear the figures 45 and 32, presumably the final totals for the division. The dashes to the right, indicating the side taken by the compiler, once again Lord Wharton, comes out correctly at 32, but the dashes to the left add up to only 40. Perhaps the lesson to be drawn is that compilers of lists were more likely to be accurate in identifying their own friends than their enemies, especially if their friends were in the minority.

This is not of course to say that the lists of those on the other side are by any means useless. If our hypothesis that such lists were often arrived at by deducting one's own number from an attendance list is correct, accuracy

---

[78] *Danby*, III, 137 n.

[79] Under 20 Nov. 1667 in Lord Robartes's (later Earl of Radnor) notebook on the proceedings in Clarendon's impeachment, it is remarked, 'B[isho]p St As[aph] wrote his name but blotted it out againe because he was not present at the passing of the vote' (B.L., Harl. MS. 2243, f. 62).

[80] For example, Lord Cholmondeley at the vote on the Place Bill, 3 Jan. 1693 (list no. 50, below): Cruickshanks *et al.*, 'Ten New Lists', table and notes 103 and 154.

[81] *Danby*, III, 134 n.3.

would depend on how nearly the attendance list corresponded to those actually present in the House at the time of the vote (a vexed question dealt with below, pp. 26–7). It might be objected that this would not allow for abstentions, but, at least in the Restoration period, contemporaries would probably not have allowed for them either, since abstention would appear to have been at that time a rare occurrence, only possible, as we have seen, if a lord withdrew from the House before the question was put.[82]

Distribution of the Lists

There was obviously great public interest in many of the divisions which generated division lists, on such newsworthy subjects as the Exclusion Bill of 1680, the attainder of Sir John Fenwick in 1696, the impeachment of Dr Sacheverell in 1710, the proceedings against the Earl of Oxford from 1715 to 1717, the repeal of the Stamp Act in 1766, the India Bill of 1783 and the Regency Crisis of 1788–9. That copies of lists survive in the private archives of so many different and widely scattered political families testifies to the extent of this interest.

A particular illustration of the distribution of parliamentary lists is afforded by the papers of Sir William Trumbull, a former Secretary of State who had retired in 1697 to his Berkshire estate and was kept in touch with events in London by his agent in the capital, Thomas Bateman, and by his nephews, John and Ralph Bridges, the latter being chaplain to the Bishop of London.[83] Their letters show that Trumbull was sent parliamentary lists, not only the published lists giving members of each House,[84] but also manuscript lists of the protesters in the Lords;[85] and manuscript copies of division lists, including a division list of which no copy is known to have survived.[86] Such practices were probably not

---

[82] See above p. 9.

[83] For a published selection from this correspondence, see Jones, "'Party Rage and Faction'", pp. 148–80 (see above note 17).

[84] On 16 Oct. 1702 Bateman reported that 'Mr Jones's List of the Parliament is not yet come out, when it does, I'le send it' (this is almost certainly a reference to the printed list entitled *A True List of the Lords Spiritual and Temporal: Together with the Knights, Citizens, and Burgesses of the Parliament which Met at Westminster the 20th of October 1702 . . .* , printed by Edward Jones); on 7 Apr. 1710, 'Nothing having happened, or been done in your affair since my last, this is just for a cover to the inclosed Lists'; and on 28 May 1712, 'I inclose you the List, I promised, with a paper of what passed to day in both Houses': B.L., Trumbull MSS. Alph. 50, 51; Trumbull Add. MS. 134.

[85] Bridges wrote on 27 June 1712, 'The little paper of the Lords Protests which I sent you last concluded with a list of the Dissentient Lords . . .': B.L., Trumbull Add. MS. 134.

[86] This so far undiscovered list was on the Land Grants Bill of 1712: 'I have got a List of the 78 on each Side (in the House of Lords) when the Grant-Bill was last read, and lost,

continued

uncommon. Other examples of politicians absent from London who were sent division lists were the Duke of Montrose, who received in 1711 from the Scottish M.P. George Baillie of Jerviswood a copy of the division list on the Hamilton peerage case,[87] the Earl of Strafford who received a list from the Earl of Abingdon,[88] and Lord Grange in Scotland who received a copy of the list for the Duke of Marlborough's bill in 1734 from the Earl of Marchmont.[89] Also there are several known manuscript lists of the vote at Dr Sacheverell's impeachment.[90]

Despite, or perhaps because of, the small number of lists published before the mid eighteenth century (only 20 - less than 10 per cent - of the lists between 1660 and 1761 given below appeared in a contemporary printed form - the first in 1680, no. 26, below),[91] the market for printed division

---

continued

but I must get it examined further before I send you a copy of it' (B.L., Trumbull Add. MS. 134, Bateman to Trumbull, 26 May 1712).

[87] See list no. 95, below. Montrose in 1727 sent Mungo Graham, his factor and a former M.P., who was in Scotland, a division list of the vote over Earl Graham's disputed patent. Earl Graham was Montrose's eldest son and heir, and the dispute almost certainly arose over whether Earl Graham was barred from sitting in the Lords by the 1711 resolution of the House which prevented Scottish peers who were granted British titles from taking their place in the Lords. As Earl Graham was not a Scottish peer at the time he was created a British peer, the 1711 resolution did not apply in his case (which was the first of its kind since 1711). See Scottish R.O., GD 220/5/858/4, 5 [Montrose to M. Graham], 20, 26 Jan. 1727; GD 220/5/1054/5 [John to Mungo Graham], 24 Jan. [1727]. Unfortunately no copy of the list seems to have survived.

[88] B.L., Add. MS. 22221, f. 3, Abingdon to [Strafford], [1712].

[89] Scottish R.O., GD 124/15/1426/1 (Mar and Kellie papers), Marchmont to [Grange], 24 Feb. 1733/4: 'You have Copys of the Bill concerning the officers of the Army, the two Motions upon it, the list of the lords Present, and Proxys and they are markt How they voted: together with the lords protests upon Both Questions, which by the by must not be printed, till the Session of Parliament is over ...' For other examples, see Edward Harley *jr* sending his aunt Abigail copies of lists nos. 122 and 124 partly in response to her enquiry as to how one peer voted: B.L., Add. MS. 70034 (formerly Loan 29/205), letters of 25 Dec. 1718 (printed in part in H.M.C., *Portland MSS.*, V, 574–5), 4, 13, 18 Jan. 1718/9; while Edward Harley *sr* sent his brother, the Earl of Oxford, two lists, one of which was a 'list of Xtian and Infidal B[ishop]s' who had opposed the Blasphemy Bill: B.L, Add. MS. 70236 (formerly Loan 29/143), 28 Jan. 1720, 6 May 1721 (quotation). In 1689, Oxford's father, Sir Edward Harley M.P., had sent him 'by Lemster [Leominster] the votes of the Lords Agreement with the H[ouse] of Commons in their great vote about the Throne's vacancy. Also the votes of the Lords nominating the prince and princes King and Queen with two oaths to which yesterday the Commons agreed ...' (B.L., Add. MS. 40621, f. 20, Sir Edward Harley to R. Harley, 9 Feb. 1688[/89]).

[90] Amongst those listed below (list no. 79) there is a manuscript copy of the printed division list, without any variations, in Nat. Lib. Wales, Ottley MS. 1706, J. Winstanley to Adam Ottley, n.d. [c. 23 Mar. 1710].

[91] In the late seventeenth century publication of lists often led to the punishment by the House of the printer and publisher for breach of privilege, see, e.g. L.G. Schwoerer, 'Press and Parliament in the Revolution of 1689', *Historical Journal*, XX (1977), 564–5, for the punishment of those responsible for publishing the list of 6 Feb. 1689 (below, list no. 39).

lists was considerable. There were even occasions when the rumour of the publication of such a list was recorded.[92] The trial of Dr Sacheverell in 1710 generated tremendous public interest, and printed lists of the guilty vote on 20 March (below no. 79) provide remarkable evidence of the speed of publication and the breadth of readership of such publications.[93] One version of the printed list on the Sacheverell case shows the Members of both Houses who voted for and against the doctor, and is illustrated with portraits of Sacheverell and the bishops who supported him, with an explanatory text in four languages: English, Dutch, French and Latin. Published in London and Amsterdam, it shows that parliamentary lists on issues of national importance could have a European as well as a domestic market.[94] Later in the eighteenth century quite complex lists were printed, listing several categories of lords and classifying them according to their voting in more than one division.[95] Sophisticated printing techniques were employed, obviously involving a good deal of expenditure in time and money for the printer and publisher, who no doubt expected to be able to recover their costs from sales.[96]

Early eighteenth-century newspapers contained little parliamentary material, including lists [97] - the first one appears to have been in 1715

[92] E.g. a Lords and Commons list on Bishop Atterbury's trial (B.L., Add. MS. 27980, f. 61, newsletter, 4 June 1723). No such list appears to have been published.

[93] A printed list of the division of 20 March 1710 was available the following day (B.L., RP 158 [Newsletters 1690–1710], newsletter sent by Sir Henry Gough and Thomas Guy, both M.P.s for Tamworth, to a Mrs Newey, 21 March 1709[/10]). The speed of distribution of printed lists is attested to by Bishop Nicolson of Derry (recently translated from Carlisle), who reported from Rose, Cumberland, on 9 Jan. 1719 as owning a printed copy of the list on the repeal of the Occasional Conformity and Schism Acts (no. 126, published in London in 1718; two further editions were published in 1719, one at Dublin), which could not have been printed earlier than 24 Dec. 1718 (Christ Church, Oxford, Wake MS. 21, f. 87, Nicolson to Wake, 9 Jan. 1719).

[94] William Salt Lib., Stafford, 'Portraits of Divines', 70. For a hint at the great Dutch interest in British parliamentary affairs as reflected in the amount of published material coming from Dutch presses, see G.C. Gibbs, 'The Contribution of Abel Boyer to Contemporary History in England in the Early Eighteenth Century', in *Clio's Mirror: Historiography in Britain and the Netherlands*, eds. A.C. Duke and C.A. Tamse (Zutphen, 1985), pp. 100–2. See also Jones, '"Party Rage and Faction"', p. 164 for a report of a Lords' protest published in the *Amsterdam Gazette* and on sale in London 'the very next mail after the Debate', and list no. 31 which was originally printed in the *Harlem Courant* in 1688. There is also a copy of *An Authentick List of the House of Peers: As they Voted For and Against the Convention* . . . [of 1 Mar. 1739: see below, list no. 166] in the Staatsarchiv, Hamburg (we owe this information to Jeremy Black).

[95] See, for example, *An Exact List of the Lords Spiritual and Temporal Distinguished by the following Marks* . . . (printed by E. Cave, jr., 1736), which not only classifies the Lords into 11 categories but also lists and classifies the Commons into seven: copy in B.L., Dept. of Printed Books, 1453. a. 17, and lists nos. 319 and 329 below.

[96] See below, p. 107.

[97] See Gibbs, 'The Contribution of Abel Boyer', p. 101.

(no. 113, below) - but, with the expansion of parliamentary news, division lists (usually, but by no means invariably, of a minority only), together with more general surveys, began to appear with increasing frequency in the press during the last quarter of the century. Press publication of Lords (and Commons) lists had been comparatively rare in mid century [98] and few have emerged for the 1760s. But from 1774–5, as W.C. Lowe has demonstrated, the Lords relaxed both their exclusion of strangers and their policy of prosecuting the more audacious of the printers.[99] The immediate result was the publication of a spate of minority lists on the American issue in 1775 and the use of such lists as a propaganda weapon by the parliamentary opposition. Thereafter, Lords lists appear frequently in the newspaper press. Some 42 have been found in the press during the 1790s alone, even excluding the 16 well-reported votes over the Hastings impeachment.

The Reliability of Division Lists

Analyses of the House, forecasts and managerial lists of various kinds all to some extent reflect the personal opinions and prejudices of their compilers, a fact which can in some respects limit and in other ways enhance their value to historians, but which must always invite scepticism as to the truth of what they say, or appear to say. On the other hand, a list naming the two sides in a specific division seems a more trustworthy document, a record of a particular action rather than an assessment of general attitudes or a prediction of future behaviour. Not necessarily so. Division lists can be beset with traps for the unwary.

By definition division lists are (until 1857) unofficial records, drawn up possibly by spectators with little understanding of the procedures of the House (even lords themselves were sometimes uncertain),[100] and little acquaintance with the members. They might have been drawn up after the event, with the official records of the House as an aid to compilation, and comparing various different accounts.[101] The most obvious official

---

[98] M. Harris, *London Newspapers in the Age of Walpole: A Study of the Origins of the Modern English Press* (1987), pp. 172–3.

[99] W.C. Lowe, 'Peers and Printers: The Beginning of Sustained Press Coverage of the House of Lords in the 1770s', *Parliamentary History*, VII (1988), 241–56.

[100] *Nicolson's London Diaries*, p. 135; *Wentworth Papers*, p. 253.

[101] Though there is, as yet, no direct evidence for the compilation of a division list in the early eighteenth century, there are some indications that such lists were the result of consultations with, and checking by, several individuals: see above, n. 76, and *Wentworth Papers*, p. 354. Lord Midleton's account of how he compiled from memory a list of a division in the Irish House of Lords in 1721 is instructive (Surrey R.O., Guilford Muniment Room, 1248/5, f. 129v, Midleton to Thomas Brodrick, 9 Nov. 1721). See also B.L., Stowe

continued

record to use, as we have seen, was the 'presence list' drawn up by the Clerk Assistant and entered by him in the manuscript minutes of the House at the beginning of each day's proceedings. (During the Restoration period there were two separate presence lists entered at different times of the day.) These purport to register all the lords present at the day's sitting. They were subsequently 'edited' to form the presence lists included at the beginning of each day's proceedings in the manuscript journals, later printed as the *Lords Journals*. But both the manuscript journals and the published versions contain mistakes which can be traced back to the original presence lists in the minutes. From what we know of the way in which these presence lists were compiled, it is not surprising that human error crept in.[102] An examination of the attendance record of Bishop Nicolson, who assiduously noted down in his diary when he was at the House, reveals that on half the occasions on which the *Journals* give him as absent he was in fact present.[103] The explanation in his case is that he often arrived late and was missed by the Clerk Assistant, who had compiled the day's list from observation of the lords present at the beginning of the sitting.[104] If the experienced clerks of the House could make mistakes on this scale, how much more inaccurate might unofficial compilers of division lists be? Often the numbers given for each side in a division list do not tally with the official figures as set down in the minutes.[105] Useful though division lists are, they must be used with extreme caution, especially in the classification of individuals into party groups. Nor do the presence lists in the *Journals* always serve as a completely reliable check.

Some light is shed on the accuracy of division lists drawn up by members of the House by evidence of the lost manuscript list of the vote by the Lords

continued

MS. 241, ff. 242–3, for consultations over the drawing up of an analysis of the peerage in relation to the succession (below, no. 70); and Royal Archives, Windsor Castle, Stuart Papers 162/81, Nathaniel Mist to James Edgar, 12 June 1733, where Mist writes, from Boulogne, 'Having got Lists of all the Lords who voted in this famous Question [below, no. 155] ... I shall here subjoyn it, There is one upon each Side I have not as yet got an Account of'.

[102] Jones, 'Seating Problems', pp. 139–42. The House of Lords was not an easy place in which to record numbers accurately. Its cramped conditions even for an average daily attendance of 60 to 70 (*ibid.*, p. 136), made such counting of heads a particularly difficult exercise on exceptional occasions when the Chamber was overflowing, as at the division on Oxford's impeachment on 1 July 1717, when no less than 136 lords voted: see Jones, 'Impeachment of the Earl of Oxford', pp. 66–87.

[103] See *Nicolson's London Diaries*, pp. 27–32.

[104] Jones, 'Seating Problems', p. 143.

[105] But who is to say that the tellers and the clerks of the House were less liable to error than the compilers of division lists? On 19 May 1712, for instance, at a division on the Land Grants Bill, when the motion to commit was carried by one, the question was only decided after the proxies had been counted twice, 'the tellers differing': H.L. R.O., Manuscript Minutes. There are also examples of the figures for the votes being entered incorrectly in the minutes: see, for example, under 14 Apr. 1714.

in Westminster Hall on 20 March 1710 on the guilt of Dr Sacheverell, which was sent the same evening by Godolphin to Marlborough. The duke's reply makes it clear that this manuscript list included the name of a least one peer, Suffolk, not named in the printed list which appeared for sale the following day.[106] As the voting on this occasion had been by the antiquated method of individual voice it had been a long-drawn out process. Moreover Lord Chancellor Cowper had declared that he needed time to make the count, which he did with care, checking and rechecking. 'Eventually, satisfied (as he put it) that he had "cast them up with as much exactness" as he could, he announced the verdict.'[107] Two points follow from this. If Cowper, who had plenty of time to record the votes, required time to recheck his figures, how accurate could any division be, with no time for deliberation, especially when one considers the crush that must sometimes have developed at the bar? Secondly, the slow process of the vote on 20 March in Westminster Hall still produced two varying lists, admittedly different by probably only one peer. If the individual voice method of voting could not give rise to an agreed list, how much more room was there for error in a list of a division taken by the normal method in a crowded House?

Even when all these qualifications are kept in mind, the importance of the various types of Lords lists, both to contemporary politicians and to later historians, is undeniable. As we have seen, those engaged in the great battles of high politics in this period expended much time and energy in the pursuit of knowledge of the disposition of the House of Lords and used the list as a principal means to this end. For historians, the knowledge of the working of the House of Lords has at times been restricted by a dearth of lists, as David Large acknowledged in his study of the half-century after 1783.[108] When available to historians, lists can illuminate the techniques of ministerial management, the sophistication or otherwise of the organization of opposition, the disposition of the ecclesiastical bench, the role of the independent peer and the opinions of the backbench (or backwoods) lord who rarely if ever spoke in the upper Chamber and whose political sympathies might otherwise remain completely obscure. Lists can illuminate the judicial and political function of the Lords and, as Stephen Farrell has shown, can be a vital source for the analysis of a particular group.[109] This introduction has highlighted the critical problems which Lords lists can pose; the *Register* is designed to render those lists more easily accessible to historians.

---

[106] *The Marlborough-Godolphin Correspondence*, ed. H.L. Snyder (3 vols., Oxford, 1975), III, 1445 n. 3; B.L., RP 158, newsletter, 21 Mar. 1711.

[107] Holmes, *Trial of Sacheverell*, pp. 223–4.

[108] D. Large, 'The Decline of the "Party of the Crown" and the Rise of Parties in the House of Lords, 1783–1837', *E.H.R.*, LXXVIII (1963), 670.

[109] S. Farrell, 'Division Lists and the Nature of the Rockingham Whig Party in the House of Lords, 1760–1785', *Parliamentary History*, XIII (1994), 170–89.

Note: Appendixes to the Lords Lists

There are three Appendixes to the Lords list below. The first (A) gives details of three lost division lists; the second (B) is of lists which, so far, we have not been able to date or identify; while the third (C) gives details of official and unofficial lists of proxies. The procedures of the House governing proxies have been described above (pp. 12–13). The only published discussions of the operation of the proxy voting system in the Lords in our period are in Holmes, *British Politics*, pp. 45–6, 307–9; J.E. Powell, 'Proxy Voting in the House of Lords', *Parliamentary Affairs*, IX (1955–6), 203–12; *Nicolson's London Diaries*, pp. 32–6; and M.W. McCahill, *Order and Equipose: The Peerage and the House of Lords, 1783–1806* (1979), pp. 16–18. For an unpublished discussion see A.J. Rees, 'The Practice and Procedure of the House of Lords, 1714–1784' (Wales [Aberystwyth] Ph.D., 1987), pp. 433–44. For the system prior to 1660, see V.F. Snow, 'The Evolution of Proctorial Representation in Medieval England', *American Journal of Legal History*, VII (1963), 319–39; *idem*, 'Proctorial Representation and Conciliar Management during the Reign of Henry VIII', *Historical Journal*, IX (1966), 1–26; *idem*, 'Proctorial Representation in the House of Lords During the Reign of Edward VI', *Journal of British Studies*, VIII, no. 2 (1969), 1–27; *idem*, 'A Rejoinder to Mr Graves's Reassessment of Proctorial Representation', *ibid.*, X, no. 2 (1971), 36–46; H. Miller, 'Attendance in the House of Lords during the Reign of Henry VIII', *Historical Journal*, X (1967), 325–51; and M.A.R. Graves, 'Proctorial Representation in the House of Lords during Edward VI's Reign: A Reassessment', *Journal of British Studies*, X, no. 2 (1971), 19–33. Though proxies were not used with very great frequency and rarely altered the result of a division (they were used in only 18 per cent of divisions between 1685 and 1761, but in 26 per cent between 1761 and 1800), they are important to the historian in helping to discern party lines and the probable party allegiance of a lord at a given time (see Holmes, *British Politics*, p. 45).

List of Lists

FIRST PARLIAMENT OF CHARLES II, 1660

1. *Spring 1660*, list of lords, drawn up by Lord Wharton in the spring of 1660, with a view to their probable attitude to the 'Presbyterian' peers.
    (a) Bodl. Lib., MS. Carte 81, f. 63.
    (c) G.F. Trevallyn Jones, *Saw-Pit Wharton: The Political Career from 1640 to 1691 of Philip, Fourth Lord Wharton* (Sydney, 1967), p. 157.

SECOND PARLIAMENT OF CHARLES II, 1661–79

2. *11 July 1661*, those for and those against Lord Oxford's case for the Great Chamberlaincy.
    (a) Bodl. Lib., MS. Carte 109, ff. 313–7: three lists, probably versions of the same division list.

3. *13 July 1663*, Wharton's prediction of the probable division on Bristol's attempt to impeach Clarendon.
    (a) Bodl. Lib., MS. Carte 81, ff. 2, 224.
    (b) G.F. Trevallyn Jones, 'The Bristol Affair, 1663', *Journal of Religious History*, V (1968–9), 29.

4. *Autumn 1669*, followers of the Duke of Buckingham.
    (b) F.R. Harris, *The Life of Edward Montague . . . 1st Earl of Sandwich* (2 vols., 1912), II, 312.

5. *Apr.–June 1675*, supporters of the non-resisting test.
    (a) B.L., Add. MS. 28091, ff. 161, 175, 177.
    (b) *Danby*, III, 122–4.
    (c) *Ibid.*

6. *20 Nov. 1675*, those for and those against the proposed address in favour of a dissolution.
    (a) H.L.R.O., Historical Collections 215/7, misdated 22 Nov.; B.L., Add. MS. 35885, f. 224 (includes absent peers and proxies); Bodl. Lib., MS. Carte 72, f. 293; Huntington Lib., MS. EL 8418 (Ellesmere papers). Variants.
    (b) H.M.C., *9th Rep.* pt. 2, p. 79; *Danby*, III, 125–6 (printing from MS. Carte 72, f. 293). Variants.
    (c) *Danby*, III, 125.

7. *1677–8*, Shaftesbury's list of lay lords.
    (a) Shaftesbury papers (the Earl of Shaftesbury, St Giles House, Wimborne St Giles, Dorset).
    (b) K.H.D. Haley, 'Shaftesbury's Lists of the Lay Peers and Members of the Commons, 1677–8', *B.I.H.R.*, XLIII (1970), 86–95.
    (c) *Ibid.*

8. *15 Nov. 1678*, those for and those against making transubstantiation part of the Test Bill.
    (a) Bodl. Lib., MS. Carte 81, f. 380.
    (b) *Danby*, III, 127–9.
    (c) *Ibid*, 127 n. 3, omitting Sturton from the Not Contents.

9. *29 Nov. 1678*, the 11 lords who voted for the address to remove the Queen from Whitehall.
    (a) Bodl. Lib., MS. Carte 81, ff. 3, 387.

10. *20 Dec. 1678*, 21 lords who protested against agreeing with the committee's amendments in the Bill for Disbanding the Army.
    (a) Bodl. Lib., MS. Carte 81, ff. 3, 455.

11. *26 Dec. 1678*, those for and those against adhering to the amendment to the Disbanding Bill.
    (a) Bodl. Lib., MS. Carte 81, ff. 3, 405. A combined list, see below 12.
    (b) *Danby*, III, 129–33.
    (c) *Ibid.*

12. *27 Dec. 1678*, those for and those against the committal of the Earl of Danby.
    (a) Bodl. Lib., MS. Carte 81, ff. 3, 405. A combined list, see above 11.
    (b) *Danby*, III, 129–33.
    (c) *Ibid.*

THIRD PARLIAMENT OF CHARLES II, 1679

13. *c. Mar. 1679*, Danby's calculations of likely supporters and opponents in the proceedings against him.
    (a) B.L., Add. MS. 28091, ff. 138, 140.
    (b) *Danby*, III, 140–4.
    (c) *Ibid.*, pp. 140–3.

14. *12 Mar. 1679*, lords absent, besides the papist lords.
    (a) Bodl. Lib., MS. Carte 81, ff. 3, 456.
    (b) *Danby*, III, 133.
    (c) *Ibid.*

15. *c. Mar.–Apr. 1679*, further calculations by Danby about likely voting in the proceedings against him.
    (a) B.L., Add. MS. 28091, ff. 136, 142.

(b) *Danby*, III, 144–8.
(c) *Ibid.*

16. *c. Apr. 1679*, those for and those against the attainder of Danby.
    (a) B.L., Add. MS. 28091, f. 134.
    (b) *Danby*, III, 148–51.
    (c) *Ibid.*

17. *4 Apr. 1679*, those for and those against the attainder of Danby.
    (a) Bodl. Lib., MS. Carte 81, ff. 4, 588.
    (c) *Danby*, III, 148–9 n. 6. Browning chose to print a list which cannot be dated precisely (see above, 16), and noted the differences.

18. *14 Apr. 1679*, those for and those against the attainder of Danby.
    (a) B.L., Add. MS. 29572, f. 112.

19. *10 May 1679*, those for and those against 'not to have a committee of both Houses to consider of the way of proceeding in the tryall of the lords'.
    (a) Bodl. Lib., MS. Carte 103, f. 270; MS. Carte 81, f. 553, minority only.
    (b) *Danby*, III, 134–7.
    (c) *Ibid.*

20. *27 May 1679*, those for and those against adhering to an earlier vote that the lords spiritual had a right to stay in court in capital cases till judgment of death came to be pronounced.
    (a) Bodl. Lib., MS. Carte 81, f. 551.
    (b) *Danby*, III, 137–40.
    (c) *Ibid.*, p. 137.

21. *6 Dec. 1679*, list of lords who addressed the King for a Parliament.
    (a) Huntington Lib., MS. HA P (Huntingdon papers).
    (b) H.M.C., *Hastings MSS.*, IV, 302.

FOURTH PARLIAMENT OF CHARLES II, 1679–81

22. *15 Nov. 1680*, those for the Exclusion Bill.
    (a) Bodl. Lib., MS. Carte 81, f. 654; B.L., Add. MS. 36988, f. 159; Northamptonshire R.O., Finch-Hatton MS. 2893A. Variants.
    (b) E.S. de Beer, 'The House of Lords in the Parliament of 1680', *B.I.H.R.*, XX (1943–5), 37. De Beer's version (Carte 81, f. 654) would appear to be confirmed by the fact that it contains all the names, and those only, on which the other two manuscripts agree.
    (c) *Ibid.*

23. *15 Nov. 1680*, those against the Exclusion Bill.
    (a) B.L., Add. MS. 36988, f. 189; Northants. R.O., Finch-Hatton MS. 2893A. Variants.

24. *15 Nov. 1680*, those absent at the division on the Exclusion Bill.
     (a) Northants. R.O., Finch-Hatton MS. 2893C.

25. *23 Nov. 1680*, those for and against a joint committee with the Commons to
     consider the state of the kingdom.
     (a) Bodl. Lib., MS. Carte 81, ff. 4, 669.

26. *7 Dec. 1680*, those for and against the attainder of Viscount Strafford.
     (a) Bodl. Lib., MS. Carte 80, f. 823; Bodl. Lib., MS. Rawlinson A 183 (Pepys
          papers), f. 62; B.L., Eg. MS. 2978, f. 55; B.L., Harleian MS. 7190, f.
          236; B.L., Add. MS. 70099 (formerly Loan 29/407); Cheshire R.O.,
          DCH/K/3/4 (Cholmondeley papers), Lord Cholmondeley to William
          Adams, [7 Dec.] 1680; *The Tryal of Viscount Strafford . . .* (1681), copy
          in Gloucestershire R.O., D340a Z/2 (Ducie Morton papers). Variants.

27. *7 Jan. 1681*, those who protested upon the previous question about
     committing Lord Chief Justice Scroggs (seven additional names to the list
     printed in *L.J.*, XIII, 738).
     (a) Bodl. Lib., MS. Carte 81, ff. 656, 657.

THE PARLIAMENT OF JAMES II, 1685–7

28. *c. May 1687*, groupings of lords according to their supposed attitudes to the
     policies of James II.
     (a) Koninklijk Huisarchief, The Hague, Bentinck archives, no. 85.
     (b) K.H.D. Haley, 'A List of English Peers, *c.* May 1687', *E.H.R.*, LXIX
          (1954), 304–6.
     (c) *Ibid.*, pp. 302–4.

29. *c. Nov. 1687*, groupings of lords according to their supposed attitudes to the
     repeal of the Test Act.
     (a) Archives du Ministere des Affaires Etrangeres, Correspondence Politique
          Angleterre, vol. 164, ff. 285–6.
     (b) D.H. Hosford, 'The Peerage and the Test Act: A List, *c.* November
          1687', *B.I.H.R.*, XLII (1969), 118–20.
     (c) *Ibid.*, pp. 166–7.

30. *1687*, groupings of lords according to their supposed attitudes to the repeal
     of the Test Act.
     (a) B.L., Add. MS. 34526, ff. 48–56, transcript taken by Sir James
          Mackintosh of an anonymous list in the 'Portland MSS.'.

31. *Jan. 1688*, list of lords for, against or 'absent' (i.e. doubtful?) on the repeal
     of the Test Act.
     (a) B.L., Dept. of Printed Books, S.P.R. 356. m. 3 (38.), a MS. copy, taken
          about 1727, of a published list, and headed 'The Names of the Peers
          for and against repealing the Tests. Taken out of the *Harlem Courant* in
          January 1688'.

32. *N.d.*, opposition to James II in the Lords, compiled by Danby.
     (a) B.L., Add. MS. 28091, f. 172.
     (b) *Danby*, III, 153–5.
     (c) *Ibid.*, pp. 152–3.

33. *16 Nov. 1688*, those subscribing the petition to James II for a free Parliament.
     (a) *To the King's Most Excellent Majesty, The Humble Petition of the Lords Spiritual and Temporal ... Presented ... the 17th of November, 1688* (1688: copy at P.R.O., S.P. 31/4, f. 196), reprinted in E. Bohun, *The History of the Desertion ...* (1689), p. 44.
     (b) R.A. Beddard, 'The Guildhall Declaration of 11 December 1688 and the Counter-Revolution of the Loyalists', *Hist. Jnl.*, XI (1968), 410.
     (c) *Ibid.*

34. *16 Nov. 1688*, those who subscribed and those who refused to subscribe the petition for a free Parliament.
     (a) B.L., Spencer papers, Savile papers, box 8.

35. *11 Dec. 1688*, those subscribing to the Guildhall Declaration.
     (a) *The Declaration of the Lords Spiritual and Temporal, In and about the Cities of London and Westminster, Assembled at Gildhall, 11 Dec. 1688* (1688: copy at P.R.O., S.P. 31/4, ff. 205–6), reprinted in Bohun, *History of the Desertion*, p. 95.
     (b) Beddard, 'Guildhall Declaration', p. 408.
     (c) *Ibid.*

THE CONVENTION PARLIAMENT, 1689–90

36. *29 Jan. 1689*, those in favour of a regency.
     (a) *Correspondence of Henry Hyde, Earl of Clarendon*, ed. S.W. Singer (2 vols., 1828), II, 256.
     (c) Horwitz, *Parliament*, p. 335.

37. *31 Jan. 1689*, those for and those against declaring William and Mary King and Queen.
     (a) Wiltshire R.O., 130/856 (Ailesbury papers).
     (b) E. Cruickshanks, D. Hayton and C. Jones, 'Divisions in the House of Lords on the Transfer of the Crown and Other Issues, 1689–94: Ten New Lists', *B.I.H.R.*, LIII (1980), 81–7.
     (c) *Ibid.*, pp. 60–5, 76–8.

38. *4 Feb. 1689*, those for and those against agreeing with the Commons over the word 'abdicated'.
     (a) Wilts. R.O., 1300/856.
     (b) Cruickshanks *et al.*, 'Ten New Lists', pp. 81–7.
     (c) *Ibid.*, pp. 60–5, 76–80.

39. *6 Feb. 1689*, those for and those against agreeing with the Commons in the word 'abdicated' etc.

(a) Wilts. R.O., 1300/856; H.L.R.O., Main papers (as printed in *L.J.*, XIV, 119); *The Names of the Lords Spiritual and Temporal who Deserted* [not Protested] *against the Vote in the House of Peers, the Sixth Instant* ... (1688/9): copies in H.L.R.O., Main papers 1689, and in the Huntington Lib., Rare Book Dept. HEH 29420.

(b) Cruickshanks *et al.*, 'Ten New Lists', pp. 81–7 (prints Wilts. R.O., 1300/856).

(c) *Ibid.*, pp. 61–5, 76–80; L.G. Schwoerer, 'Press and Parliament in the Revolution of 1689', *Hist. Jnl.*, XX (1977), 364–5.

40. *31 May 1689*, those for and against reversing the judgments on Titus Oates.
(a) Wilts. R.O., 1300/856.
(b) Cruickshanks *et al.*, 'Ten New Lists', pp. 81–7.
(c) *Ibid.*, pp. 65–8, 76–80.

41. *30 July 1689*, those for and those against adhering to amendments in Oates' case.
(a) Wilts. R.O., 1300/856.
(b) Cruickshanks *et al.*, 'Ten New Lists', pp. 81–7.
(c) *Ibid.*, pp. 65–8, 76–80.

42. *Oct. 1689–Feb. 1690*, analysis of the Lords by the Marquess of Carmarthen (formerly Danby).
(a) BL., Add. MS. 28091, f. 153.
(b) *Danby*, III, 173–6
(c) *Ibid.*

SECOND PARLIAMENT OF WILLIAM III, 1690–95

43. *6 Oct. 1690*, those for and those against discharging Earls of Peterborough and Salisbury from the Tower, with absentees; comments by Carmarthen opposite many of the names of those against.
(a) P.R.O., S.P. 8/8/2
(b) *Danby*, III, 179–81.
(c) *Ibid.*

44. *16 Dec. 1690*, marked MS. list of the committee on Earl of Ailesbury's Estate Bill.
(a) Wilts. R.O., 1300/856.

45. *20 Nov. 1691*, marked MS. list of the committee on Lord Ailesbury's Bill.
(a) Wilts. R.O., 1300/856.

46. *Mid Nov. 1692*, a list of 99 peers and 23 bishops headed 'A List of the Nobility now in Towne' (probably in the hand of a clerk of the House of Lords), with various markings; possibly an assessment by the Earl of Nottingham of pros, cons and doubtfuls in relation to the likely attack on him, as Secretary of State, over the failed descent on France.
(a) Leicestershire R.O., Finch papers, box 4960, P.P. 161.

47. *31 Dec. 1692*, those for and those against committing the Place Bill.
   (a) Wilts. R.O., 1300/856.
   (b) Cruickshanks *et al.*, 'Ten New Lists', pp. 81–7.
   (c) *Ibid.*, pp. 69–73, 76–80.

48. *31 Dec. 1692–2 Jan. 1693*, Lord Ailesbury's forecast for the Duke of Norfolk's Divorce Bill.
   (a) Wilts. R.O., 1300/856.
   (b) Cruickshanks *et al.*, 'Ten New Lists', pp. 81–7.
   (c) *Ibid.*, pp. 73–5, 76–80.

49. *2 Jan. 1693*, those for and those against the Duke of Norfolk's Divorce Bill.
   (a) Wilts. R.O., 1300/856.
   (b) Cruickshanks *et al.*, 'Ten New Lists', pp. 81–7.
   (c) *Ibid.*, pp. 73–5, 76–80.

50. *3 Jan. 1693*, those for and against passing the Place Bill, and those abstaining.
   (a) Wilts. R.O., 1300/856.
   (b) Cruickshanks *et al.*, 'Ten New Lists', pp. 81–7.
   (c) *Ibid.*, pp. 69–73, 76–80.

51. *25 Jan. 1693*, those bishops for and those bishops against committing the Bill to Prevent Dangers from Disaffected Persons.
   (a) Dr William's Lib. MS. 201.38 (Stillingfleet transcripts), f. 37, [Bishop Moore] to Bishop Stillingfleet, 26 Jan. [1693].

52. *4 Feb. 1693*, those voting Lord Mohun guilty and those voting him not guilty of murder.
   (a) H.L.R.O., Main papers, 11 Jan. 1693 (658e); Huntington Lib., MS. EL 9917.
   (b) H.M.C., *Lords MSS., 1692–3*, pp. 297–8; T.B. Howell, *A Complete Collection of State Trials* (33 vols., 1809–26), XII, 1048–9.

53. *17 Feb. 1694*, a division on the case of *Montague* v. *Bath*.
   (a) Wilts. R.O., 1300/856; Bodl. Lib., MS. Carte 79, f. 497. Variants.
   (b) Cruickshanks *et al.*, 'Ten New Lists', pp. 81–7, prints Wilts. R.O., 1300/856, which is incomplete; the division list in Carte 79 is a complete one.
   (c) Cruickshanks *et al.*, 'Ten New Lists', pp. 75–80.

THIRD PARLIAMENT OF WILLIAM III, 1695–8

54. *Feb.–Mar. 1696*, those who refused the Association at first.
   (a) *A Summary Account of the Proceedings Upon the Happy Discovery of the Jacobite Conspiracy, in a Second Letter to a Devonshire Gentleman* (1696); H.L.R.O., MS. minutes, 27 Feb., 31 Mar. 1696. Bodl. Lib., MS. Rawlinson D. 918, f. 150v, is a list of those who refused to sign 27–29 Feb.; another, though with some variations, is in Bodl. Lib., Alm. f. 1692. 1, commonplace book

of William Brome, interleaved in I. Abendana, *The Oxford Almanack for . . . 1692*. Beaufort MSS. (the Duke of Beaufort, Badminton House, Gloucestershire), 604.3.1(41), 'Lords and Commons non Associations' [*c.* 28–9 Feb. 1696] is incomplete.

(b) H.M.C., *Lords MSS.*, new ser. II, 205–13; H.M.C., *Portland MSS.*, III, 574; *Danby*, III, 188–94.

(c) *Danby*, III, 187–94.

55. *23 Dec. 1696*, those for and those against the attainder of Sir John Fenwick.
   (a) B.L., Add. MS. 17677 RR, ff. 172–3; Add. MS. 28252, f. 58; Add. MS. 47608, pt. 5, f. 138; Cornwall R.O., DDR (S) 1/1031 (Rashleigh papers), ff. 34–6; Magdalene College, Cambridge, Pepys Lib., PL 2180, pp. 11–12; Northants. R.O., Montagu (Boughton) papers, Vernon letters, I, f. 41; Bodl. Lib., Alm. f. 1692, 1, commonplace book of William Brome; St John's College, Oxford, MS. 297:2 (voting lists on 2nd and 3rd headings); Folger Shakespeare Lib., G. c. 12 (incomplete on Not Contents side). Variants.
   (b) Cobbett, *Parl. Hist.*, V, 1154–5.
   (c) Horwitz, *Parliament*, p. 335.

56. *15 Mar. 1698*, those for (marked '.') and those against (marked '-') the Bill for Punishing Charles Duncombe.
   (a) Northants. R.O., Ellesmere (Brackley) MS. 635.

FOURTH PARLIAMENT OF WILLIAM III, 1698–1700

57. *8 Feb., 1699*, those against the retention of the Dutch Guards.
   (a) Magdalene College, Cambridge, Pepys Lib., PL 2179, p. 85; Northants. R.O., Maunsell (TM) MS. 561/10.

58. *Feb. 1700*, forecast of those for (marked '+') and those against (marked '-') the East India Company Bill.
   (a) P.R.O., C.113/37.
   (b) C. Jones, '"A Fresh Division Lately Grown Up Among Us": Party Strife, Aristocratic Investment in the Old and New East India Companies and the Division of the House of Lords of 23 February 1700', *Historical Research*, LXVIII (1995).
   (c) *Ibid.*

59. *23 Feb. 1700*, division on the East India Company Bill.
   (a) P.R.O., C.113/37.
   (b) Jones, 'A Fresh Division'.
   (c) *Ibid.*

60. *After 10 July 1700*, marked printed list of the Parliament, 27 Oct. 1698, marking Whig Lords and differentiating possibly between loyal followers of the Junto and potential supporters of the new ministry.
   (a) B.L., Eg. MS. 3359, ff. 37–8.

FIFTH PARLIAMENT OF WILLIAM III, 1701

61. *17 June 1701*, those for and those against the impeachment of Lord Somers.
    (a) *The Several Proceedings and Resolutions of the House of Peers in Relation to the Lords Impeached or Charged* (1701); H.L.R.O., MS. minutes; B.L., Add. MS. 70268 (formerly Loan 29/163/61), 'Anno 1701. A List of all the Lords Spiritual and Temporall; Distinguishing which of them were absent from the Tryall of the Lord Sommers, and Earl of Orford; and which of them were not Content, and which of them were Content for the Acquittal of those Lords' (incomplete).
    (b) H.M.C., *Lords MSS.*, new ser., IV, 300, printed H.L.R.O. list.
    (c) Holmes, *British Politics*, pp. 36, 464, where reference is incorrectly given as Loan 29/160/1.

62. *23 June 1701*, those against the impeachment of Earl of Orford.
    (a) *The Several Proceedings and Resolutions of the House of Peers in Relation to the Lords Impeached or Charged* (1701); H.L.R.O., MS. minutes; B.L. Add. MS. 70268 (formerly Loan 29/163/61), 'Anno 1701. A List . . .' (incomplete).
    (b) H.M.C, *Lords MSS.*, new ser., IV, 300, prints H.L.R.O. list.
    (c) Holmes, *British Politics*, pp. 36, 434, where reference is incorrectly given as Loan 29/160/1.

FIRST PARLIAMENT OF ANNE, 1702–5

63. *20 Oct. 1702*, marked copy of a printed list of the Parliament (see below, House of Commons list 80).
    (a) B.L., Eg. MS. 3359, ff. 45–6.

64. *c. Jan. 1703*, Earl of Nottingham's estimate of support for and opposition to the Occasional Conformity Bill.
    (a) Northants. R.O., Finch-Hatton MS. 2900.
    (c) Snyder, 'Occasional Conformity', p. 187 n.1.

65. *16 Jan. 1703*, those for and those against the 'penalties amendment' to the Occasional Conformity Bill.
    (a) B.L., Blenheim papers (D.II.10) (this cannot now be found and may never have been transferred from Blenheim Palace; see above, p. xvii).
    (b) Snyder, 'Occasional Conformity', pp. 188–90.
    (c) *Ibid.*, pp. 175–6, 187–8.

66. *c. Nov. 1703*, forecast by Earl of Sunderland for the second Occasional Conformity Bill.
    (a) B.L., Add. MS. 61495, ff. 11–14 (formerly Blenheim MS. D.II.10).
    (b) Snyder, 'Occasional Conformity', pp. 188–9.
    (c) *Ibid.*, pp. 175–6, 187–8.

67. *c. 26 Nov.–8 Dec. 1703*, Sunderland's second forecast for the second Occasional Conformity Bill.
    (a) Blenheim Palace papers (the Duke of Marlborough, Blenheim Palace, Woodstock, Oxfordshire), VIII, 23 (see above, p. xvii).
    (c) Snyder, 'Occasional Conformity', pp.175–6, 190–2.

68. *14 Dec. 1703*, those for and those against the second Occasional Conformity Bill.
    (a) A. Boyer, *History of the Reign of Queen Anne, Digested into Annals* (11 vols., 1703–13), II, Appendix, pp. 27–9; and various. MS. variants are Cambridge Univ. Lib., MS. Mm.VI.42, ff. 22v-23; Carew papers (Sir Richard Carew Pole, Anthony House, Anthony, Cornwall), CZ/EE/13; and Lancashire R.O., DD Ke 82 (Kenyon papers). A printed variant is *List of the Lords Spiritual and Temporal, who Voted for and against the Bill of Occasional Conformity, to which also are Added the Proxies* (Cambridge, 1705).
    (b) Cobbett, *Parl. Hist.*, VI, 170–1.
    (c) Snyder, 'Occasional Conformity', pp. 191–2.

69. *Mid Mar. 1704*, list of lords and M.P.s, drawn up by Lord Nottingham, probably a forecast of support over the 'Scotch plot' (see below, Commons list no. 82).
    (a) Leics. R.O., Finch papers, box 4960, P.P. 161.

70. *Before 14 Apr. 1705*, analysis of the peerage 'in relation to the succession', classifying Hanoverians, Jacobites and those uncertain, and distinguishing Catholics.
    (a) B.L., Stowe MS. 224, ff. 331–2. Another copy is *ibid.*, 241, ff. 242–3.
    (b) J. Macpherson, *Original Papers: Containing the Secret History of Great Britian from the Restoration to the Accession of the House of Hanover* (2 vols., 1775), II, 643.

SECOND PARLIAMENT OF ANNE, 1705–8 (FIRST PARLIAMENT OF GREAT BRITAIN, 29 Apr. 1707–1708)

71. *4 Mar. 1707*, English lords voting for the rider to the Union Bill, that nothing in the bill should be construed as an approbation of Presbyterianism nor an acknowledgement that the religion of the Church of Scotland was 'the true protestant religion'.
    (a) Bodl. Lib., MS. Ballard 31, f. 61, William Bishop to Arthur Charlett, 17 Mar. 1707; three of 19 lords missing.

72. *1707*, analysis, by Earl of Marchmont, of the Scots representative peers in the First Parliament of Great Britain, into Court and Country, with a note of which peers influenced others.
    (a) Scottish R.O., GD 158/943 (Marchmont papers).

THIRD PARLIAMENT OF ANNE, 1708–10

73. *c. May 1708*, marked copy of a printed list of the First Parliament of Great
     Britain, with the returns at the 1708 election added in MS. (see below,
     Commons list no. 96).
     (a) *A True List of the Lords Spiritual and Temporal, Together with the Members of*
          the House of Commons Constituting the First Parliament of Great Britain . . .
          What Alterations Have Been Since Made to the 30th of March are Here
          Corrected: in private possession; photocopy in the possession of the
          History of Parliament Trust.

74. *21 Jan 1709*, those for and those against allowing Scots peers with British
     titles the right to vote in the election of representative peers.
     (a) Annandale papers (the Earl of Annandale, Raehills, Lockerbie, Dumfries-
          shire), (the original reference was, black japanned box no. 12, bundle
          'Annandale Papers, 1708': this collection has since been rearranged).
     (b) C. Jones, 'Godolphin, the Whig Junto and the Scots: A New Lords'
          Division List from 1709', *Scottish Historical Review*, LVIII (1979), 172–4.
     (c) *Ibid.*, pp. 158–72.

75. *15 Mar. 1709*, those bishops voting for and against committing the
     Naturalization Bill.
     (a) Tullie House, Carlisle, Bishop Nicolson's diary, 15 Mar. 1709 (Ware
          transcripts, XXIV, p. 111).
     (b) *Nicolson's London Diaries*, pp. 485–6.

76. *22 Mar. 1709*, those bishops voting in committee for and against an
     amendment to the Scottish Treason Bill.
     (a) Tullie House, Carlisle, Bishop Nicolson's diary, 22 Mar. 1709 (Ware
          transcripts, XXIV, pp. 115–6).
     (b) *Nicolson's London Diaries*, p. 488.

77. *25 Mar. 1709*, those bishops voting for and against resuming the House on
     the Scottish Treason Bill.
     (a) Bishop Nicolson's diary (in possession of the late Professor P.N.S.
          Mansergh's family), 25 Mar. 1709.
     (b) *Nicolson's London Diaries*, p. 489; 'Bishop Nicolson's Diaries: Part VI',
          ed. R.G. Collingwood, *Transactions of the Cumberland and Westmorland*
          Antiquarian and Archaeological Society, new ser., XXXV (1945), 83.

78. *?Early to mid Mar. 1710*, list of 53 peers and four bishops in the hand of
     Lord Nottingham; possibly a forecast of those likely to vote against Dr
     Sacheverell.
     (a) Leics. R.O., Finch papers, box 4960, P.P. 161.

79. *20 Mar. 1710*, those voting Dr Sacheverell guilty and not guilty of high
     crimes and misdemeanours, and those abstaining.
     (a) *The Tryal of Dr Henry Sacheverell before the House of Peers for High Crimes*
          and Misdemeanours (1710), pp. 451–2, and at least three variant printed
          lists. Manuscript variant copies are at B.L., Add. MS. 15574; Lancashire
          R.O., DDF 2439/9 (Farington of Worden papers); National Lib. Wales,

Bodewryd Corresp. 183, [Edward Wynne] to Margaret Wynne, 24 Mar. 1709 [/10]; Nat. Lib. Wales, Ottley MS. 1706; Cheshire R.O., Shakerley papers, DSS Drawer 3 (this collection is being rearranged).

(b) G. Holmes, *The Trial of Doctor Sacheverell* (1973), pp. 283–5; Holmes, *British Politics*, pp. 425–35.

(c) Holmes, *Trial*, p. 283 and Holmes, *British Politics*, pp. 36, 463.

80. *21 Mar. 1710*, those Scots representative peers who voted against the Court's proposal to incapacitate Dr Sacheverell from receiving further preferment during his suspension.
    (a) Bodl. Lib., MS. Carte 129, f. 445v.

81. *12 Sept. 1710*, list, in Robert Harley's hand, of 13 peers to be provided for.
    (a) B.L., Add. MS. 70333 (formerly Loan 29/10/19).
    (b) C. Jones, '"The Scheme Lords, the Neccessitous Lords, and the Scots Lords": The Earl of Oxford's Management and the "Party of the Crown" in the House of Lords, 1711–14', *Party and Management in Parliament, 1660–1784*, ed. C. Jones (Leicester, 1984), pp. 152–60.

FOURTH PARLIAMENT OF ANNE, 1710–13

82. *3 Oct. 1710*, analysis of the English lords by Robert Harley: those expected to support the ministry; Court Whigs and others doubtful; those considered certain to oppose.
    (a) B.L., Add. MS. 70333 (formerly Loan 29/10/19).
    (b) Jones, 'Scheme Lords', pp. 152–60.

83. *After 10 Nov. 1710*, analysis of the Scots representative peers in terms of their attitude to the succession and the Union.
    (a) B.L., Stowe MS., f. 20.

84. *11 Nov. 1710*, analysis of the Scots representative peers, into Court Tories, Episcopal Tories, and Presbyterian Court Tories.
    (a) Christ Church, Oxford, Wake MS. XVII, f. 269, Richard Dongworth to Bishop Wake, 11 Nov. 1710.
    (b) D. Szechi, 'Some Insights on the Scottish M.P.s and Peers Returned in the 1710 Election', *Scottish Historical Review*, LX (1981), 62–3.
    (c) *Ibid.*, pp. 61–2, 63, 66.

85. *25 Nov. 1710*, those Scots representative peers in the new Parliament who had been arrested during the invasion scare in 1708 as suspected Jacobites.
    (a) Bodl. Lib., MS. Carte 129, f. 445v.

86. *1710–11*, list of Tories in the first session of this Parliament.
    (a) *An Exact List of all those True English* [erased, 'Tory' substituted in MS.] *Patriots of the Honourable House of Commons of Great-Britain, that were for Easing the Nation of the Heavy Burden ane Taxes, by Puting an End to the Expensive and Bloody War* (1711): Kansas Univ., Kenneth A. Spencer

Research Lib., Dept. of Special Collections, 18th Century P19; photocopy in Institute of Historical Research.

(c) H.L. Snyder, 'A New Parliament List for 1711', *B.I.H.R.*, L (1977), 185–93.

87. *9 Jan. 1711*, those bishops voting for resuming the House on the state of the war in Spain.
    (a) Tullie House, Carlisle, Bishop Nicolson's diary, 9 Jan. 1711 (Ware Transcripts, XXVI, p. 10).
    (b) *Nicolson's London Diaries*, p. 531.

88. *c. Dec. 1711*, list, partly in the hand of Earl of Oxford (formerly Robert Harley); perhaps a calculation of support.
    (a) B.L., Add. MS. 70331 (formerly Loan 29/10/4).
    (b) Jones, 'Scheme Lords', pp. 152–60.

89. *?Dec. 1711*, list of 19 Whig peers, plus Nottingham and Godolphin, and four Whig bishops, in Nottingham's hand; possibly concerning Nottingham's alliance with the Whigs over the attack on the Tory peace policy, and/or the passing of the fourth Occasional Conformity Bill.
    (a) Leics. R.O., Finch papers, box 4960, P.P. 161.

90. *2 Dec. 1711*, list of 51 peers to be canvassed before the 'No Peace without Spain' motion.
    (a) B.L., Add. MS. 70332 (formerly Loan 29/10/16).
    (b) Jones, 'Scheme Lords', pp. 152–60.

91. *8 Dec. 1711*, an assessment of those against presenting the Address (vote confirming that of 7 Dec. on the 'No Peace without Spain' motion) in an abandoned division.
    (a) Bute (Loudoun) papers (the Marquess of Bute, Mount Stuart, Rothesay, Isle of Bute), bundle A 249.
    (b) C. Jones, 'The Division that Never Was: New Evidence on the Aborted Vote in the Lords on 8 December 1711 on "No Peace without Spain"', *Parliamentary History*, II (1983), 196–9; Jones, 'Scheme Lords', pp. 152–60.
    (c) Jones 'Division that Never Was', pp. 191–6.

92. *10 Dec. 1711*, list in Oxford's hand, of office-holders and pensioners who had voted against the ministry on the 'No Peace without Spain' motion, 7/8 Dec., with some suggested replacements, and a separate list, apparently of loyal peers to be rewarded (see below, Commons list no. 108).
    (a) B.L., Add. MS. 70332 (formerly Loan 29/10/16).
    (b) Jones, 'Scheme Lords', pp. 152–60.

93. *19 Dec. 1711*, forecast by Oxford for the division the next day on the Hamilton peerage case.
    (a) B.L., Add. MS. 70332 (formerly Loan 29/10/16).
    (b) Jones, 'Scheme Lords', pp. 152–60.

94. *19 Dec. 1711*, list compiled by Oxford, possibly a second forecast for the Hamilton peerage division.

(a) B.L., Add. MS. 70332 (formerly Loan 29/10/16).
(b)   Jones, 'Scheme Lords', pp. 152–60.

95. *20 Dec. 1711*, those for and those against disabling the Duke of Hamilton from sitting as an hereditary British peer, and those abstaining.
(a) B.L., Add. MS. 70269 (formerly Loan 29/163/10). Other copies are at Scottish R.O., GD 112/45/2 (Breadalbane papers); GD 220/5/256/23 (Montrose MSS.), enclosure in a letter from George Baillie to Montrose, 25 Dec. 1711; and also at Bute (Loudoun) papers, bundle A 253.
(b) Jones, 'Scheme Lords', pp. 152–60.
(c) Holmes, *British Politics*, pp. 36, 464.

96. *29 Dec. 1711*, list in Oxford's hand of lords to be contacted during the Christmas recess.
(a) B.L., Add. MS. 70332 (formerly Loan 29/10/16).
(b) Jones, 'Scheme Lords', pp. 152–60.

97. *15 Jan. 1712*, list of 15 'poor lords', together with the size of pension necessary to secure their allegiance.
(a) Niedersächsisches Staatsarchiv, Hanover, Cal.Br.24, England 109, f. 119, Bothmer to the Elector of Hanover, 15/26 Jan. 1712.
(b) E. Gregg and C. Jones, 'Hanover, Pensions and the "Poor Lords", 1712–13', *Parliamentary History*, I (1982), 176.
(c) *Ibid.*, pp. 173–6.

98. *26 Feb. 1712*, bishops voting for and against the Scottish Toleration Bill.
(a) Bodl. Lib., MS. Ballard 36, f. 122.

99. *12 Apr. 1712*, the four bishops who voted against committing the Ecclesiastical Patronage (Scotland) Bill.
(a) B.L., Trumbull Add. MS. 136, Ralph Bridges to Sir William Trumbull, 15 Apr. 1712.
(b) C. Jones, '"Party Rage and Faction" – The View from Fulham, Scotland Yard and the Temple: Parliament in the Letters of Thomas Bateman and John and Ralph Bridges to Sir William Trumbull, 1710–1714', *British Library Journal*, XIX (1993), 162.

100. *June/July 1712*, list of 22 lords, in Oxford's hand, possibly doubtful Court supporters.
(a) B.L., Add. MS. 70331 (formerly Loan 29/10/5).
(b) Jones, 'Scheme Lords', pp. 152–60.

101. *26 Feb. 1713*, list, in Oxford's hand, of lords he designed to canvass or contact before the forthcoming session.
(a) B.L., Add. MS. 70332 (formerly Loan 29/10/14).
(b) Jones, 'Scheme Lords', pp. 152–60.

102. *Mid Mar. to early Apr. 1713*, list, in Jonathan Swift's hand (with additions by Oxford), of lords expected to support the ministry and those expected to oppose.
(a) B.L., Add. MS. 70305 (formerly Loan 29/31/2).

(b) C. Jones, 'Swift, the Earl of Oxford, and the Management of the House of Lords in 1713: Two New Lists', *British Library Journal*, XVI (1990), 124–8.

(c) *Ibid.*, pp. 117–24.

103. *Late May 1713*, list, in Swift's hand, of 28 possibly doubtful supporters (plus 'Scotch peers').

(a) B.L., Add. MS. 70305 (formerly Loan 29/31/2).

(b) Jones, 'Swift . . . and the Management of the House of Lords', p. 128.

(c) *Ibid.*, pp. 117–24.

104. *c. 13 June 1713*, Oxford's estimate of voting on the French Commerce Bill.

(a) B.L., Add. MS. 70331 (formerly Loan 29/10/3).

(b) Jones, 'Scheme Lords', pp. 152–60.

(c) Holmes, *British Politics*, pp. 422–3.

105. *13 June 1713*, list of 12 Court supporters expected to desert over the French Commerce Bill.

(a) B.L., Add. MS. 70332 (formerly Loan 29/10/13).

(b) Jones, 'Scheme Lords', pp. 152–60.

(c) Holmes, *British Politics*, pp. 422–3.

106. *After July 1713*, list of 'poor lords', prepared for the Elector of Hanover, distinguishing between those who 'always will be right out of principle' and those who vote with the Court but may be bought over, and at what price.

(a) Niedersächsisches Staatsarchiv, Hanover, 91, Schutz, I, ff. 101–2.

(b) Gregg and Jones, 'Hanover, Pensions and the "Poor Lords"', pp. 176–7.

(c) *Ibid.*, pp. 173–6.

FIFTH PARLIAMENT OF ANNE, 1713–15

107. *1714–17*, list of seven peers endorsed 'Lds *etc.* pensions'.

(a) Camb. Univ. Lib., Cholmondeley (Houghton) MS. P. 53/49.

108. *Feb. 1714*, analysis of the 1713 election returns of Scots representative peers, distinguishing Jacobites and Hanoverians, sent by Lord Polwarth to Hanover, 9 Feb. 1714. (See below, Commons list no. 118.)

(a) B.L., Stowe MS. 226, ff. 121–3.

(b) J. Macpherson, *Original Papers: Containing the Secret History of Great Britain, from the Restoration, to the Accession of the House of Hanover* (2 vols., 1775), II, 560–1.

109. *27 May–c.4 June 1714*, Lord Nottingham's forecast for the Schism Bill.

(a) Leics. R.O., Finch papers, box 4960, P.P. 161.

(b) Jones, 'Scheme Lords', pp. 152–60.

(c) Holmes, *British Politics*, pp. 423–4.

110. *11 June 1714*, those bishops for and those bishops against the extension of
the Schism Bill to Ireland, and those absent.
    (a) Tullie House, Carlisle, Bishop Nicolson's diary, 11 June 1714 (Ware
        transcripts, XXX, 29).
    (b) *Nicolson's London Diaries*, pp. 612–3.
    (c) *Ibid.*, p. 607 n. 18.

111. *15 June 1714*, those bishops for and those bishops against the Schism Bill at
its third reading.
    (a) B.L., Add. MS. 70070 (formerly Loan 29/8), newsletter, 15 June 1714.
        Bodl. Lib., MS. Fol. θ 666, f. 68v is a later variant.
    (c) *Nicolson's London Diaries*, p. 607 n. 18.

112. *26 Jan. 1715*, list of Tory lords still in office (two bishops, 25 peers, and one
M.P., Lord Guernsey).
    (a) B.L., Add. 47028, f. 7.

FIRST PARLIAMENT OF GEORGE I, 1715–22.

113. *10–12 Mar. 1715*, analysis of the Parliament into Whigs and Tories, distinguishing 'Whimsicals' on either side.
    (a) *Flying Post*, 10–12 Mar. 1715. Also *An True and Correct List of the Lords
        Spiritual and Temporal . . .* (1715): copy in Huntington Lib., Rare Book
        Dept. 56928.
    (c) Snyder, 'Party Configurations', p. 52.

114. *9 Apr. 1715*, list of the peerage distinguishing between Whigs and Tories.
    (a) Scottish R.O., GD 220/6/1756/17.

115. *20–25 May 1717*, Lord Guilford's lobbying list for the committee on the
Brownlowe Estate Bill.
    (a) Bodl. Lib., MS. North b. 24, f. 93.

116. *c. 22 May 1717*, forecast by Oxford of supporters, opponents and those
doubtful, on the question as to whether his impeachment should be pro-
ceeded with.
    (a) B.L., Add. MS. 70345 (formerly Loan 29/1/2).
    (b) C. Jones, 'The Impeachment of the Earl of Oxford and the Whig Schism
        of 1717: Four New Lists', *B.I.H.R.*, LV (1982), 80–2.
    (c) *Ibid.*, pp. 70, 77–9.

117. *24 June 1717*, a division at Oxford's impeachment: those for and those
against proceeding with the articles for high crimes and misdemeanours
before judgment was given on the articles for high treason, and those
abstaining.
    (a) B.L., Eg. MS. 2543, ff. 398–9; B.L., Add. MS. 70088 (formerly Loan
        29/52 [two copies]); Royal Archives, Windsor Castle, Stuart papers 21/44;
        Harley papers (Mr Christopher Harley, Brampton Bryan Hall, Bucknell,

Shropshire; photocopy in Herefordshire R.O., C.64/117), bundle 117.
Variants.
(b) Jones, 'Impeachment of Oxford', pp. 80–7.
(c) *Ibid.*, pp. 73–5, 79.

118. *1 July 1717*, those for acquitting Lord Oxford of high treason and other crimes and misdemeanours.
(a) B.L., Add. MS. 70413 (formerly Loan 29/226/2); W. Marlwick, *The History of the Third Session of the Present Parliament with What Pass'd Most Remarkable at the Tryal of the Earl of Oxford* (1717), pp. 101–2. Variants.
(b) Jones, 'Impeachment of Oxford', pp. 80–7.
(c) *Ibid.*, p. 76.

119. *c. Nov. 1717*, list of lords summoned to the ministry's pre-sessional meeting.
(a) P.R.O., S.P. 35/10, f. 174.
(b) Jones, 'Impeachment of Oxford', pp. 80–7.
(c) J.C. Sainty, 'The Origins of the Leadership of the House of Lords', *B.I.H.R.*, XLVII (1974), 57, 67.

120. *5 Mar. 1718*, those bishops voting for appointing a date for a committee on the Bristol Workhouse Bill.
(a) Tullie House, Carlisle, Bishop Nicolson's diary, 5 Mar. 1718 (Ware transcripts, XXXII, 44).
(b) *Nicolson's London Diaries*, p. 679.

121. *10 Nov. 1718*, lords summoned to the ministry's pre-sessional meeting.
(a) P.R.O., S.P. 45/1; 35/13, f. 100. Two lists, the latter has various comments and marks.

122. *14 Dec. 1718*, list of bishops who attended a meeting with the ministers to settle the Bill for Repeal of the Schism and Occasional Conformity Acts (marked by Archbishop Wake on a printed list of those for and against the bill, see below, 126).
(a) Christ Church, Oxford, Wake MS. VIII, f. 89.

123. *19 Dec. 1718*, those for and those against the committing of the Bill for the Repeal of the Schism and Occasional Conformity Acts, with speakers on both sides marked.
(a) B.L., Add. MS. 47028, ff. 264v-65.

124. *19 Dec. 1718*, those bishops for and those bishops against committing the Bill for Repeal of the Schism and Occasional Conformity Acts.
(a) B.L., Add. MS. 70034 (formerly Loan 29/205, f. 48v), enclosure in Edward Harley *jr* to Abigail Harley, [?] 25 Dec. 1718; Nat. Lib. Wales, Ottley MSS. 2492, and 1704, Atterbury to Ottley, 3 Jan. 1719. Another copy only giving those bishops for is in Harley papers (Brampton Bryan Hall), bundle 117, folder 'odds and ends', F.P. Gwynn to Edward Harley *jr*, 27 Dec. 1718.

125. *23 Dec. 1718*, those bishops for and those bishops against the rider offered by Nottingham to the Bill for the Repeal of the Schism and Occasional Conformity Acts.
    (a) Harley papers (Brampton Bryan Hall; photocopy in Herefordshire R.O., C.64/117), bundle 117. Misdated as 22 Dec.

126. *Dec. 1718*, those for and those against the repeal of the Schism and Occasional Conformity Acts.
    (a) *A List of the Lords Spiritual and Temporal, who Voted for and against the Repeal of the Several Acts Made for the Security of the Church of England* [1718–19]. This is a composite list, giving the maximum strengths on each side; not a specific division. A marked copy is in Christ Church, Wake MS. VIII, f. 89 (see above, no. 122); another in Nat. Lib. Wales, Brogyntyn MS. 3446(a).

127. *3 Mar.–8 Apr. 1719*, analysis of the Scots peerage, recording attitudes to the Peerage Bill, and giving the votes of the representative peers (division of 3 Mar.).
    (a) B.L., Add. MS. 70269 (formerly Loan 29/163/10).
    (c) C. Jones, '"Venice Preserv'd; or A Plot Discovered": The Political and Social Context of the Peerage Bill of 1719', in *A Pillar of the Constitution: The House of Lords in British Politics, 1640–1784*, ed. C. Jones (1989), pp. 87 n. 32, 97.

128. *1720*, marked list of the House of Lords.
    (a) Huntington Lib., Rare Books Dept., HEH 280409.

129. *16 May 1721*, those voting for and against the college garden being a proper place for the dormitory of Westminster School in the case of *The Dean of Westminster* v. *The Attorney General*.
    (a) B.L., Harleian MS. 7190, f. 310.
    (b) C. Jones, 'Jacobites under the Beds: Bishop Atterbury of Rochester, the Earl of Sunderland, and the New Dormitory for Westminster School in 1721', *British Library Journal*, (forthcoming).
    (c) *Ibid.*

130. *24 May 1721*, those lords voting in favour of the reversing the decree in the cause of *Marlborough* v. *Strong*.
    (a) B.L., Add. MS. 61356, f. 103 (formerly Blenheim papers F.I.24).
    (b) F. Harris, 'Parliament and Blenheim Palace: The House of Lords Appeal of 1721', *Parliamentary History*, VIII (1989), 58.
    (c) *Ibid.*

131. *Mid Oct. 1721*, Tory lords and sympathisers summoned to the new session on 19 Oct., and those lords and M.P.s responsible for approaching them.
    (a) P.R.O., S.P. 35/40/423–4.
    (b) C. Jones, 'The New Opposition in the House of Lords, 1720–23', *Hist. Jnl.*, XXXVI (1993), 328–9.
    (c) *Ibid.*, p. 314.

132. *26 Oct. 1722*, those against sending the Duke of Norfolk to the Tower.
    (a) Lancs. R.O., DDSt (Weld of Stonyhurst papers), 'Correspondence relating to the imprisonment of the Duke of Norfolk in the Tower, 1722–3'. One lord missing.

133. *14 Mar. 1723*, list of lords summoned to the ministry's pre-sessional meeting.
    (a) P.R.O., S.P. 35/42, f. 200.

134. *8 Jan. 1724*, list of lords summoned to the ministry's pre-sessional meeting.
    (a) P.R.O., S.P. 35/48, ff. 14–16.

135. *19 Jan. 1726*, list of lords summoned to the ministry's pre-sessional meeting.
    (a) P.R.O., S.P. 45/7, f. 22.

FIRST PARLIAMENT OF GEORGE II, 1727–34

136. *26 June 1727*, list of lords summoned to the ministry's pre-sessional meeting.
    (a) P.R.O., S.P. 45/7, f. 21.

137. *19 Sept. 1727*, list headed, 'Remarks on Dr Chetwind's List of pensions' (14 peers named).
    (a) Cambridge Univ. Lib., Cholmondeley (Houghton) MS. P. 53/24.

138. *18 Mar. 1729*, partial list of 20 (out of 31) lords who voted Content on the resolution concerning the Spanish claim to Gibraltar.
    (a) Royal Archives, S.P. 126/20, copy of Lords protest with the 17 protesters and three extra names added.

139. *12 May 1729*, partial list of 17 (out of 19) lords who voted with the minority on the Corn Bill.
    (a) Royal Archives, S.P. 128/31A, copy of Lords protest with the 14 protesters and three extra names added.

140. *12 Jan. 1730*, list of lords summoned to the ministry's pre-sessional meeting.
    (a) P.R.O., S.P. 45/1.

141. *27 Jan. 1730*, lords voting against the Treaty of Seville (list of 24 protesters plus seven others 'that Voted and did not sign the Protests').
    (a) B.L., Add. MS. 22263, f. 119.

142. *Jan.–Mar. 1730*, a set of calculations; lords 'for', 'against', 'doubtful', and 'absent'; and those 'to be spoke to', with the names of persons through whom they were to be approached.
    (a) P.R.O, S.P. 36/22, ff. 142–6.

143. *20 Jan. 1731*, list of lords summoned to the ministry's pre-sessional meeting (subsequently annotated with 104 numbers to indicate who attended).
    (a) P.R.O., S.P. 45/1.

144. *2 Mar. 1731*, forecast for the vote on the Pension Bill, subsequently annotated to form a slightly incomplete division list.
    (a) P.R.O., S.P. 36/22, ff. 140–1.

145. *2 Mar. 1731*, those for and those against the Pension Bill.
    (a) B.L., Add. MS. 33033, ff. 245–6.

146. *6 May 1731*, those for and those against the clause in the Woollen Bill removing the duty on Irish yarn (Not Contents incomplete).
    (a) B.L., Add. MS. 47061, f. 22v.
    (b) H.M.C., *Egmont Diary*, I, 189–90.

147. *12 Jan. 1732*, lords summoned to the ministry's pre-sessional meeting.
    (a) P.R.O., S.P. 45/1: two lists, one of which notes certain absentees, and has other marks: '+' indicates those who were summoned, a number indicates those 107 who attended.

148. *1 Feb. 1732*, list of 13 lords with names against them, probably of those who might influence them: endorsed, 'Parlt. List' (possibly a whipping list for the Pension Bill).
    (a) P.R.O., S.P. 45/1.

149. *c. 10 Feb. 1732*, list of lords, grouped under 'Sir Robert Walpole' and 'Myself'; possibly a whipping list for the Pension Bill.
    (a) P.R.O, S.P. 45/1.

150. *17 Feb. 1732*, those for and those against the Pension Bill.
    (a) B.L., Add. MS. 33033, ff. 240–1.

151. *12/15 Jan. 1733*, lords summoned to the ministry's pre-sessional meeting.
    (a) P.R.O., S.P. 45/1: two lists, one of which notes certain absentees, and has other marks (i.e. those contacted).

152. *3 May 1733*, those for and those against laying down before the House the accounts of the South Sea Company.
    (a) Royal Archives, S.P. 162/81, Nathaniel Mist to James Edgar, 12 June 1733.
    (b) Cobbett, *Parl. Hist.*, IX, 106.

153. *24 May 1733*, those for and those against Newcastle's motion to examine a witness on the South Sea Company's affairs.
    (a) *A List of the Lords Spiritual and Temporal, who Voted for, or against, an Enquiry into the Frauds of the South-Sea Company*, appended to a printed list of those for, against and absent in a Commons division on the Excise Bill, headed *The List* [1733]; noting placemen: copies in B.L., Dept. of Printed Books, 1865. c.16. (22.), and B.L., Eg. MS. 2543, f. 410. Royal Archives, S.P. box 1/112, lists proxy voters and those who 'deserted over to the Court on the last question [i.e. on South Sea Company on 1 June'] (see below no. 155).
    (b) Cobbett, *Parl. Hist.*, IX, 115.

154. *24 May–1 June 1733*, marked list of lords 'against' and 'absent'; probably with reference to a division on the enquiry into the affairs of the South Sea Company.
   (a) Cambridge Univ. Lib., Cholmondeley (Houghton) MS. P. 66/5.
   (b) J.H. Plumb, *Sir Robert Walpole* (2 vols., 1972), II, 277 n. 2.
   (c) *Ibid.*

155. *1 June 1733*, those for and those against censuring the directors of the South Sea Company, including proxy votes: incomplete.
   (a) Cambridge Univ. Lib., Cholmondeley (Houghton) MS. Corresp. 1990, Newscastle to Walpole, 2 June 1733. Royal Archives, S.P. box 1/112 lists deserters to the Court from the 24 May 1733 vote (see above no. 153).
   (c) Plumb, *Walpole*, II, 277 n. 2.

156. *Early Jan. 1734*, a forecast, subsequently annotated.
   (a) B.L., Add. MS. 33002, ff. 420–1.

157. *Before 16 Jan. 1734*, list of lords summoned to the ministry's pre-sessional meeting.
   (a) B.L., Add. MS. 32993, ff. 36–7; Add. MS. 33002, ff. 409–10. Variants; the latter has some additional markings.

158. *16 Jan. 1734*, list of lords who attended the ministry's pre-sessional meeting.
   (a) B.L., Add. MS. 32993, f. 38.

159. *Before 13 Feb. 1734*, a forecast, subsequently annotated as an incomplete division for 13 Feb. 1734.
   (a) B.L., Add. MS. 33002, ff. 430–1.

160. *13 Feb. 1734*, those for and those against (including proxies) the Duke of Marlborough's Bill for the prevention of army officers being deprived of their commissions other than by court martial or an address of Parliament.
   (a) Scottish R.O., GD 220/5/887/16–17; B.L., Add., MS. 33002, ff. 430–1.

SECOND PARLIAMENT OF GEORGE II, 1734–41

161. *14 Jan. 1736*, list of lords summmoned to the ministry's pre-sessional meeting.
   (a) P.R.O., S.P. 36/38, ff. 62–4.

162. *12 May 1736*, those for and those against committing the Quakers' Tithe Bill.
   (a) *An Account of the Proceedings and Debates on the Tithes Bill . . . To Which is Added, A List of Those Peers Who Were For and Against Committing the Said Bill* (1737): copy in Huntington Lib., Rare Book Dept. HEH 255508.
   (b) Cobbett, *Parl. Hist.*, IX, 1219–20.

163. *Late (?31) Jan. 1737*, list of lords summoned to the ministry's pre-sessional meeting.
 (a) P.R.O., S.P. 36/38, ff. 62–4 (the 1736 list with minor alterations: see above no. 161).

164. *19 Feb. 1739*, five peers who voted that the directors of the South Sea Company do attend the House of Lords, and who on 1 Mar. 1739 voted for the Address on the Spanish Convention.
 (a) *The Protests for the Year 1739 to Which is Added, a List of the Peers who Voted against the Address to Approve the Convention March the 1st, 1738–9. Also of Those Who Voted for the Enquiry, Yet Voted for the Address* [1739], p. 5: copy in Huntington Lib., Rare Books Dept. HEH 329585, and P.R.O., S.P. 36/47/143–6.

165. *Late Feb. 1739*, forecast for the vote on the Spanish Convention of 1 March 1739, subsequently annotated for the division.
 (a) B.L., Add. MS. 35876, ff. 37–8; P.R.O., S.P. 36/47/113–14. Variants.

166. *1 Mar. 1739*, those for and those against the Address on the Spanish Convention.
 (a) Blenheim Palace papers, VIII, 23; another copy in B.L., M/687 (microfilm of letters of Sarah, Duchess of Marlborough to Earl of Stair, originals in Osborne Collection, Yale University); B.L., Add. MS. 35876, ff. 37–8; P.R.O., S.P. 36/47/112, 115; Scottish R.O., GD 158/1229, f. 79: list of minority who did not sign the protest. Printed versions are as above, no. 164; and *An Authentick List of the House of Peers: As They Voted for and against the Convention. Wherein is Shown, How Large a Sum is Visibly Paid Yearly to Several Noble Lords, besides the Secret Favours that may be Conferr'd on them, their Relations and Friends* (1739): B.L., Dept. of Printed Books, 8138. eee. 16. (4.); *An Exact List of the Lords, Spiritual and Temporal; Who Voted For and Against the Late Convention . . .* [1739]: copy in National Lib. Scotland, SPA 2. Variants.
 (b) C. Jones and F. Harris, '"A Question . . . Carried by Bishops, Pensioners, Placemen, Idiots": Sarah, Duchess of Marlborough and the Lords' Division over the Spanish Convention, 1 March 1739', *Parliamentary History*, XI (1992), 270–77.
 (c) *Ibid.*

165. *Late Feb. 1739*, forecast for the vote on the Spanish Convention of 1 Mar. Spanish Convention.
 (a) Cumbria R.O. (Kendal), D/Sen. Fleming/9 (Senhouse papers, George Fleming's diary); *The Protests for the Year One Thousand Seven Hundred Thirty Nine. To Which Is Added, a List of the Peers who Voted against an Address to Approve the Convention, March the 1st, 1738–9 . . .* [1740], p. 5: copy in Huntington Lib., Rare Book Dept., HEH 329585.
 (c) Jones and Harris, '"A Question . . . Carried by Bishops"', pp. 266–9.

168. *Mid. Dec. 1740*, a forecast.
 (a) B.L., Add. MS. 33002, ff. 407–8.

169. *28 Jan. 1741*, forecast of voting: those 'for', 'against' and those 'doubtful' (subsequently annotated for the division of 13 Feb. 1741; see below, no. 171).
    (a) B.L., Add. MS. 33034, ff. 1–3.

170. *c. Jan.–Feb. 1741*, ? list of 16 peers to be canvassed in support of the ministry.
    (a) B.L., Add. MS. 33002, f. 404.

171. *13 Feb. 1741*, those for and those against the motion for an address to the King to remove Walpole.
    (a) B.L., Add. MSS. 33034, ff. 1–3, 21–4; 35876, ff. 86–7 (also includes those who did not vote); 47000, ff. 111–12 (lists those 'neuter'); *A True and Exact List of the Lords Spiritual and Temporal, Also of the Knights Commissioners of Shires, Citizens and Burgesses, Chosen to Serve In the Parliament of Great Britain Summoned to Meet . . . the 25th Day of June 1741 . . . Distinguishing Marks at Each, to Know . . . Those Members . . . of the House of Peers who Voted for and against the Address to Remove a Certain Great Man* (1741), also marking those who were 'neuter', and distinguishing peers whose titles were created after the Revolution: B.L., Dept. of Printed Books, 8132. aa. 15. (4.).

THIRD PARLIAMENT OF GEORGE II, 1741–7

172. *After 8 Jan. 1742*, a forecast, subsequently annotated.
    (a) B.L., Add. MS. 33002, ff. 400–1.

173. *19 Jan. 1742*, those for and those against the motion to appoint a date for a Committee of the Whole House on the state of the nation.
    (a) B.L., Add. MS. 33034, f. 71.

174. *1 Feb. 1743*, those in favour of an address against the Hanoverian troops.
    (a) *A List of the Members of Parliament who Voted for and against Taking the Hanover Troops into British Pay, December 10, 1742. To Which is Added, The Lords Protest . . .* (1742[-3]). p. [23], omitting Lord Sandwich: copy in Huntington Lib. Rare Book Dept. 330535. The B.L. copy of this pamphlet (Dept. of Printed Books, 8132. a. 41.) lacks the Lords division list.

175. *1 Feb. 1743*, those who voted for the first question and against the second and who did not protest on the Hanoverian troops (nine lords).
    (a) Cambridge Univ. Lib., Add. MS. 6851 (Edward Harley's journal), vol. 2, f. 63.

176. *22 Feb. 1743*, those bishops against the second reading of the Spirituous Liquors Bill.
    (a) B.L., Add. MS. 6043 (Bishop Secker's diary), f. 162.
    (b) Cobbett, *Parl. Hist.*, XII, 1300–1.

177. *16 Apr. 1744*, those nine lords who voted against the reversal of judgment in the case of *Le Havre* v. *Norris*.
     (a) Cambridge Univ. Lib., Add. MS. 6851, vol. 2, f. 79.

178. *2 May 1746*, those 26 lords who voted for the question on the war in Flanders.
     (a) Cambridge Univ. Lib., Add. MS. 6851, vol. 2, ff. 108–9.

FOURTH PARLIAMENT OF GEORGE II, 1747–54

179. *1747*, 'List of Lords and Commons in opposition'.
     (a) Bodl. Lib., MS. D.D. Dashwood D1/3/13.

180. *24 May 1747*, those 16 lords who voted against the committing of the Heritable Jurisdiction Bill.
     (a) Cambridge Univ. Lib., Add. MS. 6851, vol. 2, ff. 118–9.

181. *1748*, 55 'Lords absent' (some listed with proxies against their names), and nine listed as 'Some Lord against': management list for the Buckingham Assizes Bill.
     (a) B.L., Add. MS. 33002, f. 411r.

182. *23 Mar. 1748*, those for and those against committing the Buckingham Assizes Bill.
     (a) B.L., Add. MS. 33002, ff. 411v-12.

183. *10 May 1748*, 32 lords who voted against the clause relating to episcopal order during the Committee of the Whole House on the Bill for Disarming the Scottish Highlands.
     (b) Cobbett, *Parl. Hist.*, XIV, 272.

184. *15 Mar. 1749*, those 16 lords who voted for the clause in the second reading of the Mutiny Bill that no punishment should be inflicted by a court martial relating to life and limb.
     (a) Cambridge Univ. Lib., Add. MS. 6851, vol. 2, ff. 130–1.

185. *20 Mar. 1750*, list of 28 lords who met at Newcastle House.
     (a) B.L., Add. MS. 32994, f. 272.

186. *10 May 1751*, those 12 lords voting against the clause giving the Regent a council in the Regency Bill.
     (b) Horace Walpole, *The Memoirs of King George II*, ed. J. Brooke (New Haven, 3 vols., 1985), I, 78–9.

187. *17 Mar. 1752*, those 12 lords who voted against committing the Forfeitures (Scotland) Bill.
     (a) B.L., Add. MS. 32994, f. 295.

188. *22 Mar. 1753*, the five lords who were to have voted in the abandoned division against Stone and Murray.
    (a) Harrowby papers (the Earl of Harrowby, Sandon Hall, Shropshire), Vol. 430, S.H. ser., Doc. 27, pt. 2b, p. 48 (Sir Dudley Ryder's diaries, 1739–56).
    (b) Walpole, *Memoirs of King George II*, I, 223.

189. *3 Mar. 1754*, lords in favour of the second reading of the Clandestine Marriages Bill.
    (a) B.L., Add. MS. 35877, f. 174.

FIFTH PARLIAMENT OF GEORGE II, 1754–61

190. *30 May 1754*, list of lords summoned to the ministry's pre-sessional meeting.
    (a) B.L., Add. MS. 32995, ff. 242–5.

191. *13 Nov. 1754*, list of lords summoned to the ministry's pre-sessional meeting.
    (a) B.L., Add. MS., 32995, ff. 344–7.

192. *12 Nov. 1755*, list of lords summoned to the ministry's pre-sessional meeting.
    (a) B.L., Add. MS. 32996, ff. 275–9.

193. *10 Dec. 1755*, those in favour of agreeing with the resolution on the treaties with Russia and Hesse-Cassel.
    (a) Huntington Lib., MS. HA 8312, Theophilus Lindsey to Lord Huntingdon, 24 Dec. 1755.
    (b) H.M.C., *Hastings MSS.*, III, 113.

194. *24 May 1756*, those against the Militia Bill, and those who 'went away'.
    (a) B.L., Add. MS. 35877, f. 308.

195. *Dec. 1756/Jan. 1757*, analysis of the House, divided into 'for' and 'against', with some queries (Newcastle management list while in opposition to the Pitt–Devonshire administration).
    (a) B.L., Add. MS. 33034, ff. 214–15.

196. *29 Nov. 1757*, list of lords summoned to the ministry's pre-sessional meeting.
    (a) B.L., Add. MS. 32997, ff. 300–3.

197. *1757*, list of peer pensioners in 'the Old Book', 9 July 1755 – 9 Nov. 1757.
    (a) B.L., Add. MS. 32997, f. 64.

198. *1757*, list of peer pensioners in the 'New Book', since 20 July 1757.
    (a) B.L., Add. MS. 32997, f. 237.

199. *1757*, list of peer pensioners 'in Old Book who have not yet been paid in New One'.
    (a) B.L., Add. MS. 32997, f. 332.

200. *1757*, list of peer pensioners 'whose private payments have lately ceas'd'.
    (a) B.L., Add. MS. 32997, f. 332.

201. *9 May 1758*, analysis of lords present (management list for the Habeas Corpus Bill).
    (a) B.L., Add. MS. 33034, ff. 265–6.

202. *9 May 1758*, list of lords absent, with some distinguishing marks (management list for the Habeas Corpus Bill).
    (a) B.L., Add. MS. 33034, ff. 259–60.

203. *24 May 1758*, analysis of the lords, divided into 'For', 'Against', 'Doubtful' and 'Absent' (management list for the Habeas Corpus Bill).
    (a) B.L., Add. MS. 33034, ff. 267–9.

204. *31 May 1758*, analysis of the lords, divided into 'For', 'Against', 'Doubtful' and 'Absent' (management list for the Habeas Corpus Bill).
    (a) B.L., Add. MS. 33034, ff. 314–16.

205. *?2 June 1758*, those lords for and those against the Habeas Corpus Bill.
    (a) B.L., Add. MS. 33034, f. 317.

206. *22 Nov. 1758*, list of lords summoned to the ministry's pre-sessional meeting.
    (a) B.L., Add. MS. 32998, ff. 187–94.

207. *12 Nov. 1759*, list of lords summoned to the ministry's pre-sessional meeting.
    (a) B.L., Add. MS. 32998, ff. 327–34.

208. *17 Apr. 1760*, those lords who voted the Earl Ferrers guilty of murder.
    (b) T.B. Howell, *A Complete Collection of State Trials.* (33 vols., 1809–26), XIX, 955–6.

209. *15 May 1760*, those against committing the Commons Qualification Bill.
    (a) B.L., Add. MS. 33034, f. 373.

210. *17 Nov. 1760*, list of lords summoned to the ministry's pre-sessional meeting.
    (a) B.L., Add. MS. 32999, ff. 80–7.

211. *17 Nov, 1760*, list of lords 'omitted in the great list [? list 210, above]'.
    (a) B.L., Add. MS. 32999, ff. 88–9.

212. *17 Nov. 1760*, list of 81 lords who attended the pre-sessional meeting.
    (a) B.L., Add. MS. 32999, ff. 90–1.

FIRST PARLIAMENT OF GEORGE III, 1761–68

213. *2 Nov. 1761*, list of 194 lords summoned to the ministry's pre-sessional meeting at Newcastle's house on 5 Nov. 1761; five lords are marked 'absent', 57 are marked 'out of town' and one is marked 'out of England'.

(a) B.L., Add. MS. 32999, ff. 341–8, with draft at ff. 334–40.

(b) The 26 bishops summoned, including the nine marked 'out of town', are listed in S. Taylor, 'The Bishops at Westminster in the Mid-Eighteenth Century', in *Pillar of Constitution*, pp. 159–60.

(c) W.C. Lowe, 'The Parliamentary Career of Lord Dunmore, 1761–1774', *Virginia Magazine of History and Biography*, XCVI (1988), 10.

214. *5 Nov. 1761*, list of the 81 lords who attended the pre-sessional meeting.
   (a) B.L., Add. MS. 32930, ff. 335–6.

215. *5 Feb. 1762*, list of the minority of 16 lords who voted for the Duke of Bedford's resolution for an end to the war in Germany.
   (a) B.L., Add MS. 33035, ff. 69, 71, with duplicate at Add. MS. 35878, f. 338; Hampshire R.O., Malmesbury papers (Harris diary).
   (b) William Cavendish, 4th Duke of Devonshire, *Memoranda on State of Affairs, 1759–1762*, eds. P.D. Brown and K.W. Schweizer (Camden 4th ser., XXVII, 1982), p. 157.
   (c) Lowe, thesis, pp. 399–400, 975; M.W. McCahill, 'The House of Lords in the 1760s', in *Pillar of Constitution*, pp. 168–9.

216. *26 Aug. 1762*, list of 189 lords, giving 85 'for' and 104 'against'.
   (a) B.L., Add. MS. 33000, ff. 107–9, with draft at ff. 103–5.
   (c) Namier, *Age of American Revolution*, pp. 361–3.

217. *20 Sept. 1762*, list of 193 lords, giving 73 'sure', 36 'doubtful', 79 'against' and five 'omitted'.
   (a) B.L., Add. MS. 33000, ff. 113–15.
   (c) Namier, *Age of American Revolution*, pp. 362–3.

218. *24 Sept. 1762*, list of 190 lords, giving 73 'sure', 34 'doubtful' and 83 'against'.
   (a) B.L., Add. MS 33000, ff. 118–9.
   (c) Namier, *Age of American Revolution*, pp. 362–3.

219. *24 Nov. 1762*, list of 16 bishops present (three of them indicated as 'with us') at, and ten absent from, the pre-sessional meeting 'at Ld. Egremont's'; the document adds that 'in all' 94 persons were present, but does not state whether or not they were all members of the House of Lords.
   (a) B.L., Add. MS 33000, ff. 173–4.

220. *30 Nov. 1762*, list of 37 lords 'to be spoke to'.
   (a) B.L., Add. MS. 33000, f. 177.

221. *30 Nov. 1762*, list of 'Lords who should meet together, upon any business, in the House of Lords, particularly those thus mark'd X'. 13 lords are listed; 10 of them are marked 'X'.
   (a) B.L., Add. MS. 33000, f. 183.

222. *6 Dec. 1762*, list of 162 lords, giving 51 'for', 109 'against' and two 'doubtful'.
   (a) B.L., Add. MS. 33000, ff. 217–8.
   (c) Namier, *Age of American Revolution*, pp. 362–3.

223. *18 Dec. 1762*, list of 44 lords named as 'sure friends'.
  (a) B.L., Add. MS. 33000, f. 239, with draft at f. 238.
  (b) P. Woodland, 'The House of Lords, the City of London and Political Controversy in the mid-1760s: The Opposition to the Cider Excise Further Considered', *Parliamentary History*, XI (1992), 79–81.
  (c) Namier, *Age of American Revolution*, pp. 362–3.

224. *28 Jan. 1763*, list of 16 lords 'to be constantly consulted & connected together'.
  (a) B.L., Add. MS. 32946, f. 230, with draft (dated 'Claremont, 17 Jan. 1763') at ff. 136–7; there is a copy at Chatsworth, 182.316 (4th Duke of Devonshire's papers).
  (b) P. Woodland, 'Opposition to Cider Excise Further Considered', pp. 79–81.
  (c) *Ibid.*, p. 60.

225. *28 Mar. 1763*, list of 40 of the minority of 41 lords who voted against the committal of the Cider Bill.
  (a) B.L. Add. MS. 32947, f. 337. Though 41 lords voted in the minority, Newcastle's list names only the 40 who did so in person (the other minority lord was Jersey, whose proxy was held by Newcastle). There is a list of nine absentees at f. 337 and a list of nine bishops 'for', 11 'against', five 'absent' and one 'went away' at f. 339; there is a list of the nine bishops in the minority in Hants. R.O., Malmesbury papers (Harris diary). W.W.M., R81/53, sometimes described as 'Rockingham's list', is an annotated presence list for 28 Mar. 1763 in which 50 lords are listed, 40 being marked 'X' (Woodland in (c) below, p. 83, puts the figure at 38) and ten being marked 'O'. Woodland's suggestion is that those marked 'X' formed the bulk of the minority vote and that those marked 'O' abstained from voting.
  (b) Debrett, *History, Debates and Proceedings*, IV, 139n.–140n.; Hardy, thesis, Appendix H; Woodland, 'Opposition to Cider Excise Further Considered', pp. 79–81, with a reconstructed list of the majority at pp. 84–6.
  (c) Lowe, thesis, pp. 975–6; Lowe, 'Bishops and Representative Peers', p. 91; McCahill, 'The House of Lords in the 1760s', in *Pillar of Constitution*, pp. 169–70; Woodland, 'Opposition to Cider Excise Further Considered', pp. 82–3; Farrell, thesis, pp. 49–50.

226. *30 Mar. 1763*, list of 43 lords who might have voted against the third reading of the Cider Bill.
  (a) *Annual Reg.* for 1763, p. 153; J. Almon, *The History of the Late Minority* (1765), p. 119. Each lists 43 lords although only 39 voted against the bill.
  (b) Cobbett, *Parl. Hist.*, XV, 1316; Hardy, thesis, Appendix H; Woodland, 'Opposition to Cider Excise Further Considered', pp. 79–81, with a reconstructed list of the majority at pp. 84–6.
  (c) Hardy, thesis, Appendix H; Lowe, thesis, pp. 449, 976–7; Woodland, 'Opposition to Cider Excise Further Considered', pp. 82–4.

227. *2 Apr. 1763*, list of 58 lords, 'adding those who were absent to those who may be depended upon in the last two Divisions' by the opposition.

(a) B.L. Add. MS. 32948, ff. 9–10, with draft at ff. 7–8.

(b) Woodland, 'Opposition to Cider Excise Further Considered', pp. 79–81, names 47 of these lords.

(c) *Ibid.*, pp. 82–3.

228. *19 Apr. 1763*, list of 41 'Sure friends' of the Duke of Newcastle in the House of Lords.

    (a) B.L., Add. MS. 32948, ff. 155–6, with duplicate at ff. 157–8.

    (b) Woodland, 'Opposition to Cider Excise Further Considered', pp. 79–81, using a somewhat different calculation, gives 44 lords. O'Gorman, *Rise of Party*, pp. 481–2, prints a list of 41 lords who voted against this bill and gives its source as B.L., Add. MS. 32948, ff. 155–8, but there are serious discrepancies between that document and O'Gorman's printed version.

    (c) Woodland, 'Opposition to Cider Excise Further Considered', p. 82.

229. *5 Oct. 1763*, list of 53 lords, with 46 'thought to be sure' and seven 'Queries'.

    (a) B.L., Add. MS. 32951, ff. 299–300, with draft at ff. 297–8; there is a copy (unannotated) at Chatsworth, 182.359 (4th Duke of Devonshire's papers).

230. *29 Nov. 1763*, list of the minority of 35 lords who voted against the Commons' resolution on parliamentary privilege.

    (a) B.L., Add. MS. 32953, ff. 109, 111; at f. 1 is a list of 46 lords 'thought to be sure', dated 22 Nov., and with marks to indicate their voting on 29 Nov. There is a list of ten lords who did not protest (as well as the 17 who did) on the Commons' resolution on parliamentary privilege in Hants. R.O., Malmesbury papers (Harris diary).

    (b) *Selections from the Family Papers Preserved at Caldwell. In Two Parts*, ed. W. Mure (Maitland Club, XXI, 3 vols., Glasgow, 1854), I, pt. 2, 206–7; Hardy, thesis, Appendix I; O'Gorman, *Rise of Party*, p. 516 n. 46. O'Gorman, using Newcastle's list, incorrectly includes Strafford as Stratford.

    (c) Lowe, thesis, pp. 477–8, 977–8, where the MS. number is incorrectly given as 31953.

231. *9 Feb. 1764*, list of 106 members of Wildman's Club, including 22 lords.

    (a) B.L., Add. MS. 32955, ff. 409–10. There is a more extensive list, including 23 lords, in Add. MS. 33000, ff. 360–1 and in J. Almon, *The History of the Late Minority* (1765), pp. 298–300.

    (b) Hardy, thesis, Appendix G; Woodland, 'Opposition to Cider Excise Further Considered', pp. 79–81.

    (c) O'Gorman, *Rise of Party*, p. 82; D.H. Watson, 'The Rise of the Opposition at Wildman's Club', *B.I.H.R.*, XLIV (1971), 65–6.

232. *21 Apr. 1764*, list of ten lords and 46 M.P.'s, endorsed 'Note to be sent'.

    (a) B.L., Add. MS. 33000, ff. 339–400.

233. *24 Apr. 1764*, list headed 'Note to be sent to'; 24 lords and 102 M.P.s are listed.

    (a) B.L., Add. MS. 33000, ff. 341–3.

234. *31 Jan. 1765*, list of 23 lords 'to be sent to, about Genl. Conway's affair'.
    (a) B.L., Add. MS. 33000, f. 374.

235. *27 Feb. 1765*, list of 54 lords, 43 'sure', 11 'doubtful', 'On the dismission of officers'.
    (a) B.L., Add. MS. 33000, f. 379.

236. *28 Mar. 1765*, list of 44 of the minority of 50 lords who opposed the motion to commit the Poor Bill.
    (a) B.L., Add. MS. 32966, f. 129; W.W.M., R53-22 lists 43 of the minority.
    (c) Lowe, thesis, pp. 504–5, 978–9.

237. *30 Mar. 1765*, list of seven lords to be canvassed by the Duke of Bedford.
    (a) B.L., Add. MS. 57810, f. 145.
    (b) *Additional Grenville Papers, 1763–65*, ed. J.R.G. Tomlinson (Manchester, 1962), p. 253.

238. *2 Apr. 1765*, list of 57 of the majority of 58 lords who voted for the amending of the Poor Bill.
    (a) B.L. Add. MS. 32966, f. 156; this list includes the speculation that the missing lord might have been one of four named peers. It also names eight lords as 'Voted against' or 'Absent' on the 'Second Question', i.e. the motion (defeated by 66 to 59) for postponement of the Committee of the Whole House on the Poor Bill. There are annotated presence lists relating to this division, giving 58 names, at ff. 152–3 and ff. 158–9. There is a draft list of bishops (nine 'against', 12 'for' (including proxies) and five 'absent') at f. 148 and a list of eight lords who 'voted against or abstained' at f. 149. W.W.M., R53-9 lists the same lords, adding three names as possibilities for the missing lord. There is a list of 57 lords 'absent or against' (ten of whom are marked 'Absent X' or 'A X', and one of whom is marked 'Q'), together with a list of 76 lords 'absent', clearly over the two divisions on the Poor Bill, in Add. MS. 32966, ff. 158–61.
    (b) Hardy, thesis, Appendix J; Turner, thesis, Appendix B; McCahill, 'The House of Lords in the 1760s', in *Pillar of Constitution*, p. 173, n. 19.
    (c) Hardy, thesis, p. 266; Lowe, thesis, pp. 979, 980–1; McCahill, 'The House of Lords in the 1760s', in *Pillar of Constitution*, p. 173.

239. *13 Apr. 1765*, list of 27 lords 'to be spoke to, to attend the Poor Bill, on Friday, 19th Inst.'
    (a) B.L., Add. MS. 32966, f. 196, with draft at f. 194.
    (c) Lowe, thesis, pp. 506–7.

240. *17 Apr. 1765*, list of the 120 lords who pronounced Lord Byron not guilty of murder but guilty of manslaughter and the four who pronounced him not guilty on both charges.
    (b) T.B. Howell, *A Complete Collection of State Trials* (33 vols., 1809–26), XIX, 1233–5.

241. *30 Apr. 1765*, list of the minority of nine lords 'who voted with Lord Temple' in opposing the committal of the Regency Bill.

(a) B.L., Add. MS. 32966, ff. 481–2; Add. MS. 51423, f. 184; Hants. R.O., Malmesbury Papers (Harris diary).

(b) Horace Walpole, *Memoirs of the Reign of George III*, ed. G.F. Russell Barker (4 vols., 1894), II, 82; Hardy, thesis, pp. 266–7 and Appendix K.

(c) Hardy, thesis, pp. 266–7; Lowe, thesis, pp. 511–2, 981; McCahill, 'The House of Lords in the 1760s' in *Pillar of Constitution*, pp. 174–5; Farrell, thesis, p. 48 n. 54.

242. *1 May 1765*, list of 31 lords who might have voted in the minority for an address to the King to name a regent.

(a) B.L., Add. MS. 33035, ff. 134–5. Newcastle's list contains 31 names; the minority numbered only 30. The list is annotated and three other names are added in pencil.

(b) Hardy, thesis, Appendix K.

(c) Hardy, thesis, p. 267; Lowe, thesis, pp. 513, 981.

243. *16 May 1765*, list of 25 lords, followed by list of 91 M.P.s, probably to be considered for office.

(a) B.L., Add. MS. 33000, f. 381.

244. *30 June 1765*, list headed 'Lords & others, for whom no Provision is yet found'; ten lords and 31 M.P.s are named.

(a) B.L., Add. MS. 33000, f. 385.

245. *?1765*, list of 190 lords, naming 74 'sure', 22 'doubtful' and 94 'against'.

(a) B.L., Add. MS. 33001, ff. 315–17.

(c) Farrell, thesis, p. 408, shows that this list must be pre-14 January 1766 and suggests that it belongs to the period immediately before the formation of the first Rockingham ministry in July 1765.

246. *?September 1765*, list of 182 lords, naming 136 'pro', 13 'contra certain', 13 'contra probable' and 20 'doubtful'. Although the list is undated, it probably belongs to the early months of the first Rockingham administration, since it includes Pitt's allies, but not Bute's allies, in opposition; a letter from Newcastle to his wife (B.L., Add. MS. 33077, ff. 148–9) implies a date of 9 Sept. 1765.

(a) W.W.M. R53-10.

(c) Farrell, thesis, p. 167 n. 149, suggests early September 1765 as a possible date for this list.

247. *16 Dec. 1765*, list of the 61 lords present at the ministry's pre-sessional meeting with a separate list of 18 'remarkable absentees'.

(b) Fortescue, *Correspondence*, I, 200–1.

248. *17 Dec. 1765*, lists of the minority of 24 lords who voted against the address.

(a) B.L., Add. MS. 33035, ff. 206–7, with duplicate at ff. 208–9; Add. MS. 51387, f. 187, with duplicate at Add. MS. 51406, f. 123. There is a presence list with 16 annotations of lords voting in the minority at Add. MS. 33035, ff. 196–7 and a list of bishops' voting on the address in W.W.M., R53-13.

(b)   *Proceedings North America*, II, 57; the bishops' list is in Turner, thesis, Appendix B.

(c)   P. Langford, *The First Rockingham Administration, 1765–1766* (Oxford, 1973), p. 134; Lowe, thesis, p. 981; Thomas, *Stamp Act Crisis*, p. 157.

249. *13 Jan. 1766*, list of 63 lords present at the ministerial meeting 'for reading the Speech', with an additional list of 22 'Remarkable Absentees'.
(b)   Fortescue, *Correspondence*, I, 222–3.

250. *30 Jan. 1766*, list of 123 lords 'for' and 63 'against' the repeal of the Stamp Act.
(a)   B.L., Add. MS. 33001, ff. 64–6; draft at ff. 67–70; list of 11 bishops 'supposed to be agt. this Days Question' at f. 71.
(c)   Lowe, 'Archbishop Secker', p. 434, and n. 1.

251. *3 Feb. 1766*, list of the five lords who voted against the declaratory resolution.
(a)   Huntington Lib., Hastings Correspondence, box 93: Sir Charles Hotham to the Earl of Huntingdon, 4 Feb. 1766. There is a copy in the Institute of Historical Research, microfilm XR 79/26, The Hastings Collection of Manuscripts from the Huntington Lib., reel 26.
(b)   Fortescue, *Correspondence*, 1, 253; *The Grenville Papers: Being the Correspondence of R. Grenville, Earl Temple, and the Rt. Hon. G. Grenville, their Friends and Contemporaries*, ed. W. Smith (4 vols., 1852–3), III, 357; *Proceedings North America*, II, 124–5; *Selections from the Family Papers Preserved at Caldwell. In Two Parts*, ed. W. Mure (Maitland Club, XXI, 3 vols., Glasgow, 1854), II, 68; Thomas, *Stamp Act Crisis*, p. 196 n. 1; Turner, thesis, Appendix B, where, following Cobbett, *Parl. Hist.*, XVI, 163–5, the list is misdated 10 Feb. 1766.
(c)   Lowe, thesis, pp. 559–60, 982.

252. *4 Feb. 1766*, lists of the majority of 63 lords and 59 of the minority of 60 lords on the motion that words stand part of a resolution to compensate victims of riots in America.
(a)   B.L., Add. MS. 33035, ff. 276–7, with draft at ff. 278–9 and annotated presence list, with 59 lords marked 'X' and 54 marked 'O' at ff. 274–5; W.W.M., R53-26. The former list (Newcastle's) names only 59 of the minority. The latter list (Rockingham's) is incomplete in its naming of majority and minority and contains discrepancies with Newcastle's; although it is headed 'House of Lords how they *voted* with regard to the *Stamp* Act', Lowe, (c) below, suggests that this list bears more relation to the division on 4 Feb. 1766. A document which appears to be a partial copy may be found in W.W.M., R153-5.
(b)   *Proceedings North America*, II, 155–6, reproduces Newcastle's list; Turner, thesis, Appendix B, reproduces Rockingham's.
(c)   Langford, *First Rockingham Administration*, pp. 156–8; Lowe, thesis, pp. 982–3; McCahill, 'The House of Lords in the 1760s', in *Pillar of Constitution*, pp. 177–8; Thomas, *Stamp Act Crisis*, p. 199; Farrell, thesis, pp. 50–1. The list published in O'Gorman, *Rise of Party*, p. 538 n. 53, though dated 4 Feb. 1766, is not for this division; some of its inaccuracies are pointed out in Lowe, 'Bishops and Representative Peers', p. 92.

253. *4 Feb. 1766*, list of 38 lords (including two proxy voters) connected with the court who voted against the ministry. Four 'proxies against us not given' are also named.
   (a) B.L., Add. MS. 33001, f. 91.

254. *6 Feb. 1766*, list of 118 lords present, 59 of whom are marked 'X'.
   (a) W.W.M., R53-6a.
   (b) Turner, thesis, Appendix B.
   (c) Lowe, thesis, pp. 983–5 and 'Archbishop Secker', p. 435, suggests that the 59 lords marked 'X' formed the majority of 59 (against a minority of 55) on an amendment in Committee to a resolution on America.

255. *7 Feb. 1766*, list of 64 lords belonging to the parties of the Earl of Bute (39) and the Duke of Bedford (25).
   (a) B.L., Add. MS. 33001, ff. 89–90.

256. *13 Feb. 1766*, list of 89 lords 'for', 78 'against' and 27 'doubtful' on the repeal of the Stamp Act.
   (a) B.L., Add. MS. 33001, ff. 96–8.
   (c) Lowe, thesis, pp. 571–2 and 'Archbishop Secker', pp. 438–9.

257. *14 Feb. 1766*, list of 90 lords 'for', 80 'against' and 24 'doubtful' on the repeal of the Stamp Act.
   (a) B.L., Add. MS. 33001, ff. 99–100.
   (c) Lowe, thesis, pp. 571–2 and 'Archbishop Secker', pp. 438–9.

258. *23 Feb. 1766*, list of 85 lords 'for', 73 'against' and 33 'doubtful or absent' on the repeal of the Stamp Act.
   (a) B.L., Add. MS. 33001, ff. 104–5, with draft at ff. 102–3.
   (c) Lowe, thesis, pp. 571–2 and 'Archbishop Secker', pp. 438–9.

259. *23 Feb. 1766*, list of 88 lords 'for', 72 'against' and 32 'doubtful or absent' on the repeal of the Stamp Act.
   (a) W.W.M., R53-21.
   (b) Turner, thesis, Appendix B.
   (c) Lowe, thesis, pp. 571–2 and 'Archbishop Secker', pp. 438–9.

260. *27 Feb. 1766*, list of 88 lords 'for', 70 'against' and 34 'doubtful or absent' on the repeal of the Stamp Act.
   (a) B.L., Add. MS. 33001, ff. 113–5.
   (c) Lowe, thesis, pp. 571–2, and 'Archbishop Secker', pp. 438–9.

261. *4 Mar. 1766*, list of 101 lords 'for', 75 'against' and 16 'doubtful or absent' on the repeal of the Stamp Act.
   (a) B.L., Add. MS. 33001, ff. 128–30.
   (c) Lowe, thesis, pp. 571–2 and 'Archbishop Secker', pp. 438–9.

262. *7 Mar. 1766*, list of 101 lords 'for', 75 'against' and 16 'doubtful or absent' on the repeal of the Stamp Act.
   (a) B.L., Add. MS. 33001, ff. 148–9, compiled by Newcastle; a list of this

date in W.W.M., R53-25, listing 70 lords 'supposed for', 55 'supposed agt.' and 11 'doubtful', seems to be a shorter version of Newcastle's list.
(b) Turner, thesis, Appendix B, reproduces Rockingham's list.
(c) Lowe, thesis, pp. 571–2, and 'Archbishop Secker', pp. 438–9.

263. *9 Mar. 1766*, list of 104 lords 'for', 74 'against' and 16 'doubtful or absent' on the repeal of the Stamp Act.
(a) B.L., Add. MS. 33001, ff. 151–3.
(c) Lowe, thesis, pp. 571–2, and 'Archbishop Secker', pp. 438–9.

264. *Mar. 1766*, list of 84 lords 'pro', 47 'con' and 45 'doubtful' on the repeal of the Stamp Act.
(a) W.W.M., R53-30; W.W.M., R53-27, R53-28 and R53-29 together form an exact copy. There is an almost identical list, with slightly different annotations, at W.W.M., R53-24.
(c) Lowe, thesis, pp. 571–2.

265. *11 Mar. 1766*, lists of the 105 lords who voted for and the 71 who voted against the motion to commit the Stamp Act Repeal Bill.
(a) B.L., Add. MS. 33035, ff. 385–7, with what appears to be a draft at ff. 389–91; there are incomplete lists of the majority in W.W.M., R53-20 and R53-23. There is a list of 19 lords who voted in the minority and were office-holders in B.L., Add. MS. 33001, f. 204. On 14 Mar. 1766 Newcastle classified the 71 lords in the minority as friends either of the Earl of Bute (41) or of the Duke of Bedford (30): Add. MS. 33001, ff. 161–2, with draft at ff. 165–6.
(b) List of the minority only, indicating office-holders, in Debrett, *History, Debates and Proceedings*, IV, 374–5 and in J. Almon, *Correct Copies of the Two Protests against the Bill to Repeal the American Stamp Act, of Last Session, with Lists of the Speakers and Voters* (Paris, 1766), pp. 23–4, and J. Almon, *Second Protest, with a List of the Voters against the Bill to Repeal the American Stamp Act of Last Session* (Paris, 1766), pp. 13–15. The latter two works also indicate those lords who protested. *Proceedings North America*, II, 344–6, prints the versions in Add. MS. 33035, ff. 385–7 and in Debrett. The list in Turner, thesis, Appendix B, is based on the lists in W.W.M., cited in (a) above. The list of 19 lords who were office-holders and who voted against repeal (in Add. MS. 33001, f. 204) is printed in D.A. Winstanley, *Personal and Party Government: A Chapter in the History of the Early Years of the Reign of George III, 1760–1766* (Cambridge, 1910), p. 307.
(c) Langford, *First Rockingham Administration*, pp. 193–4 and n. 187; Lowe, thesis, pp. 581–4, 985–6; McCahill, 'The House of Lords in the 1760s', in *Pillar of Constitution*, pp. 177–9; Thomas, *Stamp Act Crisis*, p. 246.

266. *28 May 1766*, list of 53 of the 57 lords who voted for and the 16 who voted against the committal of the Window Lights Bill.
(b) Fortescue, *Correspondence*, I, 343–4.
(c) Lowe, thesis, p. 986.

267. *10 Nov. 1766*, list of 68 lords present at the Grafton ministry's pre-sessional meeting.

(b) Fortescue, *Correspondence*, I, 411–12.
(c) Farrell, thesis, p. 180 n. 224.

268. *2 Jan. 1767*, list headed 'Lords & Gentlemen to be wrote to by the Duke of Richmond and Lord George Lennox'; 24 lords and 134 Sussex gentlemen are named.
    (a) B.L., Add. MS 33001, ff. 336–7, with draft at ff. 308–9 (naming 12 lords) and ff. 311–12 (dated 28 Dec. 1766).
    (c) Farrell, thesis, p. 49 n. 55.

269. *14 Jan. 1767*, list of 197 lords, divided into 'Last administration' [i.e. that of Rockingham] 43; 'Bedford' 17; 'Temple' 14; 'Court' 103; 'Doubtful' 20.
    (a) B.L., Add. MS. 33001, ff. 313–14.
    (c) Lowe, thesis, pp. 631–3; McCahill, 'The House of Lords in the 1760s', in *Pillar of Constitution*, p. 184.

270. ?*14 Jan. 1767*, list of 133 lords friendly to and 68 opposed to the Chatham administration.
    (a) B.L., Add. MS. 32979, ff. 230–3.
    (c) Farrell, thesis, p. 409; the list is endorsed 14 Jan. 1767 and internal evidence shows that it must have been compiled between Aug. 1766 and July 1767.

271. *31 Jan. 1767*, list headed 'Particular Friends in Both Houses of Parliament': 44 lords and 79 M.P.s are listed.
    (a) B.L., Add. MS. 33001, ff. 344–7.

272. *25 Feb. 1767*, list headed 'Lords & Commons to be invited to dinner'; 37 lords and 56 M.P.s are named.
    (a) B.L., Add. MS. 33001, ff. 350–2, with draft at ff. 354–5.

273. *27 Mar. 1767*, list headed 'Lords & Members of the House of Commons now in employment'; 55 lords and 156 M.P.s are named.
    (a) B.L., Add. MS. 33001, ff. 371–5.

274. *28 Mar. 1767*, list headed 'Lords to be considered', naming 12 of 'our friends', with possible offices to be held; 'Duke of Bedford's friends' (10) and 'Mr Grenville's friends' (7).
    (a) B.L., Add. MS. 33001, f. 377, with draft at f. 366.

275. *10 Apr. 1767*, lists of 36 lords who supported and 74 who possibly opposed the Duke of Bedford's motion regarding the Massachusetts Indemnity Act, along with 15 opposition lords who abstained or went away and six who voted with the administration. The actual voting figures were Contents 36, Not Contents 63.
    (a) B.L., Add. MS. 32981, ff. 109–110, 112–3. Newcastle's list of the friends of the administration contains 74 names; he does not indicate which of these lords did not vote in the majority of 63. The list of lords voting for Bedford's motion is duplicated in B.L., Add. MS. 33036, ff. 423–4, which contains a draft list of those who went away without voting.

(b) *Proceedings North America*, II, 452–4, prints a reconstructed list of the majority.

(c) J. Brooke, *The Chatham Administration, 1766–1768* (1956), pp. 127–30; Lowe, thesis, pp. 626–31, 986–7; McCahill, 'The House of Lords in the 1760s', in *Pillar of Constitution*, p. 184; Thomas, *Stamp Act Crisis*, pp. 315–18.

276. *16 Apr. 1767*, list of 197 lords, divided into 'Friends to the late Administration' [i.e. that of Rockingham] 40; 'Duke of Bedford's friends' 30; 'Court' 91; 'Doubtful' 36.
   (a) B.L., Add. MS. 33001, ff. 379–81.
   (c) Lowe, thesis, pp. 631–3; McCahill, 'The House of Lords in the 1760s', in *Pillar of Constitution*, p. 184.

277. *6 May 1767*, list of 44 of the 49 lords who voted for and 52 of the 71 who voted against Lord Gower's motion for papers regarding the Massachusetts Indemnity Act; the proxy voters are omitted.
   (a) B.L., Add. MS. 33036, ff. 451–4, indicating 'R[ockingham]' and 'B[edford]' voters; drafts and duplicates at ff. 461–2, 465–6, 471–2; list of the bishops' voting at ff. 457–8.
   (b) *Proceedings North America*, II, 459–61.
   (c) Lowe, thesis, p. 987; Farrell, thesis, p. 43.

278. *16 May 1767*, list of 198 lords, divided into 'Friends to the last Administration' [i.e. that of Rockingham] 43; 'Friends to the Duke of Bedford' 17; 'Friends to Lord Temple & Mr Geo. Grenville' 14; 'Friends to the Court' 104; 'Doubtful' 20.
   (a) B.L., Add. MS. 33001, ff. 384–6, with duplicate (bearing different annotations) at ff. 387–9. There is another copy in W.W.M., R1-786.
   (b) Turner, thesis, Appendix B.
   (c) Lowe, thesis, pp. 631–3; McCahill, 'The House of Lords in the 1760s', in *Pillar of Constitution*, p. 184.

279. *21 May 1767*, list of 12 'Lords to be sent to for proxies tomorrow'.
   (a) B.L., Add. MS. 33001, f. 390.

280. *22 May 1767*, list of the 56 lords who voted for and the 62 who voted against Lord Gower's motion to put questions to the judges regarding the Massachusetts Indemnity Act.
   (a) B.L., Add. MS. 33037, ff. 17–20, with drafts and duplicates at ff. 21–4, 27–8, 29–30, 31–2, 41–2. There is a list of the minority only in Add. MS. 32982, ff. 97–8.
   (b) *Proceedings North America*, II, 494–6.
   (c) Lowe, thesis, p. 988; Thomas, *Stamp Act Crisis*, p. 332; Farrell, thesis, pp. 42–3, 52.

281. *23 May 1767*, list of 14 'Lords who may be desired to attend the committee on Tuesday' [i.e. 26 May 1767].
   (a) B.L., Add. MS. 33001, f. 394, with draft at f. 392.

282. *25 May 1767*, list of 24 'Lords (supposed on the side of the Court) absent'.
  (a) B.L., Add. MS., 33001, f. 396.

283. *26 May 1767*, list of lords who voted for and against the two separate motions to put questions to the judges regarding the Massachusetts Indemnity Act, and to resume the House.
  (a) B.L., Add. MS. 33037, ff. 51–4, with duplicate of the majority list at ff. 55–6. In each of the two divisions 65 lords voted with the administration and 62 with the opposition. There is a draft of the minority list at ff. 41–2; Newcastle compiled it by annotating the copy of the list of 22 May 1767 (see 280(a) above) and 58 lords are listed, although there are also illegible annotations which might be additional names. There is an annotated presence list in Nottingham Univ. Lib., PwF 9790 (Portland papers).
  (b) Turner, thesis, Appendix B; *Proceedings North America*, II, 499–501.
  (c) Brooke, *Chatham Administration*, p. 146–7; Lowe, thesis, pp. 647–8, 988; McCahill, 'The House of Lords in the 1760s', in *Pillar of Constitution*, p. 185; O'Gorman, *Rise of Party*, p. 205; Thomas, *Stamp Act Crisis*, p. 333; Farrell, thesis, pp. 50, 52.

284. *26 May 1767*, list of 62 lords, divided into 'Friends' 27; 'D. of Bedford's' 15; 'Ld. Temple's &c.' 11; and nine others.
  (a) B.L., Add. MS. 33001, f. 398, with duplicate at f. 400.

285. *26 May 1767*, list of ten lords, composed of four 'absent (who voted for the Question the 22d Instant)' [i.e. for Lord Gower's motion on the Massachusetts Indemnity Act]; and six 'who were absent on the 22d that were present & voted for the Question on the 26th Inst'.
  (a) B.L., Add. MS. 33001, ff. 402–3.

286. *26 May 1767*, list of eight lords described as 'Additional voters agt. the Question &c.'
  (a) B.L., Add. MS. 33001, ff. 404–5.

287. *1 June 1767*, list of 15 lords 'to be sent to'.
  (a) B.L., Add. MS. 33001, f. 406.

288. *2 June 1767*, list of the 73 lords who voted for and the 61 who voted against the Duke of Grafton's motion to resume the House.
  (a) B.L., Add. MS. 33037, ff. 73–4, 77–8, with annotated presence list at ff. 81–2.
  (b) *Proceedings North America*, II, 507–8.
  (c) Brooke, *Chatham Administration*, p. 153; Lowe, thesis, pp. 653–5, 988; McCahill, 'The House of Lords in the 1760s', in *Pillar of Constitution*, pp. 185–6; Thomas, *Stamp Act Crisis*, p. 335; Farrell, thesis, p. 52.

289. *17 June 1767*, list of 52 of the minority of 57 lords who voted for and 73 of the majority of 98 who voted against the Duke of Richmond's motion for a conference with the House of Commons on the East India Company Dividend Bill. The proxy voters are omitted.

(a) B.L., Add. MS. 33037, ff. 111–12, 115–16, with drafts at ff. 75–6 and ff. 79–80 and duplicates at ff. 113–14 and 117–18.

(c) Lowe, thesis, pp. 663–5, 989; Farrell, thesis, p. 52.

290. *25 June 1767*, list of 60 lords said to have voted for and 44 who voted against an amendment to the East India Company Dividend Bill.

(a) B.L., Add. MS. 33037, ff. 149–52, 155–6. There is a copy of the majority list at ff. 151–2. The majority lists contain one extra lord; 59 voted in the majority.

(c) Lowe, thesis, p. 989.

291. *19 July 1767*, list (dated 'Claremont, July 19, 1767') headed 'To be considered'; 37 lords are listed, 24 'Friends of the late Administration', seven 'Duke of Bedford's Friends' and six 'Lord Temple's Friends & Mr Grenville's'.

(a) B.L., Add. MS. 32983, ff. 317–18.

292. *12 Nov. 1767*, list of 13 lords classified as 'doubtful'; this is part of an incomplete state of the House, giving numbers, but not names, of lords 'for the Court' and 'against'.

(a) B.L., Add. MS. 33001, f. 412.

293. *23 Nov. 1767*, list of the 52 lords present at the ministry's pre-sessional meeting.

(b) Fortescue, *Correspondence*, I, 508.

294. *?Nov. 1767*, list of 24 bishops and two archbishops, naming 14 'For', ten 'Against' and two 'Neuter'.

(a) B.L., Add. MS. 33037, ff. 161–2, with draft at ff. 153–4.

(c) Farrell, thesis, p. 192 n. 2, suggests a possible date of Nov. 1767 for this list.

295. *2 Feb. 1768*, list of 34 'Friends in the House of Lords'.

(a) W.W.M., R1-965; B.L., Add. MS. 33001, ff. 348–9.

(c) Lowe, thesis, p. 989; Farrell, thesis, p. 51 n. 65.

296. *4 Feb. 1768*, list of the minority of 35 lords who voted against the committal of the East India Dividend Bill.

(a) B.L., Add. MS. 33036, f. 285.

(c) Lowe, thesis, pp. 696–7, 989.

SECOND PARLIAMENT OF GEORGE III, 1768–74

297. *1 Dec. 1768*, list of the minority of five lords who voted against the committal to Newgate of Edward Aylett for breach of privilege, together with three who abstained and two who 'were gone'. Endorsed 'Earl of Hardwicke. St James's Square'.

(a) B.L., Add. MS. 35608, ff. 296–7.

(b) Horace Walpole, *Memoirs of the Reign of George III*, III, 188 and *Sir Henry Cavendish's Debates of the House of Commons During the Thirteenth Parliament of Great Britain*, ed. J. Wright (2 vols., 1841), I, 617, both give the minority of five.

298. *2 Mar. 1769*, list of the voting of the bishops on a motion for an address to the King assuring him of the support of the House over the Civil List. The address was carried by 73 votes to 18; the list names six bishops in the majority, one in the minority and four who left the House before the division.
(a) W.W.M., R1-1258.
(c) Lowe, thesis, pp. 352, 728–9.

299. *8 Jan. 1770* list of 48 lords present at the ministry's pre-sessional meeting.
(a) B.L., Add. MS. 33090, f. 475.
(c) Lowe, thesis, p. 739.

300. *9 Jan. 1770*, list of the 36 lords who voted for, and 89 of the 100 (the 11 proxy voters omitted) who voted against, an amendment to the address, together with 81 lords 'absent'.
(a) B.L., Add. MS. 33037, f. 438. There are lists of the minority only in *London Evening Post*, 9–11 Jan. 1770; *Lloyd's Evening Post*, 10–12 Jan. 1770; *London Chronicle*, 11–13 Jan. 1770; *Middlesex Journal*, 11–13 Jan. 1770; *Gazetteer and New Daily Advertiser*, 12 Jan. 1770. The press versions differ slightly from those in (b) below.
(b) Debrett, *History, Debates and Proceedings*, V, 143; Cobbett, *Parl. Hist.*, XVI, 666; *The Correspondence of William Pitt, Earl of Chatham*, eds. W.S. Taylor and J.H. Pringle (3 vols., 1838–40), III, 387n; *Proceedings North America*, III, 167, prints the version in Cobbett.
(c) Lowe, thesis, pp. 741, 990–1; Lowe, 'The Parliamentary Career of Lord Dunmore, 1761–1774', *Virginia Magazine of History and Biography*, XCVI (1988), 26 n. 90.

301. *2 Feb. 1770*, list of the minority of 47 lords who opposed the motion to resume the House after a debate on the state of the nation.
(a) W.W.M., R5; *London Evening Post*, 8–10 Feb. 1770, with those who signed the subsequent protest asterisked.
(b) Debrett, *History, Debates and Proceedings*, V, 162–3, with non-protesters asterisked; Cobbett, *Parl. Hist.*, XVI, 820. There are slight variations between these lists and that cited in (a) above.
(c) Lowe, thesis, pp. 991–2.

302. *2 Feb. 1770*, list of 48 of the 49 lords who voted for the motion to adjourn the debate on the privileges of the House of Commons (the one proxy voter is omitted).
(b) *Annual Reg.* for 1770, p. 70.
(c) Lowe, thesis, p. 992.

303. *2 Mar. 1770*, annotated list of lords present in the House of Lords; it is a list of the minority of the 38 lords who voted in person and the six who

voted by proxy against the motion for an address to increase the number of seamen.
- (a) W.W.M., R5.
- (c) Lowe, thesis, pp. 992–3.

304. *?14 Feb. 1771*, list of 38 lords, including three proxies; the voting figures, the presence list in *L.J.*, XXXIII, 62–3, and the number and identity of the proxies when checked against the Proxy Book for the session 1770–1 in H.L.R.O., all suggest strongly that this is a minority list for the division on the Falkland Islands, 14 Feb. 1771.
- (a) W.W.M., R1-2145.
- (c) Lowe, thesis, p. 993.

305. *22 Apr. 1771*, list of seven of the eight lords who voted for, and the four who voted against, the recommendation of the Committee of Privileges that the claim of Arthur Annesley to the Earldom of Anglesey be rejected.
- (a) P.R.O., 30/8/61, f. 105 (Chatham papers).

Note: there is no record of this division in the manuscript minutes in H.L.R.O. or in Sainty and Dewar, *Divisions in the House of Lords*.

306. *20 Jan. 1772*, list of 142 lords summoned to the ministry's pre-sessional meeting.
- (a) P.R.O. S.P. 37/9, ff. 9–10.

307. *20 Jan. 1772*, list of 61 lords present at the ministry's pre-sessional meeting.
- (a) P.R.O., S.P. 37/9, ff. 11–12.

308. *Feb.–Mar. 1772*, list of 41 lords who voted in the minority in the several divisions on the Royal Marriage Bill.
- (a) *General Evening Post*, 5–7 Mar. 1772; *Middlesex Journal*, 5–7 Mar. 1772; *Public Advertiser*, 6 Mar. 1772.

309. *19 May 1772*, list of the minority of 27 lords (including four proxies) who voted for, and the majority of 102 (including 29 proxies) who voted against, the second reading of the Dissenters' Relief Bill; there is also a list of seven lords who 'went away'.
- (a) P.R.O., S.P. 37/10, ff. 219–20.
- (b) G.M. Ditchfield, 'The Subscription Issue in British Parliamentary Politics, 1772–1779', *Parliamentary History*, VII (1988), 68–70.
- (c) *Ibid.*, pp. 55–6.

310. *25 Nov. 1772*, list of 47 lords present at the ministry's pre-sessional meeting.
- (a) P.R.O., S.P. 37/9, ff. 313–4.

311. *21 Dec. 1772*, list of the minority of five lords who voted for a motion for a conference with the House of Commons over the East India Commissioners Bill.
- (a) B.L., Add. MS. 63110, ff. 8–9; J.R.U.L.M., Miscellanea, Eng. MS. 940 (Townshend papers). The document in each source is a typed copy of a letter from Lord Townshend to Miss Ann Montgomery, dated 22 Dec. 1772.

312. *2 Apr. 1773*, list of the minority of 28 lords (including two proxies) who voted for the second reading of the Dissenters' Relief Bill.
   (a) *General Evening Post*, 3–6 Apr. 1773; *London Evening Post*, 3–6 Apr. 1773; *Public Advertiser*, 5 Apr. 1773.
   (b) Debrett, *History, Debates and Proceedings*, VI, 277–8; Cobbett, *Parl. Hist.*, XVII, 790–1.
   (c) Ditchfield, 'Subscription Issue', pp. 59–60.

313. *?17 June 1773*, list of 17 lords.
   (a) W.W.M., R81-4.
   (c) Lowe, thesis, pp. 993–4, speculates that this is a list of the minority of 17 lords who voted for an amendment to the East India Company Regulating Bill.

314. *1773*, list of 40 lords whom Matthew Boulton proposed to wait upon to solicit support for his Birmingham and Sheffield Assay Bill.
   (a) Assay Office Lib., Birmingham: Matthew Boulton Trust, Boulton papers, notebook 10, ff. 7–8.
   (c) E. Robinson, 'Matthew Boulton and the Art of Parliamentary Lobbying', *Hist. Jnl.*, VII (1964), 217–18, 220–1.

315. *18 May 1774*, list of the minority of 12 lords who voted against the third reading of the Massachusetts Justice Bill.
   (a) W.W.M., R1-1490.
   (b) B. Donoughue, *British Politics and the American Revolution: The Path to War, 1773–1775* (1964), p. 294; *Proceedings North America*, IV, 434.
   (c) Donoughue, *British Politics and the American Revolution*, pp. 100–1; Lowe, thesis, pp. 994–5.

316. *May 1774*, list of 22 'lords who voted against the American measures' (i.e. the Massachusetts Government Bill, Massachusetts Justice Bill and Quebec Government Bill, 11 to 18 May 1774).
   (a) *Gazetteer and New Daily Advertiser*, 18 May 1774; *Morning Chronicle*, 18 May 1774; *London Evening Post*, 21–24 May 1774; *Public Advertiser*, 25 May 1774. In these lists, the lords who 'spoke in the course of the debates' are asterisked; there are small variations between them.
   (b) *Proceedings North America*, IV, 434–5, prints the version in *London Evening Post*, cited in (a) above.

317. *2 June 1774*, list of the 21 lords who voted for, and the 11 who voted against, the motion to postpone the second reading of the Copyright Bill.
   (b) Debrett, *History, Debates and Proceedings*, VII, 4; Cobbett, *Parl. Hist.*, XVII, 1003.
   (c) Lowe, thesis, p. 853 n. 55.
Note: The sources in (b) above state that this list relates to a division of 22 Feb. 1774 on a motion to reverse judgment in the case of *Donaldson v. Beckett*, i.e. to reverse a decree of the Court of Chancery in favour of the perpetuity of literary property, with 21 lords in favour of reversal and 11 against. But there is no evidence of a division on that day in the manuscript minutes in H.L.R.O. or in Sainty and Dewar, *Divisions in the House of Lords*, while *Annual Reg.* for 1774, p. 95, specifically states that one did not take place. There are serious

discrepancies, moreover, between this list and the presence list for 22 Feb. 1774 in *L.J.*, XXXIV, 32. On the other hand, all 32 lords in the list were present on 2 June 1774 (*L.J.*, XXXIV, 226–7), the day of the division on the Copyright Bill, which was intended to mitigate the consequences of the Lords' decision in *Donaldson* v. *Beckett*, Lowe in (c) above argues convincingly that this was the division to which this list pertains.

318. *17 June 1774*, list of the minority of seven lords who voted against acceptance of the Commons' amendments to the Quebec Bill.
    (a) *London Evening Post*, 14–18 June 1774.
    (b) Debrett, *History, Debates and Proceedings*, VII, 14; *The Correspondence of William Pitt, Earl of Chatham*, eds. W.S. Taylor and J.H. Pringle (4 vols., 1838–40), IV, 353n.; *Proceedings North America*, V, 233.
    (c) P.D.G. Thomas, *Tea Party to Independence: The Third Phase of the American Revolution, 1773–1776* (Oxford, 1991), p. 113.

319. *June 1774*, (i.e. the end of the parliamentary session of 1774); 'the following lists were handed about at this time'; list of 140 lords 'who vote in support of the present Court measures', with 62 identified as holding a 'place' and two a 'pension'; list of 35 lords 'who do not attend, are abroad, under age, or Roman Catholics'; list of 50 lords 'who vote in opposition to the present Court measures'.
    (b) Debrett, *History, Debates and Proceedings*, VII, 16–18.

THIRD PARLIAMENT OF GEORGE III, 1774–80

320. *2 Dec. 1774*, list of 44 lords written to by Lord Rochford to remind them of business in the House of Lords on 6 Dec.
    (a) P.R.O., S.P. 37/10, ff. 353–4.

321. *20 Jan. 1775*, list of the minority of 18 lords who voted for Lord Chatham's motion for an address to the King for the withdrawal of British troops from Boston.
    (a) *London Evening Post*, 21–24 Jan. 1775; *Public Advertiser*, 23 Jan. 1775.
    (b) Almon, *Parl. Reg.*, II, 17; Cobbett, *Parl. Hist.*, XVIII, 168; *Proceedings North America*, V, 287.
    (c) Donoughue, *British Politics and the American Revolution*, pp. 233–4.

322. *1 Feb. 1775*, list of the minority of 32 lords who voted for Lord Chatham's motion for conciliation with America.
    (a) *London Evening Post*, 31 Jan.–2 Feb. 1775; *Public Advertiser*, 3 Feb. 1775.
    (b) Almon, *Parl. Reg.*, II, 33; Cobbett, *Parl. Hist.*, XVIII, 216; *Proceedings North America*, V, 338.
    (c) Donoughue, *British Politics and the American Revolution*, pp. 237–8; Lowe, thesis, pp. 995–6.

323. *7 Feb. 1775*, list of 90 of the 104 lords (the 14 proxy voters omitted) who voted to agree with the Commons on an address to the King upon the disturbances in North America and of the 29 who voted against doing so.
   (a) W.W.M., R1-1551. There are lists of the minority only, with slight variations, in *London Evening Post*, 9–11 Feb. 1775 and *Public Advertiser*, 13 Feb. 1775.
   (b) *Proceedings North America*, V, 403–4. There are lists of the minority only in Almon, *Parl. Reg.*, II, 63; Cobbett, *Parl. Hist.*, XVIII, 296; Turner, thesis, Appendix B; and E. Robinson, 'Matthew Boulton and the Art of Parliamentary Lobbying', *Hist. Jnl.*, VII (1964), 229 n. 56.
   (c) Lowe, thesis, pp. 996–7.

324. *?16 Mar. 1775*, list of the minority of 29 lords (including five proxies) who voted against the committal of the bill to restrain the fishery and trade of New England.
   (a) W.W.M., R48-4. This is an undated document headed 'L[or]ds who voted on *Thursday*'. The voting figures fit no other Thursday in this period; all those named in the list are named also in the presence list for 16 Mar. 1775 in *L.J.*, and in the manuscript minutes in H.L.R.O.; the proxy voters in the list were duly registered in the proxy books for 1774–5 in H.L.R.O. It is therefore highly probable that the list applies to this date and to this issue.

325. *21 Mar. 1775*, list of the minority of 21 lords who voted against the third reading of the bill to restrain the fishery and trade of New England.
   (b) Almon, *Parl. Reg.*, II, 99; Cobbett, *Parl. Hist.*, XVIII, 457–8; *Proceedings North America*, V, 589.
   (c) Lowe, thesis, pp. 997–8.

326. *12 Apr. 1775*, list of the minority of 24 lords (including four proxies) who voted against the third reading of the New Jersey Trading Bill.
   (a) *London Evening Post*, 13–15 Apr. 1775.
   (b) *Proceedings North America*, VI, 20–21.

327. *4 May 1775*, list of the minority of three lords who voted against the second reading of the Mitford Poor Bill.
   (a) *General Evening Post*, 4–6 May 1775.

328. *17 May 1775*, a division on Lord Camden's bill to repeal the Quebec Act; list of the minority of 28 lords (including seven proxies) who voted against Lord Dartmouth's motion for the rejection of the bill.
   (a) *London Evening Post*, 25–27 May 1775.
   (b) Almon, *Parl. Reg.*, II, 151–2; Cobbett, *Parl. Hist.*, XVIII, 676; *Proceedings North America*, VI, 58.

329. *Oct. 1775*, survey of the House of Lords, naming 99 'Peers who vote in support of Court measures', with 'place' indicated for 50 of them; 16 Scottish peers, with 'place' indicated for six; 23 bishops; 34 peers and one bishop 'who do not attend, are abroad, under age, or Roman Catholics'; 45 peers and two bishops 'who vote in opposition to the present Court measures'.
   (a) *London Evening Post*, 5–7 Oct. 1775.

330. *26 Oct. 1775*, list of the minority of 33 lords who voted against the motion for an address of thanks to the King.
    (b) Almon, *Parl. Reg.*, V, 19–20; Cobbett, *Parl. Hist.*, XVIII, 726; *Proceedings North America*, VI, 87.

331. *Nov. 1775*, list of 38 lords 'who have voted in this session of Parliament, in opposition to Administration'.
    (a) *London Evening Post*, 2–4 Nov. 1775; *Public Advertiser*, 6 Nov. 1775. In these lists, the lords who signed the protest of 26 Oct. 1775 are asterisked.

332. *22 Apr. 1776*, list of the 118 lords who pronounced the Duchess of Kingston guilty and the one who pronounced her 'guilty erroneously, but not intentionally', on a charge of bigamy.
    (a) *The Trial of Elizabeth, Duchess Dowager of Kingston, for Bigamy, before the Right Honourable the House of Peers, in Westminster Hall in Full Parliament . . . Published by Order of the House of Peers* (1776), pp. 154–6.
    (b) T.B. Howell, *A Complete Collection of State Trials* (33 vols., 1809–26), XX, 623–5.

333. *11 May 1778*, list of the minority of four lords who voted in favour of a reversal of the judgement of the Court of King's Bench in the case of *Horne* v. *The King*.
    (a) *General Evening Post*, 9–12 May 1778.

334. *6 Dec. 1778*, list of 55 lords written to by Lord Suffolk, to remind them of 'business of importance' (i.e. an opposition motion for an address to the King expressing displeasure at the recent proclamation by the ministry's peace commissioners in North America) on 7 Dec.
    (a) P.R.O., S.P. 37/27, ff. 50–1.

335. *23 Apr. 1779*, list of the minority of 39 lords (including one proxy) who voted for the removal from office of Lord Sandwich.
    (a) N.M.M., SAN/F/41/110-112 where there are several copies of the list; the list names 38 of the minority of 39 (the one proxy voter is omitted). There are complete lists of the minority of 39 (including the proxy voter) in *London Evening Post*, 24–27 Apr. 1779 and *Morning Chronicle*, 26 Apr. 1779; there is another version, with slight variations, in *Public Advertiser*, 27 Apr. 1779.
    (b) Almon, *Parl. Reg.*, XIV, 294.
    (c) Farrell, thesis, p. 43 n. 36.

336. *7 June 1779*, list of the minority of 25 lords who voted for a resolution on the Greenwich Hospital Enquiry.
    (a) N.M.M., SAN/F/41/117 (six other lords are also named, without further comment); *London Evening Post*, 8–10 June 1779.
    (b) Almon, *Parl. Reg.*, XIV, 477; Cobbett, *Parl. Hist.*, XX, 581.

337. *30 June 1779*, list of the 22 lords who voted for and the 39 who voted against the ballot clause in the Militia Augmentation Bill.
    (a) *London Evening Post*, 1–3 July 1779.
    (b) Almon, *Parl. Reg.*, XIV, 571–2.

(c) J.R. Western, *The English Militia in the Eighteenth Century: The Story of a Political Issue, 1660–1802* (1965), p. 214, and n. 3.

338. *25 Nov. 1779*, list of the minority of 41 lords who voted against the address of thanks, together with the names of six lords who 'went away'.
　　(a) P.R.O., S.P. 37/13, f. 258. There is another version, with slight variations, in *London Evening Post*, 27–30 Nov. 1779. There is an annotated list of lords, which seems to be an incomplete version of the majority and the minority in this division in N.M.M., SAN/F/22/41.
　　(b) G.M. Ditchfield, 'The House of Lords in the Age of the American Revolution', in *Pillar of Constitution*, pp. 237–9, which also includes a reconstructed list of the majority.
　　(c) *Ibid.*, p. 212.

339. *29 Nov. 1779*, list of 117 lords 'wrote to' as likely ministerial supporters.
　　(a) P.R.O., S.P. 37/13, ff. 266–7.

340. *1 Dec. 1779*, list of 76 of the majority of 82 lords who voted against, 36 of the 37 lords who voted for and six who 'went away' on the motion for an address of censure on ministers over Irish relief.
　　(a) N.M.M., SAN/F/41/132.

341. *7 Dec. 1779*, list of 33 of the minority of 36 lords (the three proxy voters omitted) who voted for the Duke of Richmond's motion for reform of Civil List expenditure.
　　(a) *London Evening Post*, 18–21 Dec. 1779; *St. James's Chronicle*, 21–23 Dec. 1779; *General Evening Post*, 28–30 Dec. 1779.
　　(b) Cobbett, *Parl. Hist.*, XX, 1266–7.

342. *?Dec. 1779*, list of 41 lords, endorsed 'List of Peers who have no Employments and who generally vote with Govt'. The list is dated 1779 and probably belongs to the first weeks of Lord Stormont's period as leader of the House of Lords, which began in Nov. 1779.
　　(a) Mansfield Papers (the Earl of Mansfield, Scone Palace, Perth, Perthshire), box 117, bundle 4 (Papers of David Murray, 7th Viscount Stormont).

343. *15 Dec. 1779*, list of the minority of 41 lords (including four proxies) who voted for the resolution on the reduction of the ordinaries.
　　(a) *London Evening Post*, 18–21 Dec. 1779; *St James's Chronicle*, 21–23 Dec. 1779. There is a list of four lords who 'went away without voting' in N.M.M., SAN/F/41/137.
　　(c) O'Gorman, *Rise of Party*, p. 628 n. 52.

344. *31 Jan. 1780*, list of 157 lords, clearly a canvassing list of likely ministerial supporters.
　　(a) P.R.O., S.P. 37/14, ff. 35–6.

345. *8 Feb. 1780*, list of 50 of the minority of 55 lords (the five proxy voters omitted) who voted for the Earl of Shelburne's motion for a committee of both Houses to enquire into public expenditure.
　　(a) *London Evening Post*, 8–10 Feb. 1780; *St James's Chronicle*, 8–10 Feb. 1780; *Morning Chronicle*, 11 Feb. 1780.
　　(b) Cobbett, *Parl. Hist.*, XX, 1364–5.

346. *14 Apr. 1780*, list of the 41 lords who voted for and the 60 who voted against the committal of the Contractors' Bill.
   (a) List of majority (with offices, pensions, etc. held) and minority in *London Evening Post*, 20–22 Apr. 1780. There is an annotated presence list, showing the 41 lords who voted in the minority in N.M.M., SAN/F/42/9; there are other versions of the minority lists (with slight variations) in *St James's Chronicle*, 15–18 Apr. 1780, *London Evening Post*, 15–18 Apr. 1780, *Public Advertiser*, 19 Apr. 1780.
   (c) Ditchfield, 'The House of Lords in the Age of the American Revolution', in *Pillar of Constitution*, p. 212.

347. *25 Apr. 1780*, list of the 44 lords who voted in person for a resolution that the House resolve itself into a C.W.H. on coastal defence; seven other lords voted by proxy for the motion; it was lost by 92-51.
   (a) N.N.M., SAN/F42/13; this is an annotated presence list.

FOURTH PARLIAMENT OF GEORGE III, 1780–1784

348. *14 June 1781*, list of the minority of four lords who voted for the re-commitment of the Kingston Enclosure Bill.
   (a) W.R.O., CR 2017 C244 (Denbigh Letterbooks), f. 266. *Morning Chronicle*, 15 June 1781; *Morning Herald and Daily Advertiser*, 15 June 1781.
   (b) Debrett, *Parl. Reg.*, IV, 318; *Political Magazine*, II (1781), 474.
Note: The manuscript minutes in H.L.R.O. reveal that there was a division on this question on 14 June 1781; the Contents numbered four and the Not Contents 24. The division, however, does not feature in Sainty and Dewar, *Divisions in the House of Lords*. The sources cited above give the same minority list but quote slightly different figures for the majority, varying from 20 to 28.

349. *3 July 1781*, list of the 15 lords who voted for and the 15 who voted against the motion that Lord Sandys leave the chair of the committee on the Phillips Powder Bill.
   (a) W.R.O., CR 2017 C244, f. 270.

350. *1 May 1782*, annotated presence list, with 63 lords 'for' and 26 'against', with seven queries.
   (a) W.W.M., R125-20. W.W.M., R125-19 is an undated list in Rockingham's hand which might relate to (or be an incomplete draft of) this list.

351. *4 Dec. 1782*, list of 163 lords 'written to for hearing the Speech read at Shelburne House'.
   (a) William L. Clements Lib., University of Michigan, Ann Arbor, Shelburne papers, vol. 166, ff. 261–2.
   (c) W.C. Lowe, 'George III, Peerage Creations and Politics, 1760–1784', *Hist. Jnl.*, XXXV (1992), 603 n. 86.

352. *c. 1782*, canvassing list of the House of Lords, naming 80 lords 'Hopeful', 67 'Con', 50 'Absent' and 27 'Doubtful'. Although the list is headed 'Canvass for

East India Bill' (i.e. December 1783), and was subsequently endorsed 'This is the canvas of the H. of Lords for the famous division on the India Bill', the presence of Rockingham (in the 'Con' column) means that it must have been compiled before July 1782.

(a) B.L., MS. Facs. 340 (2), ff. 289–92. The list is referred to (under its incorrect heading) in H.M.C., *10th Rept.*, pt. 6, p. 61.

(c) J. Cannon, *The Fox-North Coalition: Crisis of the Constitution, 1782–84* (Cambridge, 1969), p. 133, speculates that the list refers to a division on the Contractors' Bill, 1 May 1782, but the listing of the Rockinghamite peers in the 'Con' column casts some doubt on this possibility. Farrell, thesis, pp. 53–4, speculates that the list was originally compiled as a survey early in 1782 but that the subsequent annotations *do* refer to a canvas on the India Bill before Nov. 1783.

353. *17 Feb. 1783*, list of 69 of the majority of 72 lords who voted in person against, and of 55 of the minority of 59 lords who voted in person for, the amendment to the preliminary articles of peace; the proxy voters are omitted.

(a) N.M.M., SAN/F/42/66.

354. *30 May 1783*, list of the 19 lords who voted for and the 18 who voted against the reversal of the judgement of the Court of Common Pleas in the case of the *Bishop of London* v. *Lewis Disney Fytche*.

(a) *Morning Herald*, 6 June 1783; *Public Advertiser*, 6 June 1783 (with small variations).

(b) R. Watson, *Anecdotes of the Life of Richard Watson, Bishop of Llandaff, Written by Himself* (2 vols., 1817), I, 122–3, gives the division list and adds the names of four lords 'present in the House, but did not vote'.

(c) G.F.A. Best, *Temporal Pillars. Queen Anne's Bounty, the Ecclesiastical Commissioners and the Church of England* (Cambridge, 1964), p. 57 n. 3, where it is incorrectly stated that 18 bishops voted in the majority; the correct figure is 14.

355. *25 June 1783*, list of 12 of the majority of 18 lords (the six proxy voters omitted) who voted for, and 14 of the minority of 16 lords (the two proxy voters omitted) who voted against, the motion for postponing the committee stage of the Election Bribery Bill.

(a) C.K.S., U 1590 C79/2 (Stanhope papers). Two other versions of this list, namely C.K.S., U 1590 C6 and *York Chronicle*, 11 July 1783, omit the names of the bishops who took part in the division.

(b) G.M. Ditchfield, 'The House of Lords and Parliamentary Reform in the Seventeen-Eighties', *B.I.H.R.*, LIV (1981), 219–20.

(c) *Ibid.*, pp. 210–11.

356. *July 1783*, canvassing list of 33 lords, with notes on their interests and connections (followed by a similar list of 32 M.P.s).

(a) Nottingham Univ. Lib., Portland papers, PwF 9883a-b.

(b) A.S. Turberville, *A History of Welbeck Abbey and its Owners* (2 vols., 1938), II, photograph opposite p. 188, reproduces one folio of this list but incorrectly describes it as 'Notes by 3rd Duke of Portland upon rewards to be given to political adherents in Ireland, 1794'.

357. *25 Nov. 1783*, discussion of the voting intentions of 19 lords over the India
     Bill, in a letter from the Duke of Portland to the Earl of Sandwich; seven
     are classed as hostile, six as among 'our Friends' and six as having 'moved
     from the Enemy's Ranks to the Doubtfuls'.
     (a) N.M.M., SAN/F43a/12.

358. *8 Dec. 1783*, discussion of the voting intentions of ten lords over the India
     Bill, in a letter from Portland to Sandwich; five are described as favourably
     disposed, four are described as favourable proxy voters and one as a hostile
     proxy voter.
     (a) N.M.M., SAN/F/43a/20.

359. *15 Dec. 1783*, list of the 87 lords (including 18 proxies) who voted for, and
     the 79 (including 22 proxies) who voted against, the adjournment on the
     India Bill.
     (a) C.K.S., U 1590 C79/1; this list also names seven lords who 'went away';
         Public Advertiser, 20 Dec. 1783. A similar list in N.M.M., SAN/F/43a/24
         excludes the proxy voters but lists eight lords who abstained and five
         who were absent.
     (b) *Political Magazine*, V (1783), 404–5; Debrett, *Parl. Reg.*, XIV, 107–8; *New
         Annual Reg.*, V (1784), 128–9; *An Authentic Account of the Debates in the
         House of Lords . . . on the Bill for Establishing Certain Regulations for the
         Better Management of the Territories, Revenues and Commerce of this Kingdom
         in the East Indies. To which is Added, an Accurate List of the Divisions* (1783),
         pp. 150–2.
     (c) Aspinall, *Later Correspondence*, I, pp. xxv–xxvi; Cannon, *Fox-North
         Coalition*, p. 137.

360. *17 Dec. 1783*, list of the 76 lords (including 19 proxies) who voted for, and
     the 95 (including 20 proxies) who voted against, the committal of the India
     Bill.
     (a) *Public Advertiser*, 20 Dec. 1783.
     (b) *Political Magazine*, V (1783), 404–5; Debrett, *Parl. Reg.*, XIV, 107–8; *New
         Annual Reg.*, V (1784), 128–9; *An Authentic Account of the Debates in the
         House of Lords . . . on the Bill for . . . the East Indies*, pp. 150–2.
     (c) Aspinall, *Later Correspondence*, I, p. xxvi; Cannon, *Fox-North Coalition*,
         p. 139.

361. *?Dec. 1783*, undated list of 63 lords in the handwriting of George III.
     (b) Fortescue, *Correspondence*, VI, 475–6; the list is included among corres-
         pondence from Dec. 1783 and might be connected with the India Bill.

362. *3 Feb. 1784*, list of 16 'Lords to be apprized of tomorrow's business by Ld.
     North'.
     (a) B.L., Add. MS. 61862, f.35.

FIFTH PARLIAMENT OF GEORGE III, 1784–90

363. *17 June 1784*, list of the minority of five lords who voted for the Earl of Effingham's motion for a committee to consider the state of prisoners for debt.
    (a) *General Evening Post*, 17–19 June 1784; *Morning Chronicle*, 18 June 1784; *Public Advertiser*, 19 June 1784.

364. *30 July 1784*, list of the minority of four lords who voted to discharge the order for the second reading of the East India Regulation Bill.
    (a) *Morning Herald*, 31 July 1784.
    (b) *Political Magazine*, VII (1784), 197.

365. *18 July 1785*, list of the minority of 20 lords who voted in person for the motion to postpone consideration of the first of the resolutions relating to Irish commerce; the ten proxy voters are omitted.
    (a) W.R.O., CR 2017 C244, f. 332.

366. *27 July 1785*, list of the 14 lords who voted for, and the four who voted against, the discharge of the order for the committal of the County Election Registration Bill.
    (a) C.K.S., U 1590 C79/1.
    (b) Ditchfield, 'House of Lords and Parliamentary Reform', p. 220.
    (c) *Ibid.*, pp. 211–12.

367. *3 Apr. 1786*, list of six of the minority of 19 lords who voted for Earl Fitzwilliam's amendment to the East India Judicature Bill.
    (a) *General Evening Post*, 1–4 Apr. 1786; *Whitehall Evening Post*, 1–4 Apr. 1786.

368. *29 June 1786*, list of the four lords who voted for, and the 11 who voted against, the motion for postponing the committee stage of the County Election Registration Bill.
    (a) *General Evening Post*, 29 June–1 July 1786; *London Chronicle*, 29 June–1 July 1786; *Whitehall Evening Post*, 29 June–1 July 1786; *Morning Herald*, 30 June 1786; *Public Advertiser*, 1 July 1786. There are lists of the minority only in N.Y.R.O., ZFW 7/2/54/3 (Wyvill of Constable Burton papers) and in *Morning Chronicle*, 30 June 1786.
    (b) Ditchfield, 'House of Lords and Parliamentary Reform', p. 212 n. 49. There are lists of the minority only in Debrett, *Parl. Reg.*, XX, 144 and Cobbett, *Parl. Hist.*, XXVI, 184.
    (c) Ditchfield, 'House of Lords and Parliamentary Reform', p. 212 n. 49.

369. *3 July 1786*, list of the minority of six lords who voted that the chairman leave the chair in C.W.H. on the East India Company Relief Bill.
    (a) *Morning Herald*, 4 July 1786.

370. *7 July 1786*, list of the 15 lords (including three proxies) who voted for, and 37 of the 38 (one of the 21 proxies omitted) who voted against, the third reading of the County Election Registration Bill.

(a) C.K.S., U 1590 C79/1; N.Y.R.O., ZFW 7/2/54/6; W.R.O., CR 2017 C244, f. 354. The latter list excludes the proxy voters.
(b) G.M. Ditchfield, 'House of Lords and Parliamentary Reform', pp. 221–2.
(c) *Ibid.*, pp. 212–3.

371. *13 Feb. 1787*, list of the 52 lords who voted for, and 33 of the 38 who voted against, the motion in the Committee of Privileges that Lord Abercorn, having been created a peer of Great Britain, should cease to be a Scottish representative peer.
(a) C.K.S., U 1590 C80/5.
(b) G.M. Ditchfield, 'The Scottish Representative Peers and Parliamentary Politics, 1787–1793', *Scottish Historical Review*, LX (1981), 30–1.
(c) *Ibid.*, pp. 19–20.

372. *1788–1794*, table listing the lords who attended the impeachment of Warren Hastings, with the number of days attended by each, in the sessions of 1788, 1789, 1790, 1791, 1792, 1793 and 1794.
(a) B.L., Add. MS. 29223, ff. 166–179.

373. *Feb.–June 1788*, list of 173 lords who attended the impeachment of Warren Hastings in 1788, with the number of days attended by each; list of six lords who did not attend the impeachment at all in 1788.
(a) B.L., Add. MS. 29223, ff. 93–9.

374. *21 Apr. 1788*, list of the 25 lords who voted for, and the 18 who voted against, a resolution that the election of Lord Cathcart as a Scottish representative peer was an undue return.
(b) *Scots Magazine*, L (1788), 201.
(c) M.W. McCahill, 'The Scottish Peerage and the House of Lords in the Later Eighteenth Century', *Scottish Historical Review*, L1 (1972), 183; Ditchfield, 'Scottish Representative Peers', p. 26.

375. *May–June 1788*, list of 251 lords, divided into 'friends' (43), 'friendly' (31) 'well-disposed' (29), 'disinclined' (seven), 'against' (11) and 'uncertain' (130) over the County Election Registration Bill.
(a) C.K.S., U 1590 C79/1.
(b) Ditchfield, 'House of Lords and Parliamentary Reform', pp. 222–5.
(c) *Ibid.*, pp. 214–5, 218.

376. *June 1788*, list of lords who 'have generally or occasionally voted against Administration, either in Person or by Proxy, during the last session of Parliament'; 75 lords are listed, of whom 24 are asterisked, without explanation.
(a) *The Times*, 24 June 1788.

377. *26 Dec. 1788*, list of the 66 lords who voted for, and the 99 who voted against, Lord Rawdon's motion for an address to the Prince of Wales, asking that he take upon himself, as sole Regent, the administration of executive government in the King's name during the King's illness.
(a) *The Star*, 29 Dec. 1788; *The Times*, 30 Dec. 1788; *Public Advertiser*, 30 Dec. 1788; *Whitehall Evening Post*, 30 Dec. 1788–1 Jan. 1789.

(b) *Scots Magazine*, LI (1789), 76; *New Annual Reg.*, X (1789) ('Public Papers', item 65, p. 6); Debrett, *Parl. Reg.*, XXVI, 72–4; Cobbett, *Parl. Hist.*, XXVII, 890–1, Stockdale, *Debates and Proceedings*, XVIII, 190–2. There is a list of 16 of the minority, comprising the 'rat' lords and the 'armed neutrality' in *Memoirs of the Court and Cabinets of George III*, ed. Duke of Buckingham (2 vols, 1853), II, 79; there is a list of the bishops' voting in F.C. Mather, *High Church Prophet: Bishop Samuel Horsley (1733–1806) and the Caroline Tradition in the Later Georgian Church* (Oxford, 1992), p. 223.

378. *?26 Dec. 1788*, list of proxy voters for and against government, and lords absent, 'on the late important question in the House of Lords'.
    (a) *London Chronicle*, 30 Dec. 1788–1 Jan. 1789; *Whitehall Evening Post*, 30 Dec. 1788–1 Jan. 1789; *The Star*, 31 Dec. 1788; *Public Advertiser*, 1 Jan. 1789; *The Times*, 1 Jan. 1789.
Note: this list presumably refers to the division on Lord Rawdon's motion on the regency, 26 Dec. 1788, since there was no comparable vote in the period leading up to 31 Dec. 1788, the date on which the list was first published. Yet no proxy votes were cast in the division of 26 Dec. 1788 and several of the proxy voters named in this list are also named as voting in person in the division list (no. 377) of 26 Dec. 1788.

379. *c. 1788*, list of 169 lords, 44 'in office' and 125 'out of office', with annotations.
    (a) P.R.O., 30/8/196; ff. 119–20 (Chatham papers).

380. *1788/1789*, lists of independent members of both Houses of Parliament who subscribed to the 'Armed Neutrality'; the lists of its supporters in the Lords name a minimum of five and a maximum of 11 lords.
    (a) Essex R.O., D/DBy C9/44 (Braybrooke papers); William L. Clements Lib., Sydney papers, box 15, 'Proposal for a parliamentary grouping of independents, 1788'; Scottish R.O., GD 112/45/5/8 (Breadalbane papers); *The Star*, 31 Dec. 1788; *Public Advertiser*, 8 Jan. 1789.
    (b) There is a somewhat different list of 'Armed Neutrality' lords who voted against the administration on the Regency question in 1788 in Aspinall, *Later Correspondence*, I, p. xlv.

381. *?Dec. 1788–Feb. 1789*, list of 82 lords 'who have voted in the minority on the question relative to the Regency'; those who spoke in the debates are marked 'S'; those who protested are marked 'P'.
    (b) Debrett, *Parl. Reg.*, XXVI, 219–220.
Note: this seems to be a composite list of lords who voted with opposition in the six divisions on the Regency between 26 Dec. 1788 and 18 Feb. 1789, and of lords who signed one or both of the protests on the Regency, 26 Dec. 1788 and 23 Jan. 1789.

382. *?Dec. 1788–Feb. 1789*, list of 90 lords who voted for and 65 lords who voted against the administration over the Regency issue, with an estimate of the value of the property of each. Thirteen lords 'who did not vote but are friends to Administration' are included.
    (a) *The Times*, 23 Feb. 1789; *The Star*, 28 Feb. 1789.

383. *Jan. 1789*, list of five lords who 'are said to have joined the Regent'.
   (a) *The Star*, 26 Jan. 1789.

384. *Jan. 1789*, list of Pitt's supporters in the House of Lords; 26 office-holders, 37 peers created or promoted by Pitt and four bishops created by him are enumerated but not named; 15 'Dukes with Mr Pitt' and seven against him are named.
   (a) *The Star*, 31 Jan. 1789.

385. *3 Mar. 1789*, list of 21 lords (three of them marked 'Qy') supplied by the 3rd Earl Stanhope to the London Committee for the Abolition of the Slave Trade as likely supporters of abolition. The names of other individual lords canvassed by the Committee are given separately in the minutes, B.L., Add. MS. 21255, *passim*, and not in list form.
   (a) B.L., Add. MS. 21255, f. 88.
   (c) J.R. Oldfield, 'The London Committee and Mobilization of Public Opinion against the Slave Trade', *Hist. Jnl.*, XXXV (1992), 339.

386. *Apr.–June 1789*, list of 124 lords who attended the impeachment of Warren Hastings in 1789, with the number of days attended by each; list of 71 lords who did not attend the impeachment at all in 1789.
   (a) B.L., Add. MS. 29223, ff. 101–8.

387. *23 July 1789*, list of the minority of six lords who voted for the first reading of the bill for the annual commemoration in church services of the Glorious Revolution.
   (a) Lambeth Palace Lib., MS. 2103, f. 25 (Bishop Beilby Porteus, 'Occasional Memorandums and Reflexions'); *The Times*, 24 July 1789.
   (b) G.M. Ditchfield, 'Parliament, the Quakers and the Tithe Question, 1750–1835', *Parliamentary History*, IV (1985), 108 n. 31.
   (c) *Ibid.*

388. *1789*, list of 'House of Lords, 1789'; 251 lords listed in four columns; the 130 lords in the first two columns were friends of the administration; the 72 lords in the third column were opponents; the 49 lords in the fourth column were doubtful or inactive.
   (a) P.R.O., 30/8/196, ff. 92–3.

389. *Feb.–June 1790*, list of 114 lords who attended at the impeachment of Warren Hastings in 1790, with the number of days attended by each; list of 142 lords who did not attend the impeachment at all in 1790.
   (a) B.L., Add. MS. 29223, ff. 110–18.

SIXTH PARLIAMENT OF GEORGE III, 1790–96

390. *May–June 1791*, list of 92 lords who attended at the impeachment of Warren Hastings in 1791, with the number of days attended by each; list of 165 lords who did not attend the impeachment at all in 1791.
   (a) B.L., Add. MS. 29223, ff. 120–9.

391. *16 May 1791*, list of the minority of 20 lords who voted for an amendment (to the motion that the House should proceed upon the impeachment of Warren Hastings) that the question of bail for Hastings be referred to the judges.
  (a) B.L., Add. MS. 39882, f. 60. There are slightly different versions of this list in *Whitehall Evening Post*, 19–21 May 1791; *Morning Chronicle*, 20 May 1791; *Morning Post*, 21 May 1791; *Public Advertiser*, 21 May 1791.
  (b) G.M. Ditchfield, 'The House of Lords and the Impeachment of Warren Hastings', *Parliamentary History*, XIII (1994), 292–4.
  (c) *Ibid.*, pp. 284–6, 292.

392. *7 June 1791*, list of six of the nine lords who voted against the clause in the Catholic Relief Bill to repeal laws restricting Papists from practising as lawyers.
  (a) *Whitehall Evening Post*, 7–9 June 1791; *The Times*, 8 June 1791.

393. *Feb.–June 1792*, list of 102 lords who attended at the impeachment of Warren Hastings in 1792, with the number of days attended by each; list of 156 lords who did not attend the impeachment at all in 1792.
  (a) B.L., Add. MS. 29223, ff. 131–9.

394. *27 Feb. 1792*, list of the minority of 19 lords who voted for a resolution on the use of naval force.
  (a) *The Times*, 29 Feb. 1792; *London Recorder, or Sunday Gazette*, 4 Mar. 1792.

395. *Feb.–May 1793*, list of 63 lords who attended at the impeachment of Warren Hastings in 1793, with the number of days attended by each, and with annotations; list of 196 lords who did not attend the impeachment at all in 1793.
  (a) B.L., Add. MS. 29223, ff. 141–54.

396. *22 Apr. 1793*, list of the minority of seven lords who voted against the third reading of the Traitorous Correspondence Bill.
  (a) *St James's Chronicle*, 20–23 Apr. 1793; *The Times*, 23 Apr. 1793. The following newspapers give an almost identical list of 'the seven Peers from whom a Protest is expected': *Lloyd's Evening Post*, 22–24 Apr. 1793; *The Oracle*, 23 Apr. 1793; *Morning Chronicle*, 25 Apr. 1793; *Gazetteer and New Daily Advertiser*, 26 Apr. 1793.

397. *7 May 1793*, list of the minority of 14 lords who voted for the committal of the Commercial Credit Bill.
  (a) *Evening Mail*, 8–10 May 1793; *Lloyd's Evening Post*, 8–10 May 1793; *The Times*, 9 May 1793; *Morning Chronicle*, 9 May 1793; *General Evening Post*, 9–11 May 1793; *Public Advertiser*, 10 May 1793; *Gazetteer and New Daily Advertiser*, 10 May 1793. There are some variations between these sources.

398. *10 June 1793*, list of the 21 lords who voted for, and 47 of the 48 who voted against, the motion to appoint a date for further proceeding in the impeachment of Warran Hastings. Six lords who attended but did not vote

are also named. There are annotations to indicate the offices held by some peers and the record of attendance of others at the trial.
(a) B.L., Add. MS. 29219, ff. 1–2.
(b) G.M. Ditchfield, 'The House of Lords and the Impeachment of Warren Hastings', *Parliamentary History*, XIII (1994), 294–6.
(c) *Ibid.*, pp. 287–91.

399. *21 Jan. 1794*, list of the minority of 12 lords who voted for the Earl of Guilford's amendment to the address.
(a) *St James's Chronicle*, 21–23 Jan. 1794; *Morning Chronicle*, 23 Jan. 1794; *Morning Post*, 23 Jan. 1794; *The Oracle*, 23 Jan. 1794; *The Star*, 24 Jan. 1794.
(b) Debrett, *Parl. Reg.*, XXXIX, 36; Cobbett, *Parl. Hist.*, XXX, 1088; Woodfall, *Debates*, I, 51; *The Senator*, VIII, 29.

400. *Feb.–June 1794*, list of 111 lords who attended at the impeachment of Warren Hastings in 1794, with the number of days attended by each, and with annotations 'For', 'Against' and 'Doubtful'; list of 156 lords who did not attend the impeachment at all in 1794.
(a) B.L., Add. MS. 29223, ff. 156–64.

401. *10 Mar. 1794*, list of the minority of 14 lords and of the four bishops in the majority of 42 lords, on the motion that further hearings of the Slave Trade Enquiry be referred to a Committee.
(a) Lambeth Palace Lib., MS. 2103, f. 62.
(b) R. Anstey, *The Atlantic Slave Trade and British Abolition, 1760–1810* (1975), p. 317 n. 116.
(c) *Ibid.*, p. 317.

402. *30 Apr. 1794*, list of the minority of six lords who voted against the motion to agree to an address on the King's message respecting the treaty with Prussia.
(a) *The Oracle*, 1 May 1794.

403. *22 May 1794*, list of the minority of 11 lords (including two proxies) who voted to adjourn the House in debate on the Bill to suspend the Habeas Corpus Act.
(a) *Morning Chronicle*, 26 May 1794; *London Chronicle*, 27–29 May 1794.
(b) Debrett, *Parl. Reg.*, XXXIX, 335; Woodfall, *Debates*, IV, 124; *Debates on the Report of the Committee of Secrecy in the House of Commons, on the 16th and 17th of May, and in the House of Lords, on the 17th and 19th and 22d of the Same Month, 1794 . . . and a List of the Minority in both Houses of Parliament, who Voted against the Suspension of the Habeas Corpus Act* (Edinburgh, n. d. [?1794]), p. 116. There is a reconstructed list of ten bishops who might have voted in person in the majority in Mather, *High Church Prophet*, p. 223, although this could also amount to a list of bishops who voted on the same day for the motion (carried 95-7) that the Suspension Bill should pass.

404. *30 May 1794*, list of the minority of 12 lords who voted against the adjournment of the debate on the Duke of Bedford's motion for ending the war with France.

(a) *Morning Chronicle*, 2 June 1794; *The Oracle*, 3 June 1794.
(b) Debrett, *Parl. Reg.*, XXXIX, 384; Cobbett, *Parl. Hist.*, XXXI, 687–8; Woodfall, *Debates*, IV, 217; *The Senator*, X, 1371. There is a reconstructed list of seven bishops in the majority in Mather, *High Church Prophet*, p. 223.

405. *30 Dec. 1794*, list of the minority of 12 lords who voted for the Earl of Guilford's amendment to the address.
    (a) *Morning Chronicle*, 1 Jan. 1795; *Whitehall Evening Post*, 1–3 Jan. 1795; *The Oracle*, 2 Jan. 1795; *The Times*, 2 Jan. 1795.
    (b) Debrett, *Parl. Reg.*, XLII, 41; Cobbett, *Parl. Hist.*, XXXI, 994; Woodfall, *Debates*, V, 62; *The Senator*, XI, 40.

406. *27 Jan. 1795*, list of the minority of 17 lords (including two proxies) who voted against Lord Grenville's amendment to the Duke of Bedford's motion respecting peace with France.
    (a) *The Oracle*, 30 Jan. 1795, includes the two proxy voters and those lords who 'retired from indisposition before the Question was called'. *Morning Chronicle*, 29 Jan. 1795, *Morning Post*, 30 Jan. 1795 and *The Times*, 30 Jan. 1795, just list the 15 lords who voted in person in the minority.
    (b) Debrett, *Parl. Reg.*, XLII, 97 (includes proxies); Cobbett, *Parl. Hist.*, XXXI, 1279 (excludes proxies).

407. *12 Feb. 1795*, list of the minority of 15 lords (including three proxies) who voted for the Duke of Bedford's motion to open peace negotiations with France. The list adds three lords who 'went away from indisposition'.
    (a) *Morning Chronicle*, 14 Feb. 1795; *The Oracle*, 16 Feb. 1795.
    (b) Woodfall, *Debates*, VI, 124; *The Senator*, XI, 564.

408. *30 Mar. 1795*, list of 13 of the minority of 14 lords (one proxy voter omitted) who voted for the Earl of Guilford's motion for a committee on the state of the nation.
    (b) Aspinall, *later Correspondence*, II, 323, n. 4.

Note: the following 16 lists (nos. 409–424) give the voting of the House of Lords on the charges of impeachment against Warren Hastings on 23 April 1795. These charges were condensed into 16 questions which were put separately by the Lord Chancellor to the House, and to each of which those lords present, starting with the junior baron, could answer 'guilty', 'not guilty' or give no verdict. The precise wording of each question may be found in the regular parliamentary reports cited under no. 409b below. There were differences between the voting figures for each question, and the voting on each question is therefore treated as a separate list. Some sources give the voting of the lords on all 16 questions in tabular form; others list the 29 lords who voted on the first question then summarize more briefly the voting on the other 15 questions; others give the voting on the first question only. The primary sources for the first question (no. 409a) are not quite the same as those for the subsequent questions and they are accordingly presented separately for that list. For the remaining questions (nos. 410–24), the primary sources are the same and they are set out under no. 410; nos. 411–24 simply refer back to them. The secondary sources which comment on the lists are given for the first list only (no. 409) and are not repeated.

409. *23 Apr. 1795*, list of the 23 lords who pronounced Warren Hastings not guilty, and the six who pronounced him guilty, on the first question.
   (a) B.L., Add. MS. 24248, ff. 365–76; B.L., Dept. of Printed Books, 515, 1. 17. 2 (printed document, in two double sheets, headed 'Questions to be put to the Lords in Westminster Hall on the Impeachment against Warren Hastings, Esq., ordered to be printed 17th April 1795'; the document has MS. annotations giving a list of 11 lords who voted guilty on at least one article or who gave no verdict on one or more of the articles, and a list of 18 lords who voted not guilty 'upon the whole'); *Whitehall Evening Post*, 23–25 Apr. 1795; *Morning Chronicle*, 24 Apr. 1795; *Morning Post*, 24 Apr. 1795. There are very slight variations between these sources.
   (b) Debrett, *Parl. Reg.*, XLII, 399–400; Woodfall, *Debates*, VI (Supplement), 197–202; *Annual Reg.* for 1795, pp. 113–15; *New Annual Reg.*, XVI (1795), 143; *The History of the Trial of Warren Hastings, Esq., Late Governor-General of Bengal, before the High Court of Parliament in Westminster Hall* (1796), pp. 267–8, 270; *Debates of the House of Lords, on the Evidence Delivered in the Trial of Warren Hastings, Esq.*, (1797), pp. 314–6; *The Diary of Joseph Farington*, eds. K. Garlick and A. MacIntyre, (16 vols., New Haven and London, 1978–84), II, 329–30.
   (c) C.B. Cone, *Burke and the Nature of Politics: The Age of the French Revolution* (Lexington, Ky, 1964), pp. 251–2; P.J. Marshall, *The Impeachment of Warren Hastings* (Oxford, 1965), pp. 85–6; G.M. Ditchfield, 'The House of Lords and the Impeachment of Warren Hastings', *Parliamentary History*, XIII (1994), pp. 288, 291.

410. *23 Apr. 1795*, list of the 23 lords who pronounced Warren Hastings not guilty, and the six who pronounced him guilty, on the second question.
   (a) B.L., Add. MS. 24248, ff. 365–76; B.L., Dept. of Printed Books, 515. 1. 17. 2 (see no. 409 above); *Whitehall Evening Post*, 23–25 Apr. 1795; *Morning Chronicle*, 24 Apr. 1795. There are very slight variations between these sources.
   (b) Debrett, *Parl. Reg.*, XLII, 402–3; Woodfall, *Debates*, VI (supplement), 197–202; *Annual Reg.* for 1795, p. 115; *New Annual Reg.*, XVI (1795), 143; *History of the Trial of Warren Hastings*, p. 270; *Debates of the House of Lords on . . . the Trial of Warren Hastings*, pp. 320–1.

411. *23 Apr. 1795*, list of the 28 lords who pronounced Warren Hastings not guilty, *nem. con.*, and the one who gave no verdict, on the third question.
   (a) and (b) See (a) and (b) under no. 410.

412. *23 Apr. 1795*, list of the 24 lords who pronounced Warren Hastings not guilty, the four who pronounced him guilty and the one who gave no verdict, on the fourth question.
   (a) and (b): See (a) and (b) under no. 410.

413. *23 Apr. 1795*, list of the 24 lords who pronounced Warren Hastings not guilty, the three who pronounced him guilty and the two who gave no verdict, on the fifth question.
   (a) and (b): See (a) and (b) under no. 410.

414. *23 Apr. 1795*, list of the 24 lords who pronounced Warren Hastings not guilty, the three who pronounced him guilty and the two who gave no verdict, on the sixth question.
(a) and (b): See (a) and (b) under no. 410.

415. *23 Apr. 1795*, list of the 24 lords who pronounced Warren Hastings not guilty, the three who pronounced him guilty and the two who gave no verdict, on the seventh question.
(a) and (b): See (a) and (b) under no. 410.

416. *23 Apr. 1795*, list of the 22 lords who pronounced Warren Hastings not guilty, the five who pronounced him guilty and the two who gave no verdict on the eighth question.
(a) and (b): See (a) and (b) under no. 410.

417. *23 Apr. 1795*, list of the 22 lords who pronounced Warren Hastings not guilty, the five who pronounced him guilty and the two who gave no verdict, on the ninth question.
(a) and (b): See (a) and (b) under no. 410.

418. *23 Apr. 1795*, list of the 27 lords who pronounced Warren Hastings not guilty, *nem, con.*, and the two who gave no verdict, on the tenth question.
(a) and (b): See (a) and (b) under no. 410.

419. *23 Apr. 1795*; list of the 24 lords who pronounced Warren Hastings not guilty, the three who pronounced him guilty and the two who gave no verdict, on the eleventh question.
(a) and (b): See (a) and (b) under no. 410.

420. *23 Apr. 1795*, list of the 24 lords who pronounced Warren Hastings not guilty, the three who pronounced him guilty and the two who gave no verdict, on the twelfth question.
(a) and (b): See (a) and (b) under no. 410.

421. *23 Apr. 1795*, list of the 23 lords who pronounced Warren Hastings not guilty, the four who pronounced him guilty and the two who gave no verdict, on the thirteenth question.
(a) and (b): See (a) and (b) under no. 410.

422. *23 Apr. 1795*, list of the 23 lords who pronounced Warren Hastings not guilty, the four who pronounced him guilty and the two who gave no verdict, on the fourteenth question.
(a) and (b): See (a) and (b) under no. 410.

423. *23 Apr. 1795*, list of the 24 lords who pronounced Warren Hastings not guilty, the three who pronounced him guilty and the two who gave no verdict, on the fifteenth question.
(a) and (b): See (a) and (b) under no. 410.

424. *23 Apr. 1795*, list of the 25 lords who pronounced Warren Hastings not guilty, the three who pronounced him guilty and the one who gave no verdict on the sixteenth question.
(a) and (b): See (a) and (b) under no. 410.

425. *8 May 1795*, list of 21 of the 25 lords who voted for and 83 of the 100 who voted against the Duke of Norfolk's motion for papers respecting the recall of Earl Fitzwilliam from Ireland. The proxy voters are omitted.
(a) *The Oracle*, 12 May 1795; *The Times*, 13 May 1795 (minority only). There is an incomplete list of the minority in Wiltshire R.O., Ailesbury papers, Matthew Arnott memorandum to Ailesbury.
(b) Debrett, *Parl. Reg.*, XLII, 495–6; *The Senator*, XII, 1020–1 (with slight variations). There is a list of the 11 bishops who voted in the majority in Mather, *High Church Prophet*, p. 223.
(c) E.A. Smith, *Whig Principles and Party Politics: Earl Fitzwilliam and the Whig Party, 1748–1833* (Manchester, 1975), p. 217 n. 61.

426. *5 June 1795*, list of the minority of eight lords who voted for Lord Lauderdale's address for peace with France.
(a) Wilts. R.O., Ailesbury papers, M. Arnott to Ailesbury, 6 June 1795.

427. *8 June 1795*, list of the minority of eight lords who voted against the date set for the second reading of the Datchet and Isleworth Canal Bill.
(a) Wilts. R.O., Ailesbury papers, M. Arnott to Ailesbury, 8 June 1795.

428. *10 Nov. 1795*, list of the minority of eight lords (including one proxy) who voted against the second reading of the Safety of the King's Person Bill.
(a) *Morning Chronicle*, 11 Nov. 1795; *The Courier and Evening Gazette*, 12 Nov. 1795; *The Oracle*, 13 Nov. 1795. There is another version of this list in W.R.O., CR2017 C244, f. 459, misdated 11 Nov. 1796.
(b) Debrett, *Parl. Reg.*, XLV, 88; *Woodfall, Debates*, IX, 165; Cobbett, *Parl. Hist.*, XXXIII, 254; *The Senator*, XIII, 148.
Note: Cobbett, *Parl. Hist.*, in (b) above, wrongly associates this list with a division on the second reading of the Treasonable Practices Bill, 6 Nov. 1795.

429. *13 Nov. 1795*, list of the minority of seven lords (including two proxies) who voted against the third reading of the Safety of the King's Person Bill.
(a) *General Evening Post*, 12–14 Nov. 1795; *Morning Post*, 14 Nov. 1795.
(b) Debrett, *Parl. Reg.*, XLV, 117; Cobbett, *Parl. Hist.*, XXXII, 270; *The Senator*, XIII, 236.

430. *9 Dec. 1795*, list of the minority of 21 lords (including six proxies) who voted against the second reading of the Seditious Meetings Bill.
(a) *Morning Post*, 10 Dec. 1795; *The Times*, 11 Dec. 1795.
(b) Debrett, *Parl. Reg.*, XLV, 164; Woodfall, *Debates*, X, 336; *The Senator*, XIV, 755.

431. *14 Dec. 1795*, list of the minority of 18 lords (including four proxies) who voted against the third reading of the Seditious Meetings Bill.
(a) *Morning Chronicle*, 15 Dec. 1795.

(b) Debrett, *Parl. Reg.*, XLV, 206; Woodfall, *Debates*, X, 485; Cobbett, *Parl. Hist.*, XXXII, 554. There is a reconstructed list of eight bishops in the majority in Mather, *High Church Prophet*, p. 223.

SEVENTH PARLIAMENT OF GEORGE III, 1796–1802 (FIRST PARLIAMENT OF THE UNITED KINGDOM OF GREAT BRITAIN AND IRELAND FROM 1 JANUARY 1801)

432. *27 Feb. 1797*, list of the minority of five lords who voted for the Duke of Norfolk's motion for an address against the further export of bullion.
(b) *The Senator*, XVII, 621.

433. *6 Mar. 1797*, list of the minority of eight lords who voted for the Duke of Bedford's motion for a select committee to inquire into the reasons for the issuing of the Order in Council of 26 Feb. 1797.
(a) *Morning Chronicle*, 8 Mar. 1797.

434. *16 Mar. 1797*, list of 14 of the minority of 15 lords who voted for the Earl of Albemarle's motion on the protection of Ireland by naval force; the one proxy voter is omitted.
(a) *General Evening Post*, 16–18 Mar. 1797; *Morning Chronicle*, 18 Mar. 1797; *The Times*, 20 Mar. 1797. *The Oracle*, 16 Mar. 1797, gives no list but identifies the one opposition proxy voter as the Earl of Derby.
(b) Debrett, *Parl. Reg.*, XLVIII, 96; *The Senator*, XVII, 921.

435. *21 Mar. 1797*, list of the minority of 21 lords (including one proxy) who voted for the Earl of Moira's motion on the state of Ireland.
(a) *Whitehall Evening Post*, 21–23 Mar. 1797; *Morning Chronicle*, 22 Mar. 1797; *The Times*, 23 Mar. 1797.
(b) Debrett, *Parl. Reg.* XLVIII, 115; *The Senator*, XVII, 958.

436. *23 Mar. 1797*, list of 16 of the minority of 17 lords (one proxy voter omitted) who voted for the Earl of Oxford's motion for an address to the King for peace with France.
(a) *Morning Chronicle*, 24 Mar. 1797.
(b) Debrett, *Parl. Reg.*, XLVIII, 126; Cobbett, *Parl. Hist.*, XXXIII, 179–80; *The Senator*, XVII, 1003.

437. *9 Jan. 1798*, list of the minority of six lords who voted against the committal of the War Contribution Bill.
(a) *General Evening Post*, 9–11 Jan. 1798; *St. James's Chronicle*, 9–11 Jan. 1798; *Morning Chronicle*, 10 Jan. 1798; *The Oracle*, 10 Jan. 1798; *London Chronicle*, 11–13 Jan. 1798; *The Times*, 12 Jan. 1798. There are minor variations between these versions of the list.
(b) Debrett, *Parl. Reg.*, XLIX, 671; Cobbett, *Parl. Hist.*, XXXIII, 1299; *The Senator*, XIX, 571.

438. *22 Mar. 1798*, list of the minority of 11 lords who voted against the motion for the fining and imprisonment of James Perry and John Lambert of the *Morning Chronicle*.
 (a) *Morning Chronicle*, 26 Mar. 1798.
 (b) Debrett, *Parl. Reg.*, L, 355.

439. *22 Mar. 1798*, list of 11 of the minority of 13 lords who voted for the Duke of Bedford's motion for an address to the King for a change of ministers; the two proxy voters are omitted.
 (a) *General Evening Post*, 22–24 Mar. 1798; *Morning Chronicle*, 23 Mar. 1798; *The Times*, 24 Mar. 1798; *St. James's Chronicle*, 24–27 Mar. 1798.
 (b) Debrett, *Parl. Reg.*, L, 404; Cobbett, *Parl. Hist.*, XXXIII, 1352; *The Senator*, XX, 689. There is a reconstructed list of 12 bishops in the majority in Mather, *High Church Prophet*, p. 223.

440. *24 Apr. 1798*, list of the two lords who voted for and the two who voted against the bastardy clause in Twisleton's Divorce Bill in C.W.H.
 (a) *Lloyd's Evening Post*, 23–25 Apr. 1798; *The Oracle*, 25 Apr. 1798, only names the two who voted against.

441. *15 June 1798*, list of 18 of the minority of 19 lords who voted for a committee on the state of Ireland; the one proxy voter is omitted.
 (a) *Lloyd's Evening Post*, 15–18 June 1798; *Morning Chronicle*, 16 June 1798; *General Evening Post*, 16–19 June 1798; *The Oracle*, 18 June 1798; *The Times*, 18 June 1798.
 (b) Debrett, *Parl. Reg.*, LI, 401; Cobbett, *Parl. Hist.*, XXXIII, 1491. There is a reconstructed list of five bishops in the majority in Mather, *High Church Prophet*, p. 223.

442. *19 June 1798*, list of the minority of 14 lords who voted for an amendment to the motion for an address on the message respecting militia officers for Ireland.
 (a) *The Oracle*, 23 June 1798.

443. *27 June 1798*, list of 19 of the minority of 21 lords who voted for Lord Besborough's resolutions on Ireland.
 (a) *General Evening Post*, 26–28 June 1798; *Lloyd's Evening Post*, 27–29 June 1798; *Morning Chronicle*, 28 June 1798; *The Oracle*, 28 June 1798; *The Times*, 28 June 1798. There are slight variations between these versions of the list.
 (b) Debrett, *Parl. Reg.*, LI, 487; *The Senator*, XX, 1179.

444. *20 June 1799*, list of the majority of 19 lords who voted for and the 17 who voted against the clause in the Slave Trade Carrying Bill relating to the space between the decks of slave ships: the division took place in C.W.H.
 (a) Lambeth Palace Lib., MS. 2103, f. 101; *The Times*, 22 June 1799 (list of 11 of the minority only).
 (c) Anstey, *Atlantic Slave Trade*, p. 331.

445. *4 July 1799*, list of the eight lords who voted for and the four who voted against the second reading of the Treason Forfeiture Bill.

(a) *General Evening Post*, 6–9 July 1799; *Morning Chronicle*, 8 July 1799; *Morning Post*, 8 July 1799.

(b) Debrett, *Parl. Reg.*, LIV, 108.

446. *5 July 1799*, list of the minority of 61 lords (including the 36 proxies) who voted for and the majority of 68 lords (including the 36 proxies) who voted against the committal of the Slave Trade Limitation Bill.

(a) Lambeth Palace Lib., MS. 2103, ff. 102–3 omits most of the proxy voters. *St James's Chronicle*, 11–13 July 1799; *General Evening Post*, 11–13 July 1799; *The Times*, 12 July 1799; *The Courier and Evening Gazette*, 12 July 1799; *The Oracle*, 13 July 1799; *The True Briton*, 13 July 1799. These newspaper sources omit most of the proxy voters.

(b) Aspinall, *Later Correspondence*, III, 227–8; this version of the list includes all the proxy voters and there is also a list of ten proxies whose holders did not attend the debate.

(c) Anstey, *Atlantic Slave Trade*, p. 332.

447. *11 Oct. 1799*, list of the minority of two lords who voted for an address respecting treaties with Russia.

(a) *Morning Chronicle*, 12 Oct. 1799.

(b) Debrett, *Parl. Reg.*, LV, 155.

448. *28 Jan. 1800*, list of the minority of six lords who voted against a motion for further supplies.

(a) *General Evening Post*, 28–30 Jan. 1800; *Lloyd's Evening Post*, 29–31 Jan. 1800; *Morning Chronicle*, 30 Jan. 1800; *St James's Chronicle*, 30 Jan.–1 Feb. 1800; *The Oracle*, 31 Jan. 1800; *The Times*, 31 Jan. 1800.

(b) Debrett, *Parl. Reg.*, LV, 260; Cobbett, *Parl. Hist.*, XXXIV, 1241; *The Senator*, XXIV, 309.

449. *12 Feb. 1800*, list of the minority of six lords who voted for a committee to enquire into the causes of the failure of the expedition to Holland.

(a) *Morning Chronicle*, 13 Feb. 1800; *St. James's Chronicle*, 13–15 Feb. 1800; *General Evening Post*, 15–18 Feb. 1800.

450. *14 Feb. 1800*, list of the minority of three lords who voted against the address respecting advances to the Emperor of Germany.

(a) *Morning Chronicle*, 15 Feb. 1800.

(b) Debrett, *Parl. Reg.*, LV, 552.

451. *20 Feb. 1800*, list of the minority of two lords who voted for Earl Stanhope's motion for an address for peace negotiations.

(a) *Lloyd's Evening Post*, 19–21 Feb. 1800; *St. James's Chronicle*, 20–22 Feb. 1800; *London Chronicle*, 20–22 Feb. 1800; *Whitehall Evening Post*, 20–22 Feb. 1800; *Morning Post*, 21 Feb. 1800; *Morning Chronicle*, 21 Feb. 1800; *The Oracle*, 21 Feb. 1800; *The Times*, 21 Feb. 1800.

(b) Debrett, *Parl. Reg.*, LV, 678; Cobbett, *Parl. Hist.*, XXXIV, 1512; *The Senator*, XXIV, 693.

452. *27 Feb. 1800*, list of the minority of three lords who voted against the third reading of the Habeas Corpus Suspension Bill.

(a) *Lloyd's Evening Post*, 26–28 Feb. 1800; *St. James's Chronicle*, 27 Feb.–1 Mar. 1800; *Whitehall Evening Post*, 27 Feb.–1 Mar. 1800; *Morning Post*, 28 Feb. 1800; *The Times*, 28 Feb. 1800.

453. *21 Apr. 1800*, list of the minority of three lords who voted against the motion for a committee on the King's message and on the address and resolutions respecting a Union with Ireland.
(a) *St. James's Chronicle*, 19–22 Apr. 1800; *Lloyd's Evening Post*, 21–3 Apr. 1800; *Morning Chronicle*, 22 Apr. 1800; *Morning Post*, 22 Apr. 1800.
(b) Debrett, *Parl. Reg.*, LVI, 258; Cobbett, *Parl. Hist.*, XXXV, 158; *The Senator*, XXV, 1058.

454. *8 May 1800*, list of the minority of seven lords who voted against the motion to agree with the Commons on an address respecting Union with Ireland.
(a) *St. James's Chronicle*, 8–10 May 1800; *Morning Post*, 9 May 1800.
(b) Debrett, *Parl. Reg.*, LVI, 555; Cobbett, *Parl. Hist.*, XXXV, 196; *The Senator*, XXV, 1358.

455. *23 May 1800*, list of the majority of 77 lords (including 29 proxies) who voted for, and the minority of 69 lords (including 28 proxies) who voted against the third reading of the Adultery Prevention Bill.
(a) *True Briton*, 27 May 1800; *General Evening Post*, 27–29 May 1800; *Morning Post*, 28 May 1800; *Morning Chronicle*, 28 May 1800; *Lloyd's Evening Post*, 28–30 May 1800. There are small variations between these versions of ·the list.
(b) Debrett, *Parl. Reg.*, LVI, 715–6.
(c) Mather, *High Church Prophet*, pp. 293–4.

456. *?8 June 1800*, list of the possible voting intentions of 23 lords on the Earl of Carlisle's motion regarding a breach of the privileges of the House of Lords; the motion was scheduled for 10 June 1800.
(a) B.L., Add. MS. 58922, ff. 119–20.

457. *9 June 1800*, list of the 30 lords and 19 proxies likely to support the Earl of Carlisle's intended motion regarding breach of the privileges of the House of Lords, together with lists of 15 peers named as doubtful and six proxies doubtful.
(a) B.L., Add. MS. 58922, ff. 131–2.

458. *?June 1800*, undated list of 29 lords, probably compiled in anticipation of the Earl of Carlisle's motion regarding a breach of the privileges of the House of Lords.
(a) B.L., Add. MS. 58922, f. 127.

459. *9 July 1800*, list of the minority of two lords who voted for Lord Holland's motion that Parliament be not prorogued.
(a) *General Evening Post*, 8–10 July 1800; *Lloyd's Evening Post*, 9–11 July 1800.

Appendix A: Lost Lists

The following division lists are recorded in the typescript catalogue at the Wiltshire R.O. of the Ailesbury MSS. as items 12, 24 and 23 respectively of 'Lord Bruce's Collections', vol. I. This volume was not transferred to the Record Office with the rest of the manuscripts and is now reported as lost.

A1. *6 Dec. 1705*, those voting in the 'Church in Danger' debate.
    (a) Ailesbury MSS., 'Lord Bruce's Collection', vol. I, item 12, 'List of the Lords that voted upon the Question whether the Church was in danger, that it was not': 86 names headed by Prince George.

A2. *14 Apr. 1716*, those voting on whether to commit the Septennial Bill.
    (a) Ailesbury MSS., 'Lord Bruce's Collection', vol. I, 'Bill for continuing the Parliament 1716': 77 for (including the Prince of Wales), 43 against; proxies, 19 for, 18 against.

A3. *19 June 1716*, those voting in the Committee of the Whole House on whether to agree to amendments to the Forefeited Estates Bill.
    (a) Ailesbury MSS., 'Lord Bruce's Collection', vol. I, 'Question on the Register Bill 1716': 51 for, 24 against.

Appendix B: Undated and Unidentified Lists

B1. Undated list of 13 lords, probably pre-1760.
     (a) B.L., Add. MS. 33002, f. 404.

B2. Undated list of 14 lords, probably early 1760.
     (a) B.L., Add. MS. 35596, f. 79.

B3. Undated list of 16 lords, probably early 1760s.
     (a) B.L. Add. MS. 33000, ff. 337–8.

B4. Undated list of 16 bishops, probably early 1760s.
     (a) B.L., Add. MS. 33002, ff. 402–3, 418–9.

B5. Undated list of 24 bishops and two archbishops, naming 16 'in & about London' and ten 'Absent'; probably mid 1760s.
     (a) B.L., Add. MS. 33002, ff. 418–19.

B6. Undated list of 23 lords, probably early 1760s.
     (a) J.R.U.L.M., Townsend Papers, Militia, Eng. MS. 939, no. 26. The list belongs to a series of papers concerning the militia in the early 1760s.

B7. Undated list of 43 lords, clearly a list of Newcastle's friends from the early 1760s.
     (a) Dorset R.O., Fox-Strangways Papers, Box 240a, bundle 5.

B8. Undated list of 16 lords, possibly 1765.
     (a) B.L., Add. MS. 57810, f. 145. This list, in the Grenville Papers, is among correspondence dated between 30 Mar. and 19 May 1765.
     (b) *Additional Grenville Papers, 1763–65*, ed. J.R.G. Tomlinson (Manchester, 1962), p. 253.

B9. Undated list of the House of Lords, endorsed 'No. [?] Peers'. 210 lords are listed, 128 as 'Pro', six 'Hopeful', 11 'Doubtful', 35 'Con', 12 'Under age', ten 'Roman Catholics' and eight 'abroad'. The list probably belongs to the later period of North's ministry; the presence of Rockingham means that it must have been compiled before July 1782, while the absence of Thurlow from such a full canvass suggests that it was compiled before his elevation to the peerage in July 1778.
     (a) B.L., MS. Facs. 340 (3), ff. 75–80.

B10. Undated list, endorsed 'State of the House of Lords'; 62 lords are listed as 'Prob.', 13 as 'Con & hopeful' and one as 'Doubtful'. The presence of Rockingham (under 'Prob.') means that the list must have been compiled before July 1782.
     (a) B.L., MS. Facs. 340 (4), ff. 185–7.

Appendix C: Proxy Lists

C1. *1660–1800*, official Proxy Books.
    (a) H.L.R.O., Proxy Books, I (1625–6, 1660), IV-LXXIV (1662/3–1800).

C2. *1703–4* session, proxy list compiled by or for the Earl of Sunderland.
    (a) B.L., Add. MS. 61495, f. 21 (formerly Blenheim papers, D.II.10).

C3. *?1715*, proxy list compiled by Sunderland.
    (a) B.L., Add. MS. 38507, ff. 187–8.

C4. *28 Jan. 1741*, proxy list compiled by the Duke of Newcastle.
    (a) B.L., Add. MS. 33034, ff. 9–10.

C5. *24 Feb. 1741*, proxy list compiled by Newcastle.
    (a) B.L., Add. MS. 33034, f. 31.

C6. *c. 9 May 1758*, proxy list compiled by Newcastle.
    (a) B.L., Add. MS. 33034, f. 257.

C7. *26 May 1758*, proxy list compiled by Newcastle.
    (a) B.L., Add. MS. 33034, f. 270.

C8. *May 1758*, proxy list compiled by Newcastle.
    (a) B.L., Add. MS. 33034, f. 272.

C9. *2 Apr. 1765*, (Poor Bill), list of 'proxies for, April 2, 1765' (ten proxies and their holders given) and 'Proxies against or not given' (15 and four respectively, with their holders).
    (a) B.L., Add. MS. 32966, ff. 165–5, with draft at ff. 150–1.

C10. *28 Apr. 1765*, list of 22 proxies, with their holders; dated 28 Apr. but endorsed 28 Mar. 1765.
    (a) B.L., Add. MS. 33035, ff. 122–3.

C11. *17 Dec. 1765*, list of 15 proxies, with their holders.
    (a) B.L., Add. MS. 33035, ff. 194–5.

C12. *7 Feb. 1766*, list of 36 proxies, with their holders; four other proxies are deleted as 'vacated'.
    (a) B.L., Add. MS. 33035, ff. 294–5.

C13. *20 Feb. 1766*, list of 34 proxies, with their holders.
    (a) B.L., Add. MS. 33035, ff. 327–8.

C14. *24 Feb. 1766*, list of 28 proxies, with their holders.
    (a) W.W.M., R53–7.

C15. *6 Mar. 1766*, list of 43 proxies, with their holders; seven other proxies listed and deleted as 'vacated'.
    (a) B.L., Add. MS. 33035, ff. 361–2. Each proxy on this list is numbered; there is a partial list of these proxies, by number, as 'For' (29) and 'Against' (12), headed 'Proxies this moment brought from the office' and dated 6 Mar. 1766 at Add. MS. 33001, f. 147.

C16. *11 Mar. 1766*, list of 46 proxies, with their holders; further list of 32 proxies for and 11 against the Stamp Act Repeal Bill and its committal.
    (a) B.L., Add. MS. 33035, ff. 392–3, 394–6 respectively.
    (c) Lowe, 'House of Lords', p. 986, comments on the latter of these lists.

C17. *26 Mar. 1766*, list of 52 proxies, with their holders.
    (a) B.L., Add. MS. 33035, ff. 440–1.

C18. *26 May 1766*, list of 51 proxies, with their holders.
    (a) B.L., Add. MS. 33036, ff. 120–1.

C19. *28 May 1766*, list of 55 proxies, with their holders.
    (a) B.L., Add. MS. 33036, f.130.

C20. *12 Nov. 1766*, list of eight proxies, with their holders.
    (a) B.L., Add. MS. 33036, ff. 161–2.

C21. *6 Dec. 1766*, list of 17 proxies, with their holders.
    (a) B.L., Add. MS. 33036, f. 217.

C22. *?early 1767*, undated list of 27 proxies, with their holders.
    (a) B.L., Add. MS. 33037, ff. 39–40.

C23. *26 Jan. 1767*, list of 16 proxies, with their holders.
    (a) B.L., Add. MS. 33036, ff. 255–6.

C24. *7May 1767*, list of 30 proxies, with their holders.
    (a) B.L., Add. MS. 33036, f. 467.

C25. *15 May 1767*, list of 38 proxies, with their holders; the list is endorsed 'Court 28. Against 10'.
    (a) B.L., Add. MS. 33036, f. 491.

C26. *22 May 1767*, list of 42 proxies, with their holders.
    (a) B.L., Add. MS. 33037, ff. 37–8.

C27. *3 June 1767*, list of 39 proxies, with their holders.
    (a) B.L., Add. MS. 33037, ff. 93–4.

C28. *20 June 1767*, list of 39 proxies, with their holders.
    (a) B.L. Add. MS. 33037, f. 133.

C29. *24 Nov. 1767*, list of 14 proxies, with their holders.
    (a) B.L. Add. MS. 33037, ff. 189–90.

C30. *?10 June 1800*, undated list of 56 proxies and their holders; correlation between the list and the House of Lords proxy book for the session of 1800 suggests that it was compiled on 9 June 1800, in anticipation of the Earl of Carlisle's motion regarding a breach of the privileges of the House of Lords the following day.

    (a) B.L., Add. MS. 59375, ff. 164–5.

C31. *N.d.*, five proxy lists.

    (a) B.L., Add. MS. 33002, ff. 415–16, 424–9, 434–5 (Newcastle Papers). The fifth list (ff. 434–5) is marked, probably indicating those in favour and against.

II

THE HOUSE OF COMMONS, 1660–1761

Introduction

David Hayton and Eveline Cruickshanks

Leaving aside a small number of lists upon whose nature and purpose we can only speculate, the following types of Commons list occur in this period:[1] 'management lists', by far the highest proportion at about half, and almost all deriving from Court or ministerial sources; the associated lists of pre-sessional meetings, which amounted to a rudimentary attempt at 'whipping'; analyses of election returns, into 'parties' or more simply into those who could be relied on to support administration and those who could not; forecasts for divisions, and of course division lists proper, which form about a third of the total. Some division lists were compiled for private purposes, often, once again, as an aid to parliamentary management; others, recording the more important votes, or covering issues in which public interest was high, were intended for publication, usually with a view to influencing the electorate for or against prospective candidates. In this category we should place the various lists of placemen and pensioners, starting with *Flagellum Parliamentarium* in about 1673, and attaining a high point during the so-called 'Officers' Parliament' of 1690–5. (Subsequently, in the eighteenth century, the practice of publishing lists of placemen and pensioners *as such* seems to have been abandoned; instead, printed division list on crucial votes often identified these venal dependants on the Court side, implying that their votes had been bought and paid for in a corrupt cause.)

Such 'white' and 'black lists' were especially common in the early eighteenth century, before the Septennial Act rendered elections less frequent. The effectiveness of the so-called 'black list', published before the second general election of 1701 (and probably based on a division the previous February on an address to enter into alliances necessary for the peace of Europe), which stigmatized the Tories as favourers, and indeed tools of, the French, was such that in the following session senior Tory politicians avoided a division on a similarly delicate issue rather than run similar risk: when the Whig Lord Hartington moved 'that it be an instruction to the committee that is to consider rights, liberties and privileges of this House that they consider the rights and liberties of the commons of England', Sir Edward Seymour and his friends refrained

---

[1] This section is a revised version of the introduction contributed by Eveline Cruickshanks to the Commons section of the first edition of this *Register* (pp. 65–76).

from pressing home their opposition, since according to a Whig diarist, 'had they divided the House . . . it would have [been] a worse list for them than the black list, viz that they had been against the rights and liberties of the [commons] of England'.[2] 'White lists', on the other hand, gloried in the parliamentary deeds of those whom they named. Typical are two broadsheet lists of Tories from 1711, one of 'true English patriots' who 'were for easing the nation of the heavy burden [of] taxes, by putting an end to the expensive and bloody war'; the other of 'worthy patriots' who in the first session of the new Parliament had exposed the mismanagements of the previous ministry 'and provided for the payment of all national debts; and preserved the Church of England from being overturned by fanatics'.

The predominance of lists compiled by and for parliamentary managers is reflected in the chronological spread of the lists, the lulls and the peaks of activity. The paucity of such lists can be accounted for by low levels of party-political activity, as in the closing years of the Parliament of 1749–54. Conversely a clustering of lists will often occur in a period of tension, as in 1716–19, 1729–34 and 1739–42, and earlier in 1678–81, when, as Narcissus Luttrell recorded, 'the parties were so even that it was carried sometimes by one side and sometimes by the other, not by above four or five voices'.[3]

Alternatively, the number of lists can also reflect the accidents of survival. On the one hand there is the curious absence of any significant number of management lists in the archive of Sir Robert Walpole; on the other, the proliferation of lists of Court supporters and of placemen in the 1670s stems from the new 'system' of Commons management being developed by Sir Thomas Osborne, Earl of Danby, based on disciplining a large body of office-holders and pensioners. When Danby took up the reins of management again after the Revolution, his papers contain another clutch of lists. Later managers whose calculations are well documented in this way include Robert Harley (1st Earl of Oxford and Lord Treasurer 1711–14), who organized first the 'New Country Party' opposition of the 1690s, then the mixed or 'moderate' Court party of 1704–8, and finally, as 'premier minister', attempted to sit astride the headstrong Tory majority in the Commons after 1710; and Charles Spencer, 3rd Earl of Sunderland, who cut his political teeth as a member of the Whig Junto in the reign of Anne and subsequently became first minister to George I. The plethora of lists in the Duke of Newcastle's papers for the years 1753–61 is partly to be accounted for by Newcastle's habit of hoarding papers, and partly by his unfamiliarity with the House

---

[2] Bodl. Lib., MS. Eng. hist. b. 210, f. 5 (Sir Richard Cocks' diary). David Hayton has edited this diary for publication.

[3] N. Luttrell, *A Brief Historical Relation of State Affairs* (6 vols., Oxford, 1857), I, 3.

of Commons, from the management of which his brother Henry Pelham had previously excluded him.

Procedure in Relation to Divisions

As in the Lords, the first means used for testing opinion on a question was the 'collective voice', when the Speaker would declare the result on the basis of the relative volume of noise made by each side. Any Members could then force a division after the Speaker had given his decision, simply by saying 'the contrary voice has the question'. A division might even be contrived in this way to expose the minority, as happened in the famous division of 5 February 1689 on the vacancy of the throne, when it was 'thought by some that many of those who were hearty for the vote joined with others in the noes on purpose to sift them as afterwards it did appear'.[4] The incident was then used as the basis for an early 'black list' of supposed Jacobites circulated before the general election in 1690.

There were no separate division lobbies. Divisions were taken by sending one side out of the House to be counted by two tellers on their return through the lobby door, which was kept closed until those who had remained in their seats (and who were not allowed to move about) had been counted by the other two tellers. The principle applied by the Speaker, to decide which side should go out and which remain, was that those who were 'for the preservation of the orders of the House' should stay in, and those 'introducing any new material or any alteration' should go out. Anyone unfortunate enough to be locked outside the lobby when the division was called could not vote, a rule which produced a notable embarrassment for the ministry in April 1714, when the Tobacco Drawbacks Bill was lost in frustrating circumstances:

> This matter was very nice, for the votes being equal, the Speaker gave it against the Court, which he would not have had the opportunity of doing, if Mr Lowndes had not been obliged to go to the house of office, and he ran with his breeches in his hand, but they would not let him in.

Similarly, anyone left inside the House when the doors were closed was reckoned as having given a vote, whether or not his staying in had been intentional. The octogenarian William Sloper, who fell asleep during the debate on the Spanish Convention in 1739, and did not awaken until the division had begun, thus 'voted against his own inclinations', while George Gage, an Irish peer, was 'shut in by mistake' in 1747, and was

---

[4] Dr Williams' Library, Morrice MS. Q, p. 459 (Roger Morrice's 'Entr'ing Book'), quoted in E. Cruickshanks, J. Ferris and D. Hayton, 'The House of Commons Vote on the Transfer of the Crown, 5 February 1689', *B.I.H.R.*, LII (1979), 38.

Fig. 3. St Stephen's Chapel (House of Commons) in the Eighteenth Century

Sources: Plan of the Palace of Westminster by William Benson, c. 1719, from a copy dated 1793 (Sir John Soane Museum: 35.5.25); 'Plan of the House of Lords and Commons with the Benches of Accommodation' by Sir Christopher Wren, c. 1710 (Westminster City Library: Extra-illustrated copy of T. Pennant, *Some Account of London*, III [1925], f. 105).

1: Speaker's chair. 2: Clerk's table. 3: South side of the House showing benches on the floor of the House, with Gallery over as on north side. 4: North side of the House showing Gallery with benches, seating underneath as on south side. 5: Passage, known as 'Solomon's Porch'. 6: Stairs leading to Gallery. 7: Speaker's Withdrawing Room. 8: Clerks' closet. 9: Bar of the House. 10: Lobby. 11: Bog House. 12: Stairs to the Speaker's Chamber. 13: Speaker's Chamber. 14: Stairs to the Commons. 15: Gallery to the Painted Chamber. 16: West Gallery for 'strangers'. 17: Probably site of stairs leading to Strangers' Gallery. 18: Seat 'below the Bar'.

Notes on Plan
The seating arrangements in the Galleries is based on:

1. Sir Christopher Wren's designs for refitting the House of Commons in 1692 (All Souls College, Oxford, Wren Drawings, IV, 91), which shows four benches in the west or end Gallery (or 'Gallery below the Bar' as it was often known). This end Gallery had been built in 1621, and had originally been painted with 'rance', a mottled red (P.R.O., E 351/3254, quoted in E.R. Foster, 'Staging a Parliament in Early Stuart England', *The English Commonwealth, 1547–1640: Essays in Politics and Society Presented to Joel Hurstfield*, eds. P. Clark, A.G.R. Smith and N. Tyacke [Leicester, 1979], pp. 132, 241 n. 21).
2. A painting of the interior of the House of Commons, c. 1710, by Peter Tillemans, which shows two rows of Members sat in the north and south Galleries.

New stairs were constructed in 1670 to reach the end Gallery where 'strangers' sat (*The History of the King's Works*, ed. H.M. Colvin [6 vols, 1963–82], V, 400). The probable siting of these stairs is taken from Wren's plan of c. 1710 (see sources for plan above). The Gallery ran the full width of the west wall. The north and south Galleries were constructed by Wren in 1692. Each had a row of benches, but in 1707 the Galleries were widened to take two rows to accommodate the extra M.P.s brought into the House by the Anglo-Scottish Union (*History of the King's Works*, V, 400–4).

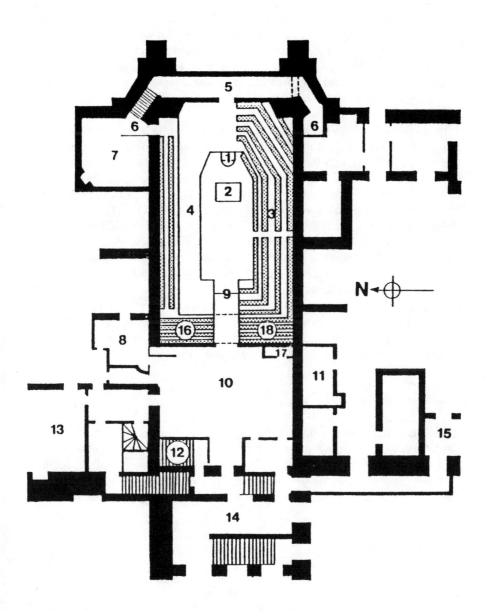

counted as voting against his own son's election petition.[5] To abstain, a Member had to leave the House altogether, or retire to the Speaker's room on the north side of the House through a door at the back of the Chamber into a passage known as 'Solomon's porch', to which William Shippen, for example, betook himself in 1741 to avoid voting for the motion to dismiss Walpole.[6] A Scots Member unseated on petition in February 1711 noted that in the critical vote 'several . . . Scots people, who had been resolved to be against me, could not prevail with themselves to go to the length to vote against me, so they went up to the galeries and skulked there, as did a good many other of the English'.[7]

In divisions in Committee of the Whole House, when the Speaker was not in the Chair, the Members filed pased either side of the Chair and there was only one teller on each side. (A rare list of a division in Committee available for this period is that of the Bewdley election dispute of 1706.) The same procedure was used in the election of the Speaker, the clerk of the House acting as Speaker *pro tem*. In 1705, when John Smith was chosen in a party-political showdown with the High Tory William Bromley, a list of the division was made by or for the back-bencher Thomas Conyers. In the case of a 'secret' committee, or a parliamentary commission, such as the commission of accounts in the early 1690s, no list of voters could be compiled, for Members were chosen by ballot: 'The clerk, and the clerk assistant, went on each side of the House with glasses, to receive from Members the lists of persons' names to be the said committee: and the said lists, being received, were brought up to the clerks' table', and taken on to a committee appointed to scrutinize the lists and declare the result.[8]

Who Could have Compiled Division Lists?

The most likely compilers were Members themselves. Ignoring the prohibition on bringing pens and paper into the Chamber, many M.P.s took notes during proceedings: one, the future Whig Lord Chancellor William Cowper, even made notes on debates in 1698–9 while seated in the chair of the committee of supply and ways and means.[9] Nor were they

---

[5] *Wentworth Papers*, p. 372; Sedgwick, I, 2; B.L., Add. MS. 33058, ff. 477–80.

[6] Sedgwick, I, 2; P.D.G. Thomas, *The House of Commons in the Eighteenth Century* (Oxford, 1971), pp. 245, 252–4; H.M.C., *Egmont Diary*, III, 192.

[7] Scottish R.O., GD 220/5/808/18 (Montrose papers), Mungo Graham to Montrose, 13 Feb. 1711.

[8] *C.J.*, XV, 5; XXII, 126; E. May, *A Treatise of the Law, Privileges, Proceedings and Usage of Parliament* (1924 edn.), p. 155.

[9] 'Debates in the House of Commons, 1697–1699', ed. D.W. Hayton, *Camden Miscellany XXIX* (Camden 4th ser., XXXIV, 1987), pp. 392–401.

shy of communicating their notes to others. In 1712 Peter Wentworth, a 'stranger' who regularly frequented the gallery, reported:

> The day I was in the House of Commons to hear the debate about the Barrier Treaty. I did not set myself to remember as much as I might, because I was promised by a Member that he would give me the notes he had taken, from whence I thought I should have been able to have writ you the whole debate from the beginning to the ending; but the gentleman has not kept his word with me, so I shall entertain you with a little more of it, tho' it won't be so methodical.[10]

Members may thus have drawn up lists themselves; usually by marking names on one of the many published broadsheet lists of the House, a conclusion dictated by the fact that surviving manuscript lists tend to follow the order of the published lists – county by county and within counties by borough in order of precedence.[11] These published lists naturally formed a good basis on which to construct a 'management list'. In the period after 1689 Lord Carmarthen, the former Danby, who headed William III's first ministry, seems invariably to have used these printed lists to make calculations of likely supporters and opponents. Another relatively simple way to record a division could have been to note only the names of those voting contrary to their normal practice, but although some lists of cross-voters survive there is no explicit evidence of this method of compilation actually having been used. The telling and noting of names would have been made easier by the practice which grew up in the eighteenth century of the Court or ministerial party sitting themselves to the right of the Chair (with the well-known exception of William Pulteney), and the anti-courtiers, or 'opposition' as they were coming increasingly to be called, on the left, a practice which probably developed from the natural habit of sitting with one's friends, and the necessity of concerting parliamentary tactics. Earlier in the period, seating patterns may have reflected regional groupings: in 1699 Henry Vincent was said to belong to the 'Saxon corner' of the Chamber, presumably where the west country Members congregated.[12]

Even so, most lists were probably compiled after the event, and in consultation with other witnesses. Defoe wrote in March 1705:

> We all know it is impossible for any man, though a Member of the House, to be able to give an exact list. This or that Member, or several together, concerting

---

[10] *Wentworth Papers*, p. 268.

[11] I.F. Burton and P.W.J. Riley, 'Division Lists of the Reigns of William III and Anne: What Are They? How Were They Compiled?', in *The Parliamentary Lists of the Early Eighteenth Century: Their Compilation and Use*, ed. A. Newman (Leicester, 1973), pp. 22–7.

[12] *Letters Illustrative of the Reigns of William III from 1696 to 1708 . . .*, ed. G.P.R. James (3 vols., 1841), II, 344–5.

and recollecting, may have a great many, but I appeal to the world, whether any man in England, nay, though he were one of them appointed for telling noses, could charge his memory with 134 names at one view and be able to be positive of his men.[13]

From at least the reign of George II, and probably earlier, the peers had a special place below the bar allocated to them to hear Commons proceedings.[14] They could also sit in the galleries, and there are several references from Anne's reign to peers attending incogniti in the galleries:[15] even, in the case of the Duke of Roxburghe in 1707, to direct his followers and the other adherents of the Scottish faction known as the *Squadrone*, in debating tactics.[16] One of the division lists on the transfer of the Crown in 1689 may have been compiled by Lord Ailesbury, in whose papers it was found.

Many of the Commons lists, however, originated with persons who were not Members of either House of Parliament. Outsiders could spectate from the Strangers' Gallery, though they were usually excluded, often at the request of the ministerial side, during sensitive debates.[17] Regular access was obtained by journalists such as John Dyer, Edward Cave and Nathaniel Mist, through bestowing 'constant fees upon their doorkeepers and officers' or through being met by Members at the door. Cases brought against them for breach of parliamentary privileges met with little success.[18] It was even easier for anyone with parliamentary connexions to get in. Lord Egmont, an Irish peer and a former Member of the Commons, but out of the House since 1734, simply 'went into the gallery of the House of Commons to hear the debate upon the army' in 1737.[19]

Because of the large number of Members (513 before the Union with Scotland and 558 thereafter), and especially with the rapid turnover in the period of the Triennial Act (1693–1716), it was not particularly easy to spot strangers. The order to clear the Strangers' Gallery was sometimes strictly enforced, but not invariably. Indeed, strangers were known to have sat on occasion in the body of the Chamber, and conceivably may have even participated in divisions. One such instance occurred in February 1694, when, it was reported, 'a Frenchman got privately into the House

---

[13] *A Review of the Affairs of France*, II, no. 7 (20 Mar. 1705), quoted in Speck, thesis, p. 91.

[14] Thomas, *House of Commons in the Eighteenth Century*, p. 150.

[15] Atholl MSS. (the Duke of Atholl, Blair Castle, Blair Atholl, Perthshire), 45/7/190, James Murray to [Atholl], 5 Dec. 1707; Scottish R.O., GD 124/5/259/3 (Mar and Kellie papers), William Cleland to [James Erskine], 6 Dec. 1705.

[16] Roxburghe MSS. (the Duke of Roxburghe, Floors Castle, Kelso, Roxburghshire), bundle 739, William Bennet to Countess of Roxburghe, 16 Dec. 1707.

[17] Thomas, *House of Commons in the Eighteenth Century*, p. 143.

[18] Sedgwick, I, 16; *D.N.B.* (Cave, Edward); *C.J.*, II, 48; XIV, 207–8.

[19] H.M.C., *Egmont Diary*, II, 350.

of Commons and sat down some time before he was discovered'.[20] Since Members were then engaged in listening to a report from the Secretary of State, Lord Nottingham, of secret intelligence of the Brest fleet, it is hardly surprising that the intruder was arrested and sent into the custody of the serjeant-at-arms, and not merely escorted from the House, as was the normal practice. The lobby of the House was frequently crowded with outsiders seeking to speak to Members on particular bills, or just coming for news. Such was the thirst for parliamentary gossip that in the spring of 1698, at the time of the inquiry into accusations of bribery of ministers by the Old East India Company, one Richard Froggatt was discovered to have stolen hundreds of 'post-letters directed at Members of the House' by breaking open 'the boxes at the lobby door', and to have sold some of the contents.[21]

Distribution of the Lists

Curiosity about parliamentary affairs ensured a wide circulation for parliamentary lists. Sir Thomas Meres declared in 1673 that the way Members had voted on the Declaration of Indulgence was quickly 'known about the town', and 20 years later another M.P., Paul Whichcote, was told that, 'when it comes to a party cause everybody knows how the votes run in both Houses'.[22] The names of those who voted in 1689 against the transfer of the Crown were public knowledge within a fortnight.[23] A zenith of interest was reached in 1704 by the issue of the 'Tack' (of the third Occasional Conformity Bill to a supply measure), since at least nine different versions of the crucial Commons division have survived. The vote in 1744 on keeping Hanoverian troops in British pay, which occurred in a Chamber as full as at any time since the fall of Walpole, was also very widely circulated, one copy even being printed in three colours to denote, respectively, those for, those against and those absent, a method of printing which demanded three separate processes and was thus very expensive.[24] In contrast, the division on the same issue two years later, when party conflict had died down, appears not to have been published at all.

[20] Folger Shakespeare Library, Newdigate newsletter, 10 Feb. 1694.

[21] *C.J.*, XII, 259–61, 287–8.

[22] A. Grey, *Debates of the House of Commons from the Year 1667 to the Year 1694* (10 vols., 1763), II, 51–2; Speck, thesis, p. 59.

[23] Cruickshanks *et al.*, 'Transfer of the Crown', p. 39.

[24] *A List of the Members of the House of Commons, Jan. 18 1743/4* ([1744], sold by J. Morgan, in Paternoster Row). The publication of division lists in the mid eighteenth century is discussed in M. Harris, *London Newspapers in the Age of Walpole: A Study in the Origins of the Modern English Press* (1987), pp. 171 *et seq.*; and R. Harris, *The Patriot Press: National Politics and the London Press in the 1740s* (Oxford, 1993), pp. 24–6.

The Reliability of Division Lists

Without an official system of recording the names of those voting in divisions one cannot regard any of these lists as being entirely accurate. We have already heeded Defoe's warning that the best that might be expected, even from 'several . . . concerting and recollecting' was 'a great many' but not 'an exact list'. At times, when the light inside the House was poor, it might be difficult for a teller even to count heads, let alone recognise faces. One eye-witness account of a division in 1711 concluded, 'I cannot be positive but there might be one or two more, for it was dark, and Jo[hn] Cockburn [a teller] could hardly well discern them'.[25] A number, the 'black' and 'white lists' especially, were in fact composite lists, giving only the general disposition of Members towards a particular question, and not the voting at a specific division. These of course left considerable room for error and scope for abuse. There are several composite lists, for example on the Sacheverell impeachment, which are among the least reliable of any lists for the period.[26] William Blathwayt was to complain bitterly of his having been included in a published list of 'those who voted against Dr Sacheverell', since it induced the Duke of Beaufort 'to oppose his election' at Bath later in the year. As he informed Lord Dartmouth, 'the report is altogether untrue . . . by reason of his illness he never once attended any of the debates, much less was in any division on the subject'.[27] Election 'black lists' such as this were notorious for including persons not even Members of Parliament at the time of the division in which they were alleged to have taken part, and were sometimes freely adapted for local purposes.[28] 'White lists', for the same reason, were equally prone to distortion and error.[29] Thus the gradual disappearance of these generalized propaganda lists in the course of the eighteenth century, combined with an apparent increase in the numbers of hack reporters paid to haunt the galleries, would suggest that the standard of accuracy, at least in published division lists, might well have improved with the passage of time. However, the techniques employed in the compiling of lists for private consumption, and the awareness and political astuteness of the compilers, probably remained unchanged.

[25] Scottish R.O., GD 220/5/808/18, Mungo Graham to Montrose, 13 Feb. 1711. See also Cambridge University Library, Add. MS. 6851, vol. I, f. 53 (Edward Harley's parliamentary journal), for the case of an inexperienced teller mistaking voting figures. Clyve Jones and Stephen Taylor are editing this text for publication.

[26] Speck, thesis, p. 73.

[27] H.M.C., *Dartmouth MSS.*, I, 297.

[28] See for example, Cruickshanks *et al.*, 'Transfer of the Crown', pp. 40–1.

[29] H.L. Snyder, 'A New Parliament List for 1711', *B.I.H.R.*, L (1977), 186–90, 193.

List of Lists

FIRST PARLIAMENT OF CHARLES II, 1660

1. *1660*, 'Names of the members of the Commons howse, 1660' (those who would oppose the exception of Lord Wharton from the Bill of Indemnity).
   - (a) Bodl. Lib, MS. Carte 81, ff. 74–7.
   - (b) G.F. Trevallyn Jones, 'The Composition and Leadership of the Presbyterian Party in the Convention', *E.H.R.*, LXXIX (1964), 332–47.
   - (c) *Ibid.*, pp. 307–30, who identifies this list as members of the Presbyterian party.

2. *6 Nov. 1660*, 'List of Persons to whom papers are delivered in and to be delivered' (those expected to speak in the debate on modified episcopacy).
   - (a) Bodl. Lib., MS. Carte 80, f. 559 (Wharton papers).
   - (b) Trevallyn Jones, 'Presbyterian Party', pp. 348–9.
   - (c) *Ibid.*, pp. 307–53.

SECOND PARLIAMENT OF CHARLES II, 1661–79

3. *1661*, Wharton's friends.
   - (a) Bodl. Lib., MS. Carte 81, ff. 79–80.
   - (b) Trevallyn Jones, 'Presbyterian Party', pp. 350–2.
   - (c) *Ibid.*, pp. 307–53.

4. *1661*, list, by Wharton, of 'Moderate men'.
   - (a) Bodl. Lib., MS. Carte 81, f. 83.
   - (b) Trevallyn Jones, 'Presbyterian Party', p. 354.
   - (c) *Ibid.*, pp. 307–53.

5. *1664*, 'Court Dependants'.
   - (a) P.R.O., 30/24/34/19 (Shaftesbury MSS.).
   - (b) J.R. Jones 'Court Dependants in 1664', *B.I.H.R.*, XXXIV (1961), 84–91.

6. *11 May 1668*, followers of the Duke of Ormond.
   - (a) Bodl. Lib. MS. Carte 36, f. 320.
   - (b) *Danby*, III, 34–44.
   - (c) *Ibid.*, I, 75 n.2.

7. *Autumn 1669*, followers of the Duke of Buckingham.
   - (b) F.R. Harris, *The Life of Edward Montagu . . . 1st Earl of Sandwich* (2 vols., 1912), II, 312.
   - (c) *Danby*, I, 75 n.3.

8. *Sept.–Nov. 1669*, Court supporters.
   (a) B.L., Add. MS. 28091, ff. 147–8, 163–4.
   (b) *Danby*, III, 34–44.
   (c) *Ibid.*, p. 33.

9. *c. May 1671*, list of Court supporters with satirical notices (a precursor of
   Flagellum Parliamentarium: see below no. 10).
   (a) B.L., Harl. MS. 7020, ff. 33–48.
   (c) *Ibid.*, p. 33.

10. *c. 1673*, list of the Court party with satirical notices.
    (a) B.L., Lansd. MS. 805, ff. 83–9.
    (b) *Flagellum Parliamentarium* . . . , ed. Sir N. Harris Nicolas (1827).
    (c) E.S. de Beer, 'Members of the Court Party in the House of Commons,
        1670–1678', *B.I.H.R.*, XI (1933–4), 1–2.

11. *Nov. 1673–Feb. 1674*, list of Court supporters, probably compiled by
    Sir Robert Paston.
    (a) B.L., Add. MS. 27448, f. 395.
    (b) B.D. Henning, *The House of Commons, 1660–1690* (3 vols., 1983), I,
        p. xxv.

12. *Midsummer 1674*, list of M.P.s receiving pensions from the Excise.
    (a) B.L., Add. MS. 28078, f. 165.
    (b) *Danby*, III, 44–5.
    (c) *Ibid.*, p. 44.

13. *Apr.–Dec. 1675*, Court 'dependants'.
    (a) B.L., Add. MS. 28091, ff. 169–70.
    (b) *Danby*, III, 65–8.
    (c) *Ibid.*, pp. 61–2.

14. *Apr. 1675–Feb. 1676*, 'King's servants and dependants'.
    (a) P.R.O., SP. 29/281A/255.
    (b) *Danby*, III, 62–5.
    (c) *Ibid.*, pp. 61–2.

15. *May 1675–Apr. 1676*, Sir Joseph Williamson's list of 'Government speakers'.
    (a) P.R.O., S.P. 29/387/240.
    (b) *Danby*, III, 94–6.
    (c) *Ibid.*, p. 93.

16. *May 1675–May 1676*, those to be canvassed.
    (a) B.L., Add. MS. 28091, f. 183.
    (b) *Danby*, III, 72–4.
    (c) *Ibid.*, p. 72 n.1.

17. *Midsummer 1675*, list of M.P.s receiving pensions from the Excise.
    (a) B.L., Add. MS. 28080, ff. 17–18.
    (b) *Danby*, III, 45–7.
    (c) *Ibid.*, p. 44.

18. *Sept. 1675*, those to be sent the Court 'whip'.
    (a) P.R.O., S.P. 29/373/179–81.
    (b) *Danby*, III, 58–61.
    (c) *Ibid.*, pp. 56–8.

19. *c. Oct. 1675*, 'Servants and Officers'.
    (a) B.L., Add. MS. 28091, f. 144.
    (b) *Danby*, III, 68–71.
    (c) *Ibid.*, pp. 61–2.

20. *c. Oct. 1675*, those 'to be remembered'.
    (a) B.L., Add. MS. 28091, f. 146.
    (b) *Danby*, III, 78–9.
    (c) *Ibid.*, p. 78 n.1.

21. *Nov. 1675*, those to be canvassed on the bill against bribery.
    (a) B.L., Add. MS. 28091, f. 158.
    (b) *Danby*, III, 74–7.
    (c) *Ibid.*, p. 74 n.1.

22. *Autumn 1675*, management list.
    (a) P.R.O., S.P. 29/237/238.
    (b) *Danby*, III, 82–4.
    (c) *Ibid.*, p. 82 n.1.

23. *Autumn 1675*, management list.
    (a) P.R.O., S.P. 29/376/153–4.
    (b) *Danby*, III, 79–82.
    (c) *Ibid.*, p. 79 n.1.

24. *1676*, Sir Richard Wiseman's account of the Commons.
    (a) B.L., Eg. MS. 3359, ff. 15–16.
    (b) *Danby*, III, 96–111.
    (c) *Ibid.*, p. 96.

25. *1676*, Wiseman's list of non-dependent Court supporters.
    (a) B.L., Add. MS. 28091, ff. 151–2.
    (b) *Danby*, III, 87–93.
    (c) *Ibid.*, p. 87 n.1.

26. *1677*, list of Court supporters with satirical comments.
    (a) *A Seasonable Argument to Persuade all the Grand Juries in England to Petition for a New Parliament* (1677).
    (b) Cobbett, *Parl. Hist.*, IV, Appendix, pp. xxi-xxxiv.
    (c) de Beer, 'Court Party', pp. 1–2.

27. *1677*, list of Court supporters, giving places and pensions.
    (a) B.L., Add. MS. 30170, f. 32.
    (b) W.C. Trevelyan, 'On the Court Party in the House of Commons in 1677', *Archaeologia Aeliana*, I (1822), 173–81.

28. *1677–8*, the Earl of Shaftesbury's list of supporters and opponents of the Court.
    (a) Shaftesbury papers (the Earl of Shaftesbury, St Giles House, Wimborne St Giles, Dorset).
    (b) K.H.D. Haley, 'Shaftesbury's Lists of the Lay Peers and Members of the House of Commons, 1667–8', *B.I.H.R.*, XLIII (1970), 95–105.
    (c) *Ibid.*, pp. 86–92.

29. *Jan.–Apr. 1678*, Sir Joseph Williamson's list of doubtful Court supporters.
    (a) P.R.O., S.P. 29/408/149.
    (b) *Danby*, III, 84–6.
    (c) *Ibid.*, p. 84 n.2.

30. *1678*, Court supporters.
    (a) P.R.O., S.P. 29/408/148.
    (b) *Danby*, III, 112–20.
    (c) *Ibid.*, pp. 111–13.

31. *May 1678*, the principal Court supporters expected in the debate on disbanding the army.
    (a) *Calendar of State Papers Domestic*, 1678, pp. 193–4.

32. *1678*, Court supporters.
    (a) *A List of One Unanimous Club of Voters in His Majesties Long Parliament Dissolved in '78'* [1679].
    (c) de Beer, 'Court Party', p. 2.

THIRD PARLIAMENT OF CHARLES II, 1679

33. *1679*, Shaftesbury's 'Worthy Men', those likely to support the Exclusion Bill.
    (a) P.R.O., 30/24/6A/348 (Shaftesbury papers).
    (b) J.R. Jones, 'Shaftesbury's "Worthy Men": A Whig View of the Parliament of 1679', *B.I.H.R.*, XXX (1957), 236–41.
    (c) *Ibid.*, pp. 232–5.

34. *21 May 1679*, those against the Exclusion Bill.
    (a) Dr Williams' Lib., Morrice MS. P, f. 238; P.R.O., S.P. 29/417/232 (i). Variants.
    (b) The former is printed in A. Browning and D.J. Milne, 'An Exclusion Bill Division List', *B.I.H.R.*, XXIII (1950), 207–25; the latter in K. Feiling, *A History of the Tory Party, 1640–1714* (Oxford, 1924), pp. 494–5.
    (c) Browning and Milne, 'An Exclusion Division List', pp. 205–7.

35. *21 May 1679*, those absent at the division on the Exclusion Bill.
    (a) Dr Williams' Lib., Morrice MS. P, ff. 239–40.
    (b) Browning and Milne, 'An Exclusion Bill Division List', pp. 207–25.
    (c) *Ibid.*, pp. 205–7.

THE PARLIAMENT OF JAMES II, 1685–7

36. *17 Nov. 1685*, the principal Court supporters expected in the debate on the dismissal of Roman Catholic officers.
   (a) *Calendar of Treasury Books*, VIII, 430–1.

37. *1686–7*, Danby's list of the opposition to James II in Parliament.
   (a) B.L., Add. MS. 28091, f. 172.
   (b) *Danby*, III, 155–7.
   (c) *Ibid.*, pp. 152–3.

THE CONVENTION PARLIAMENT, 1689–90

38. *5 Feb. 1689*, the Earl of Ailesbury's list of those in favour of agreeing with the second of the Lords' amendments to the resolution that the throne was vacant.
   (a) Wiltshire R.O., 1300/856 (Ailesbury papers). Variants to be found in [Anthony Rowe], *A Letter to a Friend, upon the Dissolving of the Late Parliament, and the Calling of a New One. Together with a List of Those that were against Making the Prince and Princess of Orange, King and Queen* (1690); Cambridge Univ. Lib., MS. Mm.vi.42, ff. 24–29; H.L.R.O., Historical Collection 82, 'A compleat List of all the Members who were elected to serve in the Several Parliaments of England, from the Long Parliament summond the 3d November 1640 to the Convention Parliament under King William 3d which met the 22d Jan. 1688/9', compiled by the Earl of Egmont (probably in the 1730s), which marks those that 'Voted against making the Pr[ince] of Orange king'.
   (b) E. Cruickshanks, J. Ferris and D. Hayton, 'The House of Commons Vote on the Transfer of the Crown, 5 February 1689', *B.I.H.R.*, LII (1979), 41–7, prints both the Ailesbury and Rowe lists.
   (c) *Ibid.*, pp. 37–41.

39. *19 Oct. 1689*, marked copy of a printed list of the Commons.
   (a) B.L., Dept. of Printed Books, 112. f. 43 (21).

40. *19 Oct. 1689*, marked copy of a printed list of the Commons.
   (a) B.L., Eg. MS. 3359, ff. 23–4.

41. *Jan. 1690*, those in favour of the disabling clauses of the Corporation Bill.
   (a) *Some Queries Concerning the Election of Members for the Ensuing Parliament* (1690).
   (b) *Danby*, III, 164–72.
   (c) *Ibid.*, p. 164; Walcott, 'Division-Lists', pp. 25–6.

42. *c. Feb. 1690*, Anthony Rowe's black list of those who had voted on 5 Feb. 1689 in favour of agreeing with the second of the Lords' amendments on the vacancy of the throne (see above, no. 38).

(a) *A Letter to a Friend, upon the Dissolving of the Late Parliament, and the Calling of a New One* (1690); the Huntington Lib. copy (Rare books HEH 29405) has manuscript markings.

(b) Cruickshanks *et al.*, 'Transfer of the Crown', pp. 41–7.

(c) *Ibid.*, pp. 39–41.

SECOND PARLIAMENT OF WILLIAM III, 1690–95

43. *c. Mar. 1690*, lists of possible supporters drawn up by the Marquess of Carmarthen.

(a) B.L., Add. MS. 28091, f. 149.

(b) *Danby*, III, 176–8.

(c) *Ibid.*, p. 176.

44. *20 Mar. 1690*, marked copy of a printed list of the Commons, classifying Members as Whigs ('1'), Tories ('2'), or doubtful ('3'), and some probably as Court ('x').

(a) B.L., Eg. MS. 3359, ff. 27–8.

45. *20 Mar. 1690*, marked copy of a printed list of the Commons, classifying some Members possibly as Court supporters.

(a) B.L., Eg. MS. 3359, ff. 25–6.

46. *Before 25 Nov. 1690*, likely Court supporters.

(a) P.R.O., S.P. 8/8/26.

(b) *Danby*, III, 178–9.

47. *16–22 Dec. 1690*, marked copy of printed list of the Commons in Oct. 1690, classifying some Members possibly as Court; perhaps compiled by Lord Carmarthen in connection with the projected attack on him in the Commons (see Horwitz, *Parliament*, p. 65).

(a) B.L., Eg. MS. 3359, ff. 31–2.

48. *Aft. 23 Dec. 1690*, marked copy of a printed list of the Commons, classifying some Members possibly as Court supporters.

(a) B.L., Eg. MS. 3359, ff. 29–30.

49. *26 Dec. 1690*, marked MS. list of the committee on Lord Ailesbury's Estate Bill.

(a) Wilts. R.O., 1300/856.

50. *7 Apr. 1691*, marked MS. copy of a list of the Commons, with subsequent additions and corrections, classifying Members possibly as Court ('.') and opposition ('/').

(a) Nottingham Univ. Lib., Pw2 Hy 403 (Portland [Harley] papers).

51. *31 Oct. 1691*, marked MS. list of the committee on the bill to maintain and secure the rights of corporations, with three names added; on the dorse a separate list of 19 members of the committee.
    (a) B.L., Add. MS. 42592, ff. 167–8.

52. *30 Nov. 1691*, marked MS. list of the committee on Lord Ailesbury's bill.
    (a) Wilts. R.O., 1300/856.

53. *1692*, list of 94 placemen.
    (a) Nottingham Univ. Lib., Pw2 2392 (Portland [Bentinck] papers).
    (c) Horwitz, *Parliament*, p. 358.

54. *Mar.–Dec. 1692*, working list of Court supporters and those whom they could be expected to influence.
    (a) P.R.O., S.P. 8/8/25.
    (b) *Danby*, III, 182–3.

55. *May–Nov. 1692*, list of 103 placemen.
    (a) P.R.O., S.P. 8/14.
    (b) *Danby*, III, 184–7.

56. *1693*, list of 97 placemen.
    (a) B.L., Add. MS. 70035 (formerly Loan 29/206, ff. 170–1).

57. *Spring 1693*, Samuel Grascome's analysis of the Commons.
    (a) Bodl. Lib., MS. Rawlinson D. 846, f. 5.
    (c) Horwitz, *Parliament*, p. 339.

58. *1693*, Grascome's list of 137 placemen.
    (a) Bodl. Lib., MS. Rawlinson D.846, ff. 1–3.

59. *1693–4*, list of 85 placemen.
    (a) B.L., Harl. MS. 6846, ff. 268–71.

60. *Dec. 1694–Apr. 1695*, list compiled by Henry Guy, M.P., of 'friends' (possibly supporters of the Earl of Sunderland), with some marked 'd[oubtful]'.
    (a) B.L., Trumbull Add. MS. 13, no. 68 (Add. MS. 13 was a bundle of miscellaneous material from various periods; it has now been split up and its contents incorporated chronologically with other Trumbull material).
    (b) D. Rubini, *Court and Country, 1688–1702* (1967), pp. 262–7 (without satisfactory explanation).
    (c) *Ibid.*, pp. 51–2, 111–13; Horwitz, *Parliament*, p. 340.

THIRD PARLIAMENT OF WILLIAM III, 1695–8

61. *31 Jan. 1696*, probable forecast for a division on the proposed Council of Trade.
    (a) B.L., Add. MS. 70305 (formerly Loan 29/31/1).

(b) Burton *et al.*, 'Political Parties', pp. 41–52.

(c) *Ibid.*, pp. 6–13.

62. *Feb.–Mar. 1696*, those who refused to sign the first voluntary Association.

    (a) *A Summary Account of the Proceedings upon the Happy Discovery of the Jacobite Conspiracy, in a Second Letter to a Devonshire Gentleman* (1696) and various. A variant, with three extra names, is B.L., Add. MS. 28252, f. 53. Huntington Lib., HEH 130297, *A Copy of the Association Agreed upon by the Honourable House of Commons, on Monday the 24th of February 1695/6* (1696), has 93 names, plus one other unnamed.

    (b) *Danby*, III, 194–213 (from *A Summary Account . . .*).

    (c) Walcott, 'Division-Lists', p. 26; de Beer, 'Addenda', p. 66; *Danby*, III, 187 *et seq.*; Horwitz, *Parliament*, p. 338.

63. *?26 Mar. 1696*, those for and those against fixing the price of guineas at 22*s.* (may be a consolidated list with the division of 20 Mar., which inserted 25*s.* into a clause rather than 22*s.*).

    (a) [S. Grascome], *An Account of the Proceedings in the House of Commons in Relation to the Recoining of Clipp'd Money and Falling the Price of Guineas, together with a Particular List of the Names of Members Consenting and Dissenting* (1696).

    (b) Burton *et al.*, 'Political Parties', pp. 41–52.

    (c) *Ibid.*, pp. 14–19; E.S. de Beer, 'Division Lists of 1688–1715: Some Addenda', *B.I.H.R.*, XXX (1942–3), 65–6;. Horwitz, *Parliament*, p. 338; L. Davison and T. Keirn, 'John Locke, Edward Clarke and the 1696 Guineas Legislation', *Parliamentary History*, VII (1988), 239 n.52.

64. *25 Nov. 1696*, those for and those against the Attainder of Sir John Fenwick.

    (a) B.L., Add. MS. 47608 (unfol.); Bodl. Lib., MS. Rawlinson D. 198, f. 150 is a partial MS. list of those voting against the bill, with some variations.

    (b) Burton *et al.*, 'Political Parties', pp. 41–52.

    (c) *Ibid.*, pp. 20–6.

65. *July 1698*, list of 95 placemen.

    (a) *A Letter to a Country-Gentleman: Setting forth the Cause of the Decay and Ruin of Trade* (1698).

    (b) *The Harleian Miscellany* (10 vols., 1808–13), VIII, 506–13.

FOURTH PARLIAMENT OF WILLIAM III, 1698–1700

66. *c. Aug. 1698*, list of the House of Commons, with 110 placemen marked.

    (a) *A Compleat List of the Knights, Citizens and Burgesses of the New Parliament* (B.L., Dept. of Printed Books, 1850, c.6. (16); another copy in Add. MS. 40772, f. 8).

67. *c. Aug. 1698*, forecast of the balance of parties in the new House, probably on the issue of the standing army.

(a) B.L., Add. MS. 70306 (formerly Loan 29/35/12).

(b) H. Horwitz, 'Parties, Connections and Parliamentary Politics, 1689–1714: Review and Revision', *Journal of British Studies*, VI, no. 1 (1966–7), 62–9.

(c) *Ibid.*; Burton *et al.*, 'Political Parties', p. 33 n.2.

68. *c. Aug. 1698*, list of 78 'Q[ueries]', compiled by author of list 67 above, as a subsequent calculation: confined to Members marked '+' or 'x' [?Court], or 'q', or left unmarked, in original list.

(a) B.L., Add. MS. 70306 (formerly Loan 29/35/12).

69. *27 Oct. 1698*, marked copy of a printed list of the Parliament, probably a forecast of those opposed to a standing army (see below, no. 70).

(a) B.L., Eg. MS. 3359, ff. 35–6.

(b) D. Hayton. 'The Country Party in the House of Commons, 1698–1699: A Forecast of the Opposition to a Standing Army?', *Parliamentary History*, VI (1987), 145–60.

(c) *Ibid.*, pp. 141–4.

70. *18 Jan. 1699*, those against disbanding the army.

(a) B.L., Add. MS. 28091, f. 167, and various. One variant, identifying placemen, is Magdalene College, Cambridge, Pepys Lib., PL 2179, pp. 71–4.

(b) *Danby*, III, 213–7.

(c) Horwitz, *Parliament*, pp. 358–9.

71. *Jan.–May 1700*, analysis of the House, assigning Members to various interests, including 'Lord Som[ers] etc', 'O[ld] E[ast India] Company', 'Places', and 'Q'.

(a) B.L., Add. MS. 70306 (formerly Loan 29/35/12).

(c) Horwitz, *Parliament*, p. 340.

FIFTH PARLIAMENT OF WILLIAM III, Feb.–Nov. 1701

72. *1701–13*, composite list of the Members of the last two Parliaments of William III and the first four Parliaments of Anne, noting, *inter alia*, which were placemen.

(a) Bodl. Lib., MS. Carte 129, ff. 427v-43.

73. *10 Feb. 1701* marked copy of a printed list of the Parliament.

(a) B.L., Eg. MS. 3359, ff. 43–4.

74. *22 Feb. 1701*, list of Members, possibly of those who would support the Court on agreeing with the committee of supply to make provision from time to time to make good the principal and interest due on parliamentary funds granted since the King's accession.

(a) B.L., Add. MS. 28091, ff. 179–80.

(b) Rubini, *Court and Country*, pp. 269–78.

(c) *Ibid.*, p. 268; Horwitz, *Parliament*, p. 340 (where it is suggested that this is a list of those who supported Robert Harley's plan for the succession).

75. *After 24 June 1701*, black list of Tories, prepared for the general election of Nov. 1701, allegedly of those who had opposed making preparation for war; probably based on the division of 14 Feb. 1701, on whether the Commons would support the King and take measures for the safety of England, the preservation of the Protestant religion and the peace of Europe.
    (a) [Tristram Savage], *A List of One Unanimous Club of Members of the Late Parliament Dissolved Nov. 11, 1701, that Met at the Vine Tavern in Long Acre; who Ought to be Opposed in the Ensuing Elections, by All that Intend to Save their Native Country from being Made a Province of France; by Reason of their Constant Voting with Davenant, Hamond, and Tredenham, who were Caught with Monsieur Poussin the French Agent* (1701). A MS. copy of this list, with a few MS. annotations, is Bodl. Lib., MS. Rawlinson D. 918, ff. 165–6; another version, with some variations, marked in MS. on a printed list of the Commons, is in the possession of Eveline Cruickshanks.
    (c) Walcott, 'Division-Lists', pp. 26–7.

SIXTH PARLIAMENT OF WILLIAM III, 1701–2

76. *c. Dec. 1701*, list, annotated by Lord Spencer, of the election returns.
    (a) Blenheim Palace papers B.I.1.
    (b) Snyder, 'Party Configurations', pp. 54–8.
    (c) *Ibid.*, pp. 41–4, 54.

77. *c. Dec. 1701*, list of the new House of Commons, annotated by Robert Harley; perhaps a forecast for the division on the choice of Speaker, 30 Dec. 1701, between Harley and Sir Thomas Littleton.
    (a) B.L., Harleian MS. 7556, ff. 96–100.
    (c) Horwitz, *Parliament*, p. 339.

78. *26 Feb. 1702*, those in favour of the resolution vindicating the Commons proceedings in the impeachment of William III's ministers.
    (a) [James Drake], *Some Necessary Considerations relating to All Future Elections of Members to Serve in Parliament, Humbly Offer'd to All Electors* (1702).
    (b) *Somers' Tracts*, XII, 215–18, and various.
    (c) Walcott, 'Division-Lists', p. 27.

FIRST PARLIAMENT OF ANNE, 1702–5

79. *c. Aug. 1702*, list of some Members of the new Parliament, annotated by Lord Spencer.
    (a) Blenheim Palace papers B.I.1.
    (b) Snyder, 'Party Configurations', p. 58.
    (c) *Ibid.*, pp. 41–3, 44, 58.

80. *20 Oct. 1702*, marked copy of a printed list of the Parliament, perhaps a forecast for the Tack, Nov. 1704.
    (a) B.L., Eg. MS. 3359, ff. 45–6.

81. *13 Feb. 1703*, those for and those against agreeing with the Lords' amendment to the bill extending the time for taking the Abjuration.
    (a) Various, including Lancashire R.O., DDKe 6/53 (Kenyon MSS.); and a printed list in Hertfordshire R.O., D/EP F.187, f. 16 (Panshanger MSS.).
    (b) J. Oldmixon, *The History of England* (1735), pp. 283–4.
    (c) Walcott, 'Division-Lists', pp. 27–8; Speck, thesis, pp. 62–4, 442.

82. *Mid Mar. 1704*, list of lords and M.P.s drawn up by the Earl of Nottingham, probably a forecast of support over the 'Scotch plot' (see above, Lords list 69).
    (a) Leicestershire R.O., Finch MSS., box 4960, P.P. 161.

83. *30 Oct.–24 Nov. 1704*, forecast for the Tack.
    (a) B.L., Add. MS 70306 (formerly Loan 29/35/12).

84. *c. 28 Nov. 1704*, Harley's lobbying list for the Tack.
    (a) B.L., Add. MS. 70230 (formerly Loan 29/138).
    (b) P.M. Ansell, 'Harley's Parliamentary Management', *B.I.H.R.*, XXXIV (1961), 92–7.
    (c) *Ibid.*

85. *28 Nov. 1704*, those for and those against the Tack, and those absent in the division.
    (a) Various. One variant of those for is in George Parker, *Parker's Ephemeris for the Year of our Lord 1713* (1713) [copy in Univ. of London Lib.].
    (b) *Somers' Tracts*, XII, 474–6, and various.
    (c) Walcott, 'Division-Lists', pp. 28–9; Speck, thesis, pp. 64–5, 442–3.

86. *1705*, list of 126 placemen.
    (a) *A List of Gentlemen that are in Offices, Employments, &c.* (Cambridge, 1705).

SECOND PARLIAMENT OF ANNE, 1705–8 (FIRST PARLIAMENT OF GREAT BRITAIN, 29 Apr. 1707–1708)

87. *c. June 1705*, list of the election returns, annotated by the Earl of Sunderland (formerly Lord Spencer).
    (a) Blenheim Palace papers B.I.1.
    (b) Snyder, 'Party Configurations', pp. 59–63.
    (c) *Ibid.*, pp. 41–3, 46, 58–9.

88. *c. June 1705*, analysis of the election returns.
    (a) Staffordshire R.O., D. 539/P/16/2/4/19 (Dartmouth papers).

89. *c. June 1705*, an analysis of the Parliament, into 'Churchmen', 'True Church', 'High Church', 'Low Church', 'High Church Courtiers', 'Low Church Courtiers', 'No Church' and 'Sneakers'.
   (a) *A Numerical Calculation of the Honourable Members as were Elected for the Ensuing Parliament* (1705); B.L., Stowe MS. 354, ff. 161–2; Eg. MS. 3359, ff. 51–2.
   (c) Speck, thesis, pp. 82–3.

90. *25 Oct. 1705*, division on the Speaker.
   (a) Durham Univ., Prior's Kitchen, Baker Baker MSS. Collection, 8/17.
   (b) W.A. Speck, 'The Choice of a Speaker in 1705', *B.I.H.R.*, XXXVII (1964), 36–46.
   (c) *Ibid.*, pp. 20–36.

91. *Feb. 1706*, those supporting the Court over the 'place clause' in the Regency Bill.
   (a) *A List of Moderate Patriots who . . . Voted for the Repeal of a Clause in an Act . . . Intituled 'An Act for the Further Limitation of the Crown, and Better Securing the Rights and Liberties of the Subject . . .'* (1708).
   (b) Walcott, 'Division-Lists', pp. 30–3.
   (c) *Ibid.*, pp. 29–30; Speck, thesis, pp. 68–71.

92. *16 Feb. 1706*, those placemen voting in committee against setting a date to hear the Bewdley election petition.
   (a) B.L., Add. MS. 61495, f. 22 (formerly Blenheim papers D.II.10b), dated Tuesday 19 Feb. 1705[/6].
   (b) Snyder, 'Party Configurations', p. 48.
   (c) *Ibid.*

93. *c. 19 Feb. 1706*, those voting on the Tory side in committee on the Bewdley election.
   (a) Blenheim Palace papers, VIII, 23.
   (b) Snyder, 'Party Configurations', pp. 48–9.
   (c) *Ibid.*

94. *1707*, analysis, by the Earl of Marchmont, of the Scots Members in the First Parliament of Great Britain, into Court and Country, with a note of which were influenced by particular representative peers.
   (a) Scottish R.O., GD 158/943 (Marchmont papers).

95. *1707/1708*, analysis of the House, into Whigs ('=') and Tories ('x').
   (a) Cambridge Univ. Lib., MS. Mm. VI. 42, ff. 14–20.

THIRD PARLIAMENT OF ANNE, 1708–10

96. *1708*, marked copy of a printed list of the First Parliament of Great Britain, with the returns at the 1708 election added in MS.: Members classified as Whig, Tory, Court Whig, Court Tory or Tacker (see above, Lords list 73).

(a) *A True List of the Lords Spiritual and Temporal, Together with the Members of the House of Commons Constituting the First Parliament of Great Britain . . . What Alterations have been Since Made to the 30th of March 1708 are here Corrected*: original in private possession; photocopy in the possession of the History of Parliament Trust.

97. *c. May 1708*, pre-election list of Scottish constituencies (with names of likely Members or proprietors of controlling interests) divided into 'Court', 'Country' and 'Squadrone'.
   (a) Annandale papers (the Earl of Annandale, Raehills, Lockerbie, Dumfriesshire), bundle 397.

98. *c. May 1708*, list of election returns, annotated by Lord Sunderland.
   (a) B.L., Add. MS. 61497A (formerly Blenheim papers C.I.44).
   (b) Snyder, 'Party Configurations', pp. 63–6.
   (c) *Ibid.*, pp. 41–3, 50–1, 63.

99. *Feb.–Mar. 1709*, those in favour of the Bill for Naturalizing Foreign Protestants.
   (a) *A List of Those Members of the late Parliament that Voted for the Passing of the Act for Naturalizing Foreign Protestants; and Consequently, for the Bringing over the Palatines* (1710).
   (b) *A Collection of White and Black Lists* (1715), pp. 12–15.
   (c) Walcott, 'Division-Lists', p. 33; Speck, thesis, pp. 72–3.

100. *Feb.–Mar. 1710*, those for and those against the impeachment of Dr Sacheverell.
   (a) Various.
   (b) Oldmixon, *History of England*, pp. 439–42.
   (c) Walcott, 'Division-Lists', pp. 33–5; Speck, thesis, pp. 73, 444.

101. *12 Sept. 1710*, list, in Robert Harley's hand, of nine Members to be 'provided for before their elections'.
   (a) B.L., Add. MS. 70333 (formerly Loan 29/10/19).

FOURTH PARLIAMENT OF ANNE, 1710–13

102. *c. Nov. 1710*, analysis of the new House, into Whigs, Tories, and those 'doubtful' (subdivided into: [i] those who have not yet appeared; [ii] those who voted with the Court; [iii] those of whom little is known).
   (a) B.L., Stowe MS. 223, ff. 453–6.
   (c) Speck, thesis, pp. 84–5.

103. *11 Nov. 1710*, analysis of the Scots Members, into Court Tories, Episcopal Tories and Whigs.
   (a) Christ Church, Oxford, Wake MS. XVII, f. 269, Richard Dongworth to Bishop Wake, 11 Nov. 1710.
   (b) D. Szechi, 'Some Insights on the Scottish M.P.s and Peers Returned in the 1710 Election', *Scottish Historical Review*, LX (1981), 63–6.
   (c) *Ibid.*, pp. 61–2, 63, 66–8.

104. *1710–11*, list of Tories in the first session of this Parliament.
    (a) *An Exact List of all those True English* [erased, 'Tory' substituted in MS.]
        Patriots of the Honourable House of Commons of Great-Britain, that Were for
        Easing the Nation of the Heavy Burden ane Taxes, by Puting [sic] *an End to*
        the Expensive and Bloody War (1711): University of Kansas, Kenneth A.
        Spencer Research Lib., Dept. of Special Collections, 18th Century P19;
        photocopy in Institute of Historical Research.
    (c) H.L. Snyder, 'A New Parliamentary List for 1711', *B.I.H.R.*, L (1977),
        185–93.

105. *1711*, list of Tories, and members of the October Club.
    (a) *A True and Exact List of those Worthy Patriots who, to their Eternal Honour,*
        have, in one Session, Detected the Mismanagements of the Late M[inist]ry ...
        (1711).
    (b) List of members of the October Club published by H.T. Dickinson, 'The
        October Club', *Huntington Library Quarterly*, XXXIII (1969–70), 170–2,
        from a list printed in Feb. 1712 by Abel Boyer, *The Political State of Great*
        Britain (60 vols., 1714–40), III, 117–22, probably derived from (a).
    (c) Dickinson, 'October Club', pp. 172–3; Snyder, 'Party Configurations',
        p. 38.

106. *25 May 1711*, those supporting the amendments to the South Sea Bill.
    (a) B.L., Add. MS. 70163 (formerly Loan 29/45/C/5).
    (b) J.G. Sperling, 'The Division of 25 May 1711, on an Amendment to the
        South Sea Bill: A Note on the Reality of Parties in the Reign of Anne',
        Hist. Jnl., IV (1961), 193.
    (c) *Ibid.*, pp.191–202.

107. *7 Dec. 1711*, those supporting the motion of 'No Peace without Spain'.
    (a) B.L., Add. MS. 70319 (formerly Loan 29/29/2).
    (b) G.S. Holmes, 'The Commons' Division on "No Peace without Spain",
        7 December 1711', *B.I.H.R.*, XXXIII (1960), 233–4.
    (c) *Ibid.*, pp. 223–33.

108. *10 Dec. 1711*, list of office-holders and pensioners who had voted against
    the ministry on the 'No Peace without Spain' motion, with some suggested
    replacements; in the hand of the Earl of Oxford (formerly Robert Harley)
    (see above, Lords list 92).
    (a) B.L., Add. MS. 70332 (formerly Loan 29/10/16).

109. *21–3 Jan. 1712*, canvassing list for the attack on the Duke of Marlborough.
    (a) B.L., Add. MS. 70331 (formerly Loan 29/10/3).
    (b) Holmes, *British Politics*, pp. 310, 505 n. 77.

110. *7 Feb. 1712*, Scots Members voting for and against the bill for toleration of
    episcopacy in Scotland and those absent (gives also those 'absent from the
    House who were in town').
    (a) Nat. Lib. Scotland, Advocates' papers, Wodrow Letters, Quarto VI,
        f. 107; Nat Lib. Scotland, MS. 1392, f. 80, Robert Munro to John
        Mackenzie, 9 Feb. 1711/12 (giving absentees 'in town', in Scotland and
        abroad).

111. *?6 May 1713*, fragmentary list, probably of the minority in a division on the French Wines Duty Bill.
     (a) B.L., Harl. MS. 7190, f. 316.

112. *23 May 1713*, list of 22 Scots M.P.s who met and agreed to call a conference with the Scottish representative peers over the proposed dissolution of the Union.
     (a) Aberdeen Univ. Lib., Duff House (Montcoffer) MS. 3175/2380.

113. *4 June 1713*, Scots Members voting on the committal of the French Commerce Treaty Bill: those for, those against, those who 'went out' and those who were absent.
     (a) Mellerstain papers (the Earl of Haddington, Mellerstain, Gordon, Berwickshire), ser. 1, bundle 343.
     (b) G. Holmes and C. Jones, 'Trade, the Scots and the Parliamentary Crisis of 1713', *Parliamentary History*, I (1982), 68–70.
     (c) *Ibid.*, pp. 63–4, 76 n. 119.

114. *18 June 1713*, those for and those against the French Commerce Treaty.
     (a) *A Letter from a Member of the House of Commons relating to the Bill of Commerce . . .* (1713) and various.
     (b) *White and Black Lists*, pp. 23–30.
     (c) Walcott, 'Division-Lists', pp. 35–6; Speck, thesis, pp. 78–80, 444.

115. *18 June 1713*, Scots Members voting on the French Commerce Treaty Bill: those for, those against and those absent.
     (a) Mellerstain papers, ser. 1, bundle 343.
     (b) Holmes and Jones, 'Parliamentary Crisis of 1713', pp. 68–70.
     (c) *Ibid.*, pp. 63–5.

FIFTH PARLIAMENT OF ANNE, 1713–15

116. *1713–14*, list of the House, giving placemen.
     (a) Chandler, VIII, Appendix.

117. *1713–14*, analysis of the House elected in 1713, compiled for George I after the 1715 election.
     (a) Lincolnshire Archives Office, Worsley papers, I.
     (b) Sedgwick, I, 164–87.
     (c) *Ibid.*, I, 162–3.

118. *Feb. 1714*, analysis of the 1713 election returns of Scots Members, distinguishing Jacobites and Hanoverians, sent by Lord Polwarth to Hanover, 9 Feb. 1714.
     (a) B.L., Stowe MS. 226, ff. 121–2.
     (b) J. Macpherson, *Original Papers; Containing the Secret History of Great Britain, from the Restoration, to the Accession of the House of Hanover* (2 vols., 1775), II, 559–61.

119. *18 Mar. 1714*, those opposed to the expulsion of Steele.
  (a) *Mr Steele's Apology for himself and his Writings Occasioned by his Expulsion from the House of Commons* (1714), and various.
  (b) Cobbett, *Parl. Hist.*, VI, 1282–3.

120. *12 May 1714*, Scots Members voting for and against extending the Schism Bill to cover popery.
  (a) Nat. Lib. Scotland, Advocates' papers, Wodrow Letters, Quarto VIII, f. 118, [Thomas Smith] to Robert Wodrow, [?19 May] 1714.

FIRST PARLIAMENT OF GEORGE I, 1715–22

121. *1714–15*, marked copy of a list of the First Parliament of Anne, with the returns to the First Parliament of George I added in MS.
  (a) Univ. of California, Berkeley, Lib., Rare Books Dept., CS/420/p3.
  (b) Snyder, 'Party Configurations', pp. 67–72.
  (c) *Ibid.*, pp. 51–3, 67.

122. *1715–22*, list of the House, noting placemen.
  (a) Chandler, VIII, appendix.

123. *Feb.–Mar. 1715*, analysis of the new House, compiled for George I (see above, no. 117).
  (a) Lincs. Archives Office, Worsley papers, I.
  (b) Sedgwick, I, 164–87.
  (c) *Ibid.*, I, 162–3.

124. *10–12 Mar. 1715*, analysis of the new Parliament.
  (a) *Flying Post*, 10–12 Mar. 1715.
  (c) Snyder, 'Party Configurations', p. 52.

125. *17 Mar. 1715*, list of the old and the new Parliaments, classifying Members of the new House of Commons as Whigs (marked '*') and Tories (marked '+'), and noting some placemen.
  (a) *A Correct List of the Lords Spiritual and Temporal, as Also of the Knights . . . Citizens and Burgesses of the Last and Present Parliaments of Great Britain . . . With Remarks* (1715): 24 pages bound between pp. 170 and 171 of Boyer, *Political State of Great Britain*, IX: Institute of Historical Research copy.

126. *24 Apr. 1716*, division on the Septennial Bill.
  (a) *An Exact and Correct List of the Members of the House of Commons who Voted for and against the Bill for Repealing the Triennial Act, 24 Apr. 1716. Also of the Absent Members, which Makes this a Complete List* (1716), and various, including the *Stamford Mercury*, 22, 29 Mar. 1722 (see G.A. Cranfield, *The Development of the Provincial Newspaper, 1700–1760* [Oxford, 1962], p. 161).
  (b) Cobbett, *Parl. Hist.*, VII, 367–74.
  (c) Sedgwick, I, 126–7; Ransome, 'Division-Lists', pp. 1–2.

127. *c. 24 Apr. 1716*, marked copy of a printed list of the House of Commons relating to a division or divisions on the Septennial Bill; possibly a forecast, subsequently amended, of those for and against the bill: similar to list 126 but with some variations.
    (a) Durham Univ., Priors' Kitchen, Baker Baker MS., 8/27.

128. *4 June 1717*, those who voted with the government on the charges of fraud against Cadogan in the transport of Dutch troops sent for during the '15.
    (a) B.L., Add. MS. 61495, ff. 86–7 (formerly Blenheim papers D.II.13); two duplicates at ff. 88–91.

129. *4 June 1717*, office-holders voting against the government on the charges of fraud against Cadogan, divided into 'military', 'Prince', 'civil'.
    (a) Leices. R.O., Finch MSS., box 4951.
    (b) Sedgwick, I, 82.
    (c) *Ibid.*, pp. 81–2.

130. *4 June 1717*, Scots Members voting for and against the government on the charges against Cadogan.
    (a) Scottish R.O., GD 248/214/1/42.

131. *After 4 June 1717*, list of 13 Members, followers of Walpole and Townshend, who were to be removed, with suggested replacements: compiled by Sunderland after the division of 4 June 1717 (see above, nos. 129–30).
    (a) Blenheim Palace papers D. II. 10b.
    (c) Sedgwick, I, 83.

132. *13 June 1717*, list of Members summoned by Joseph Addison to confer about the impeachment of the Earl of Oxford.
    (a) P.R.O., S.P. 35/9/19.
    (c) C. Jones, 'The Impeachment of the Earl of Oxford and the Whig Schism of 1717: Four New Lists', *B.I.H.R.*, LV (1982), 71 n. 30.

133. *Jan. 1719*, those for and those against the repeal of the Occasional Conformity and Schism Act, and those absent.
    (a) *An Exact and Correct List of the Members of the Honourable House of Commons, who Voted for and against the Bill for Repealing the Acts to Prevent Occasional Conformity, and to Hinder the Growth of Schism: In January 1718. Also of the Absent Members, which Makes this a Complete List* (1719).
    (b) Chandler, VIII, Appendix; Cobbett, *Parl. Hist.*, VIII, 585–8.
    (c) Sedgwick, I, 127; Ransome, 'Division-Lists', pp. 2–3.

134. *c. 28 Feb. 1719*, forecast, by James Craggs, for the Peerage Bill.
    (a) B.L., Stowe MS. 247, ff. 184–91.
    (c) Sedgwick, I, 84–5.

135. *c. 28 Feb. 1719*, canvassing list, compiled by Craggs, for the vote on the Peerage Bill.
    (a) B.L., Stowe MS. 247, ff. 193–200.

136. *8–26 Mar. 1719*, forecast by Sunderland for the Peerage Bill.
  (a) B.L., Add. MS. 61495, ff. 188–93 (formerly Blenheim papers D.II.9, 10).
  (c) Sedgwick, I, 84–5.

137. *Apr. 1719*, marked MS. list of Scottish M.P.s; possibly concerned with the Peerage Bill.
  (a) B.L., Add. MS. 70269 (formerly Loan 29/163/10).

138. *c. Sept. 1719*, list of Tories compiled by Sunderland.
  (a) B.L., Add. MS. 61496, f. 26 (formerly Blenheim papers D.II.5).

139. *Dec. 1719*, those for and those against the Peerage Bill.
  (a) *A Guide to the Electors of Great Britain, Being Lists of All Those Members in the Last Parliament who Voted for and against Such Bills as were of the Greatest Importance Either to the Prerogatives of the Crown, or to the Privileges of the People. To which is added a List of the Projectors, Erectors of Certain COMPANIES which Flourished in the Year of the BUBBLES ... together with a List of the Members that Were for [and] against the Peerage Bill* (1722); Chandler, VIII, appendix.
  (b) Cobbett, *Parl. Hist.*, VII, 624–7.
  (c) Sedgwick, I, 128; Ransome, 'Division-Lists', p. 3.

140. *Dec. 1719*, 'Whigs against the Peerage Bill upon the division' (see above, list 139).
  (a) Mellerstain papers, ser. 1, bundle 425.

141. *24 Mar.–10 Apr. 1721*, list of 125 names: partial division list?
  (a) Nottingham Univ. Lib., Pw2 Hy 865 (Portland [Harley] papers).

142. *1722–27*, list of the House giving placemen.
  (a) Chandler, VIII, appendix.

143. *28 Mar. 1722*, marked list of some election returns, apparently distinguishing between Whigs ('-') and Tories ('+').
  (a) H.M.C., *Townshend MSS.*, pp. 136–7.

144. *Mid Dec. 1722–mid Mar. 1723*, list of regular Court supporters 'against' and absent, probably at a specific division.
  (a) Cambridge. Univ. Lib., Cholmondeley (Houghton) MS. P. 66/1.
  (c) A. Hanham, 'An Early Walpolian Division List: The Wells Election Case of 1723', *Parliamentary History* (forthcoming, 1996).

145. *2 May 1723*, those who voted for and against the return of Edwards and Gwyn in the disputed Wells election, divided into Whigs, Tories, and those absent.
  (a) Somerset R.O., Somerset Archaeological and Natural History Soc. Papers, DD/SAS 62 C/909.
  (b) Hanham, 'Early Walpolian Division List'.
  (c) *Ibid.*

FIRST PARLIAMENT OF GEORGE II, 1727–34

146. *1727–34*, list of the House, giving placemen.
   (a) Chandler, VIII, appendix.

147. *1727–8*, printed list of the House of Commons with MS. markings against
   some names of M.P.s for English and Welsh constituencies, perhaps
   indicating supporters of the opposition.
   (a) Boyer, *Political State*, XXXIII, Appendix, pp. 16–62: Institute of
   Historical Research copy.

148. *1 Aug. 1727*, Scots Members who were placemen.
   (a) Cambridge Univ. Lib., Cholmondeley (Houghton) MS. P. 68/6.

149. *5 Apr. 1728*, those regular Court supporters absent and voting against the
   Court candidate, in the disputed return for Flint boroughs.
   (a) Cambridge Univ. Lib., Cholmondeley (Houghton) MS. P. 66/2.

150. *?10 Apr. 1728*, those regular Court supporters absent and voting against
   the Court candidate in the committee of elections, in the disputed return
   for Flint.
   (a) Cambridge Univ. Lib., Cholmondeley (Houghton) MS. P. 66/2.
   (c) Hanham, thesis, pp. 10, 28–9, 142.

151. *c. May 1728*, list of regular Court supporters 'against' and 'absent': endorsed,
   'Sr P[aul] M[ethuen?]'s Lists'.
   (a) Cambridge Univ. Lib., Cholmondeley (Houghton) MS. P. 66/2.
   (c) Hanham, thesis, pp. 10, 28–9.

152. *23 Apr. 1729*, those for and those against making good the arrears in the
   Civil List.
   (a) *Who is Who: Being a List of Those who Voted for and against Granting
   £115,000 for Making Good the Arrears of the CIVIL LIST*, in *Caleb's
   Seasonable Exhortation* (1730); Chandler, VIII, appendix.
   (b) Cobbett, *Parl. Hist.*, VIII, 703.
   (c) Sedgwick, I, 128; Ransome, 'Division-List', p. 3; Hanham, thesis, pp.
   29–30, 169–70.

153. *4 Feb. 1730*, those for and those against paying for the Hessian troops.
   (a) *A True List of such Gentlemen of the House of Commons, as Voted for and
   against the Question for Granting the Sum of £241,259. 1s. 3d. for Defraying
   the Expense of Twelve Thousand Hessian Troops in the Pay of Great Britain
   for the year MDCCXXX* (1730). Huntington Lib., copy (HEH 318911) has
   MS. markings.
   (b) Chandler, VIII, appendix.
   (c) Sedgwick, I, 128–9; Ransome, 'Division-Lists', p. 4; Hanham, thesis, pp.
   29–30, 183–4.

154. *26 Jan. 1732*, division in the committee of supply on the army estimates.
   (a) *Supplement to the Protests of the Lords: Being a List of All Such Gentlemen of*

the House of Commons as Voted for, or against the Present Number of Standing Forces in this Kingdom (1732).
(c) Sedgwick, I, 129; Hanham, thesis, p. 33.

155. *8 Feb. 1732*, list of 21 M.P.s chosen by ballot for the committee appointed to investigate the Charitable Corporation, and includes the names of others not chosen, but who featured on the 'Court' and 'Bedford Head' (i.e. opposition) lists for the inquiry.
(a) Northamptonshire R.O., Isham papers, IC. 3522.
(c) Hanham, thesis, pp. 314–17.

156. *?9 and 10 Feb. 1732*, absent Court supporters on the divisions on the ministry's proposal to revive the salt duties.
(a) Cambridge Univ. Lib., Cholmondeley (Houghton) MS. P. 66/6.
(c) Hanham, thesis, pp. 292–4.

157. *14 Mar. 1733*, division in the committee of supply on the Excise Bill.
(a) *A List of Those who were for and against Bringing in the Excise Bill, for 266, Against 205, Each Including One Teller* (1733) and various. Chandler, VIII, appendix, also marks those for the bill who 'afterwards voted against' it. Another version also shows (i) M.P.s absent from the call of the House taken on 13 Mar.; and (ii) M.P.s who voted against the Excise in subsequent, but unspecified divisions: B.L., Eg. MS. 2543, ff. 409–10; Northants R.O., C(A)7552 (Cartwright of Aynho papers); and *Gentleman's Magazine*, III (1733), 575–80.
(b) Cobbett, *Parl. Hist.*, VIII, 1308–13.
(c) Sedgwick, I, 129; Ransome, 'Division-Lists', pp. 4–5; P. Langford, *The Excise Crisis* (Oxford, 1975), pp. 173–4; Hanham, thesis, pp. 34, 342–8.

158. *16 Mar. 1733*, those for and those against agreeing with the resolution of the committee of supply to end the customs duty on tobacco, with placemen marked; list of voting on the 16th by Lord Perceval, amended (very confusingly) to show voting on the 14th.
(a) B.L., Add. MS. 47000, ff. 67–8.
(c) Langford, *Excise Crisis*, p. 174; Hanham, thesis, pp. 34, 342–6.

159. *10 Apr. 1733*, Court supporters absent from a vote against hearing counsel for the City of London against the Excise Bill.
(a) Cambridge Univ. Lib., Cholmondeley (Houghton) MS. P. 66/7.
(b) Langford, *Excise Crisis*, pp. 175–6.
(c) *Ibid.*, pp. 175–9; Hanham, thesis, pp. 348–50.

160. *24 Apr. 1734*, 'Court' and 'opposition' lists for the ballot for the committee of inquiry into customs frauds.
(a) H.M.C., *15th Report*, Appendix VI (Carlisle MSS.), pp. 112–13.
(c) Hanham, thesis, pp. 366–71.

161. *13 Mar. 1734*, those for and those against giving leave for the bill for the repeal of the Septennial Act, with placemen marked.
(a) *A Complete List of the Members who Voted for and against the Bill for Repealing the Septennial Act* (1734) and various.

(b) Cobbett, *Parl. Hist.*, IX, 479–82, without placemen.

(c) Sedgwick, I, 129; Ransome, 'Division-Lists', pp. 4–5; Hanham, thesis, pp. 34, 391–2.

162. *13 Mar. 1734*, list of Yorkshire Members who voted for and against Repeal of the Septennial Act.

(a) B.L., Add. MS. 31142, f. 147.

SECOND PARLIAMENT OF GEORGE II, 1734–41.

163. *1734–41*, list of the House, giving placemen.

(a) Chandler, XII, 454–65.

164. *1734–41*, analysis of the House, into those 'for the Court measures' and those 'against the Court measures': in the hand of Earl of Egmont.

(a) H.L.R.O., Hist. Collections 82, 'Compleat List of members of Parl[iamen]t Summond to meet in Parl[iamen]t on the 7th June 1734, but prorogued to 16 Jan[uar]y 1734/5 when it sat to do busi[ness] and was dissolved 25 April 1741'.

165. *25 Mar. 1735*, list of 41 Members, headed 'Wells'; probably a forecast for the division on the disputed election for Wells.

(a) Cambridge Univ. Lib., Cholmondeley (Houghton) MS. P. 66/9.

166. *31 Mar. 1736*, list of the 12 Members who voted in favour of passing the Westminster Bridge Bill.

(a) Cambridge Univ. Lib., Add. MS. 6851, vol.1, f. 36v (Edward Harley's journal).

167. *1736–7*, partial division list for the debate on the Prince of Wales' income.

(a) Bodl. Lib., MS. Don.b.18., ff. 156–7.

168. *8 Mar. 1739*, those for and those against the address on the Spanish Convention, with placemen marked.

(a) *The Publick having been Imposed on by Several Very Imperfect and Erroneous Lists of the Members of the House of Commons who Voted for and against the Late Convention with Spain . . . it has been Thought Proper to do that Justice to the Gentlemen on Both Sides they Deserve by Giving a More Exact One* (1739), and various, including Northants R.O., C(A)7548b, printed *List of the Members who Voted for and against the Convention, March 1738[/39]*, with MS. corrections and additions by Thomas Cartwright M.P., which simply update it in accordance with the division as printed in Chandler and the *Gentleman's Magazine*, IX (1739), 304–10.

(b) Chandler, XII, appendix.

(c) Sedgwick, I, 129–30; Ransome, 'Division-Lists', pp. 6–7.

169. *21 Nov. 1739*, list of Members absent, classified as for and against, at a division on an address respecting the right to navigate in American seas.

(a) Cambridge Univ. Lib., Cholmondeley (Houghton) MS. P. 66/10.
(c) Sedgwick, I, 130.

170. *20 Jan. 1740*, those for and those against the Place Bill, and those absent,
with placemen marked.
(a) Chandler, XII, appendix.
(c) Sedgwick, I, 130; Ransome, 'Division-Lists', p. 7.

171. *18 Nov. 1740*, list of Members absent, classified as for and against, at a
division on an amendment to the Address.
(a) Cambridge Univ. Lib., Cholmondeley (Houghton) MS. P. 66/11.
(c) Sedgwick, I, 130.

172. *13 Feb. 1741*, opposition defectors and abstainers at a division on an address
for the removal of Sir Robert Walpole.
(a) *Gentleman's Magazine*, XI, 232; B.L., Add. MS. 4107, f. 235; Add. MS.
47071, f. 13.
(b) W. Coxe, *Memoirs of the Life and Administration of Sir Robert Walpole,
Earl of Orford* (3 vols., 1798), III, 563; H.M.C., *Egmont Diary*, III, 192
(printing B.L., Add. MS. 47071, f. 13).
(c) Sedgwick, I, 130; Ransome, 'Division-Lists', p. 7.

173. *c. Apr. 1741*, analysis in Egmont's hand of the old Members not re-elected
in 1741; into those 'for the Court' and 'Anti-Courtiers'.
(a) H.L.R.O., Hist. Collections 82, 'Members of the last Parliam[en]t at its
dissolution 1741 not returned in the present'.

THIRD PARLIAMENT OF GEORGE II, 1741–4

174. *c. May 1741*, analysis of the new House, recording, *inter alia*, which Members
were 'said to be chosen on the Country interest'.
(a) *Gent. Mag.*, XI, 227–31.

175. *c. May 1741*, analysis in Egmont's hand of the new Members, into 'Supposed
Courtiers' and those 'Supposed against the Court'.
(a) H.L.R.O., Hist. Collections 82, 'Persons returned to serve in the New
Parl[iamen]t Summond to meet who did not Serve in the last Parliam[en]t'.

176. *?July 1741*, list of all Members distinguished as ministerial supporters and
opposition.
(a) *The Craftsman*, 25 July 1741.
(c) M. Harris, 'Print and Politics in the Age of Walpole', in *Britain in the Age
of Walpole*, ed. J. Black (1984), pp. 207, 251 n. 58.

177. *16 Dec. 1741*, division on the election of the chairman of the Committee of
Privileges.
(a) Chandler, XIII, pt. 1, pp. 55–60.
(c) Sedgwick, I, 130; Ransome, 'Division-Lists', pp. 7–8.

178. *May–Dec. 1741*, list of 80 Whig M.P.s, classified 'For', 'Against' and 'Doubtful'; calculation of support gained and lost following the 1741 general election.
  (a) B.L., Add. MS. 33002, f. 454.

179. *c. Dec. 1741–Jan. 1742*, list of 265 M.P.s, endorsed 'list of votes against Sir Robert Walpole, 1741', including a category headed 'persons that voted with us in the last Parliament, sometimes in this to be hoped for'; a likely calculation of overall voting strength against Walpole before his fall in Feb. 1742.
  (a) Bodl. Lib., MS. Eng. Misc. b.48, ff. 137–8.

180. *Feb. 1742*, opposition Members who met at the Fountain Tavern.
  (a) *London Evening Post*, 6 Feb. 1742.
  (c) Harris, 'Print and Politics', pp. 207, 251 n. 59.

181. *9 or 23 Mar. 1742*, those in favour of an inquiry into the conduct of Walpole's administration.
  (a) Chandler, XIV, appendix, marked on a list of those who voted for the Hanoverian troops, 10 Dec. 1742 (see below, no. 185).
  (c) Sedgwick, I, 130.

182. *26 Mar. 1742*, the 'Court' and 'Country' lists for the election of the committee of inquiry into Walpole's administration.
  (a) B.L., Add. MS. 61479, ff. 70, 71 (formerly Blenheim papers D.II.13, F.I.25); B.L., Add. MS. 6043, f. 112v.; Morrab Lib., Penzance, Borlase papers, William Borlase's letterbook, pp. 46–7; Hamilton papers (the Duke of Hamilton, Lennoxlove, East Lothian), TD 86/11/1/C3/348/2 ('old Courtiers' distinguished on one list), in a letter from B. Murray to the Duke of Hamilton, 25 Mar. 1742.
  (b) *Horace Walpole's Correspondence*, ed. W.S. Lewis *et al.* (48 vols., London, New Haven and Oxford, 1937–83), XVII, 383–6: from a different source; heads the lists 'Court' and 'Opposition'.

183. *25 May 1742*, the 'Court' and 'Country' lists for the election of the commissioners of accounts.
  (a) B.L., Add. MS. 61479, f. 69 (formerly Blenheim papers D.II.13).

184. *Oct. 1742*, the 'Cockpit list': 294 government supporters who were to be invited to hear the final draft of the King's Speech, with the names of suitable intermediaries through whom the invitation might be sent.
  (a) B.L., Add. MS. 32699, ff. 467–8.
  (c) Sedgwick, I, 130.

185. *10 Dec. 1742*, those for and those against the Hanoverian troops.
  (a) *A List of the Members of Parliament who Voted for and against Taking the Hanover Troops into British Pay, 10 Dec. 1742, and those Absent at the Vote* (1742); copy in *Westminster Journal*, LXIV, 12 Feb. 1743; Nat. Lib. Scotland, Advocates' papers, MS. 80.7.1 (Dundas of Dundas papers), f. 54 (printed list with MS. markings, including 'those . . . [who] changed their opinions in the vote upon the said troops the 18 Jan. 1743/4' and various calculations); Chandler, XIV, appendix.

(b) Cobbett, *Parl. Hist.*, XII, 1053–8.
(c) Sedgwick, I, 130; Ransome, 'Division-Lists', p. 8.

186. *18 Jan. 1744*, those for and those against the Hanoverian troops.
(a) *The Lords' Protest, to which is Added a List of the Members of Parliament who Voted for and against Continuing the Hanover Troops in British Pay, Jan. 18 1743[-4]* (1744); copy in circulation in which 'the yellow voted for the Hanover troops, the red against, the black were neuter': Dyfed Archives Service, Carmarthen, Cawdor Muniments, Box 138, John to Pryse Campbell, 6 Mar. 1744; Nat. Lib. Scotland, Advocates papers 80.7.1, f. 54 (see above, no. 185).
(c) Sedgwick, I, 131.

187. *11 Apr. 1746*, those voting for and against the Hanoverian troops, and probable government supporters who were absent.
(a) B.L., Add. MS. 33034, ff. 110–11: the Members grouped under various headings; Bodl. Lib., MS. D.D. Dashwood B.6/1. There is a differing opposition list of those voting for the Hanoverians after having previously been against them, in Nat. Lib. Scotland, MS. 17498 (Fletcher of Saltoun papers), ff. 222–3, 'Voters agt the Hanoverians Ap. 1746', which also has a sub-category of 'Querry'.
(c) Sedgwick, I, 131.

FOURTH PARLIAMENT OF GEORGE II, 1747–54

188. *c. July 1747*, list of 'Members chose', divided into 'For' and 'Against'.
(a) B.L., Add. MS. 33002, ff. 440–6.

189. *20 Nov. 1747*, those for and those against hearing the Seaford election petition at the bar of the House.
(a) B.L., Add. MS. 33058, ff. 477–80.

190. *1747*, 'List of Lords and Commons in opposition'.
(a) Bodl. Lib., MS. D.D. Dashwood D1/3/13.

191. *c. 20 Mar. 1750*, list of 33 Members summoned to be at Sir T. Robinson's on 20 Mar. 1750.
(a) B.L., Add. MS. 32994, f. 271.

192. *14 Nov. 1750*, list of 77 'sure votes', dated from 'Claremont'.
(a) B.L., Add. MS. 32994, ff. 211–12.

193. *c. 1750*, list of 50 Members 'sure upon any question' and 91 Members 'probable' upon any question.
(a) B.L., Add. MS. 32994, ff. 207–9.

194. *7–14 Mar. 1753*, marked list of the committee on the Banbury Turnpike Bill.
(a) Bodl. Lib., MS. North b. 24, f. 181.

195. *6 Apr. 1753*, list of those 18 M.P.s who attended the Drayton Lane Turnpike committee.
    (a) Bodl. Lib., MS. North b. 24, f. 180.

196. *c. Apr. 1754*, list compiled by the Viscount of Dupplin, of army officers in the House not re-elected in 1754.
    (a) B.L., Add. MS. 33034, f. 193.

FIFTH PARLIAMENT OF GEORGE II, 1754–61

197. *c. May 1754*, analysis, by Dupplin, of the election returns: 'the present Parliament as returned compared with the last as it stood, at the time of the dissolution', giving gains and losses by constituency.
    (a) B.L., Add. MS. 33034, f. 195.

198. *c. May 1754*, analysis of the new House into those 'for' the government, those 'against' and those 'doubtful'.
    (a) B.L., Add. MS. 32995, ff. 158–69.

199. *c. May 1754*, analysis, by Dupplin, of the new House, into 'for', 'against' and 'doubtful', with six double returns not included.
    (a) B.L., Add. MS. 33034, ff. 183–8.

200. *c. May 1754*, Dupplin's list of the new House, with the Members divided into 'for', 'against Whigs', 'against Torys' and 'doubtful', and those 'for' further subdivided into their professions and political groups.
    (a) B.L., Add. MS. 33034, ff. 173–81.
    (c) *The House of Commons, 1754–1790*, eds. Sir L. Namier and J. Brooke (3 vols., 1964), I, 524.

201. *c. May 1754*, list by Dupplin, of 'country gentlemen': 314 names.
    (a) B.L., Add. MS. 33034, ff. 169–71.

202. *c. May 1754*, list by Dupplin, of placemen, military and naval officers, merchants and planters.
    (a) B.L., Add. MS. 33034, ff. 189–92.

203. *c. May 1754*, list, by Dupplin, of army officers in the new House.
    (a) B.L., Add. MS. 33034, ff. 193.

204. *10 June 1754*, list of Members described as possessing 'Employments in the House of Commons'.
    (a) B.L., Add. MS. 32995, f. 256.

205. *1754*, list of 31 government supporters.
    (a) B.L., Add. MS. 32995, f. 170.

206. *4 Mar. 1755*, list of speakers, headed 'the Question for fifteen years was carried without a Division. The Noes very few'. On the navy.
   (a) B.L., Add. MS. 32996, ff. 42–3.

207. *Before 24 Mar. 1755*, list of Members applied to about the Mitchell election petition.
   (a) B.L., Add. MS. 33002, f. 458.

208. *24 Mar. 1755*, list of Tories at a meeting at the Horn Tavern about the Mitchell election.
   (a) Warwickshire R.O., CR/136/A (585) (Newdigate papers), Sir Roger Newdigate's diary.
   (c) L. Colley, 'The Mitchell Election Division, 24 March 1755', *B.I.H.R.*, XLIX (1976), 83 n.3.

209. *24 Mar. 1755*, the Mitchell election division (first division of the day).
   (a) Cambridge Univ. Lib., Add. MS. 6575.
   (b) Colley, 'Mitchell Election Division', pp. 83–107.
   (c) *Ibid.*, pp. 80–3; J.C.D. Clark, 'The Decline of Party, 1740–1760', *E.H.R.*, XCIII (1978), 506 n. 2.

210. *24 Mar. 1755*, Tory voters on each side in the Mitchell election division.
   (a) B.L., Add. MS. 33002, f. 438; Add. MS. 35877, f. 237.
   (c) Colley, 'Mitchell Election Division', p. 82; Clark, 'Decline of Party', p. 506 n. 2.

211. *28 Mar. 1755*, list of 16 Members headed 'State of the House of Commons'.
   (a) B.L., Add. MS. 32996, f. 67.

212. *26 Sept. 1755*, 'persons to be wrote or spoke to' by the Duke of Newcastle.
   (a) B.L., Add. MS. 32996, ff. 231–6.

213. *27 Sept. 1755*, list of Members with 'particular connections'.
   (a) B.L., Add. MS. 32996, ff. 237–8.

214. *Sept. 1755*, list of Members to be 'wrote or spoak to' by Newcastle.
   (a) B.L., Add. MS. 32996, f. 229.

215. *20 Oct. 1755*, list of Members 'to be wrote to'.
   (a) B.L., Add. MS. 32996, f. 251.

216. *25 Oct. 1755*, list of Members with comments.
   (a) B.L., Add. MS. 32996, f. 257.

217. *13 Nov. 1755*, Whigs who voted against the address of thanks for the subsidy treaties with Russia and Hesse.
   (a) B.L., Add. MS. 33034, f. 208.
   (c) Namier and Brooke (eds.), *House of Commons, 1754–1790*, I, 524.

218. *1755*, Members who voted against or 'went off'.
   (a) B.L., Add. MS. 33002, f. 460.

219. *c. 1755*, list of Scottish Members divided into five groups: 'D[uke of] Argyll while in power', 'D. Argyll if out of power', 'Last Ministry or Mr Pitt', 'D[uke of] Newcastle', 'Not to be relied on at present. To be treated with'.
    (a) B.L., Add. MS. 32995, f. 383.

220. *3 Mar. 1756*, those against the second reading of the Silver Plate Duty Bill.
    (a) B.L., Add. MS. 32997, f. 82.

221. *20 Mar. 1756*, list of Members 'desired to attend on Monday'.
    (a) B.L., Add. MS. 32996, f. 381.

222. *22 Mar. 1756*, some of those against committing the Silver Plate Duty Bill.
    (a) B.L., Add. MS. 35877, f. 244.

223. *3 Apr. 1756*, list of 'Members of the House of Commons proper for employment'.
    (a) B.L., Add. MS. 32996, ff. 387–8.

224. *c. Nov. 1756*, list of Members, assigned to Fox, Newcastle and 'doubtful'.
    (a) B.L., Add. MS. 51430, f. 38.

225. *27 Dec. 1756*, list, compiled by Newcastle, of supporters of Pitt and those of Fox.
    (a) B.L., Add. MS. 32997, ff. 66–7.

226. *1756*, list of Members 'to be spoke to' by Mr West.
    (a) B.L., Add. MS. 32996, f. 383.

227. *6 Feb. 1757*, list, compiled by Newcastle, of government supporters.
    (a) B.L., Add. MS. 32997, ff. 101–11; fair copy at ff. 113–21.

228. *26 Apr. 1757*, some of those who voted against, in a division on 'the Invasion' [14 names].
    (a) B.L., Add. MS. 35877, f. 363.

229. *2 May 1757*, government supporters who deserted in a division on an enquiry into the loss of Minorca.
    (a) B.L., Add. MS. 34034, ff. 218–9; Add. MS. 35877, f. 373: Devonshire papers (the Duke of Devonshire, Chatsworth House, Bakewell, Derbyshire), 330/202, Henry Fox to Devonshire, n.d. Variants.

230. *2 May 1757*, 'List of Scotch Members who voted for and against the amendment': 19 for, 13 against, plus one on each side added in pencil.
    (a) B.L., Add. MS 33034, f. 232.

231. *30 May 1757*, list of speakers in the Commons, divided into those attached to Newcastle, Fox and Pitt.
    (a) B.L., Add. MS. 32997, ff. 203–4.

232. *1757*, list of pensioners in the 'Old Book', 9 July 1755–9 Nov. 1757.
    (a) B.L., Add. MS. 32997, f. 64.

233. *1757*, list of pensioners in the 'New Book' since 20 July 1757.
    (a) B.L., Add. MS. 32997, f. 237.

234. *1757*, list of pensioners 'in Old Book who have not yet been paid in New One'.
    (a) B.L., Add. MS. 32997, f. 330.

235. *1757*, list of pensioners 'whose private payments have lately ceas'd'.
    (a) B.L., Add. MS. 32997, f. 332.

236. *21 Nov. 1758*, list of 28 Members who met at Mr Secretary Pitt's to discuss the speech and heads of Address and to choose who would move and second them.
    (a) B.L., Add. MS. 32998, f. 185.

237. *24 Feb. 1760*, list of 170 placemen.
    (a) B.L., Add. MS. 33034, ff. 327–30.

238. *5 Apr. 1760*, government management list, naming Members with their constituencies, and giving the initials of persons through whom they might be approached.
    (a) B.L., Add. MS. 33034, ff. 342–50.

239. *7 Apr. 1760*, those to be spoken to by Newcastle before the second reading of the Scottish Militia Bill on 15 Apr.
    (a) B.L., Add. MS. 33034, ff. 351–4.

240. *11 Apr. 1760*, government management list, giving the names of persons through whom Members were to be approached.
    (a) B.L., Add. MS. 33034, ff. 355–62.

241. *11 Apr. 1760*, a second management list, naming those through whom Members were to be approached.
    (a) B.L., Add. MS. 33034, ff. 365–72.

III

THE PARLIAMENT OF SCOTLAND, 1660–1707

Introduction

Patrick Riley

The Scottish parliamentary lists recorded here belong in the main to the official record of parliamentary transactions and can be approached with relative peace of mind. Without necessarily assuming that official status implies accuracy, at least we do know how, why and by whom such lists were produced.

Surviving Scottish lists fall into three main categories: official records, formal addresses, and lists privately compiled. The majority of lists were entered in the minutes of the Scottish Parliament from 1689 to the Union and are printed in the *Acts of the Parliament of Scotland*.[1] There are lists of subscribers to formal documents (nos. 2, 3, 22); division lists were printed on extraordinary occasions, during the Darien debates in the session of 1700–1 and then again during the Union Parliament of 1706–7; Members' protests, registering formal dissent from one parliamentary measure or another, were recorded;[2] and names were entered in the minutes as Parliament resolved to discipline Members for prolonged absence or failure to qualify to take their seats. From William's reign the lists survive of those who subscribed to two opposition addresses to the King: that of the Club in 1689 (no. 7); and of the Country Party opposition in 1700 (no. 23). Finally there are unofficial lists of votes or of special categories of Members produced, for either record or propaganda, by persons for the most part unknown.[3]

[1] *A.P.S.*, IX-XI, *passim*.

[2] Not all protests have been listed. There seemed little point in noting individual protests over questions of precedence and privilege, nor dissent registered by one or two Members only. But some protests amount to a register of the bulk of the parliamentary opposition at that time. Only such substantial protests have been included. It should be noted, though, that even such heavily subscribed protests as that against the address over Darien (no. 27) or that against the Wine Act of 1703 (no. 35) are incomplete as lists of the minority since, for one reason or another, more Members were prepared to vote against the Court than would go to the length of registering formal dissent.

[3] The clutch of lists relating to the trial for treason of the Earl of Breadalbane in 1695 (nos. 13–20), found since this introduction was first written by Patrick Riley, represents not only a major new source for Scottish political history in William's reign but also the most highly concentrated collection of Scottish private working parliamentary lists in the period covered by this register. No. 8, like 13–20, is also a private list produced possibly by, but certainly for the use of, Breadalbane.

Private compilations apart, the reliability of the lists must be rated extremely high. There is no reason whatsoever to doubt the authenticity of the signatures on the two addressess. Both were subscribed with relative publicity. No allegations of forgery were made. Alexander Gordon, Provost of Aberdeen and Member for the burgh, excused his signature by claiming to have been drunk at the time and whilst the Earl of Sutherland's having signed was generally looked on as quite inexplicable nobody doubted the genuineness of his signature.[4] Signatories of other formal documents, the Convocation's letter to William, for example (no. 3), or the Asssociation (no. 22), would seem to be above suspicion. Nor need one agonise over the lists in the *Acts of the Parliament of Scotland* of those fined or expelled. They are Parliament's official record of its intentions.

Parliamentary voting lists deserve some attention since Scottish voting practice differed markedly from that in both the English and Irish Parliaments. In the Scottish Parliaments the clerks called out the roll and each Member gave his vote individually and aloud. Apart from Middleton's attempt in 1662 to introduce, for dubious reasons of his own, voting by ballot,[5] public and individual voting seems to have been the rule in the Scottish Parliament. A precise formulation of the practice appeared in the regulation of 26 May 1703: 'Ordered that when the rolls are called for a vote of parliament all Members stand upright in their places and give their vote audibly and that none presume to answer for another.'[6] So in theory and, up to a point, in practice, it was possible to compile a more accurate list of voters in the Scottish Parliament than under the English system with its main exodus of one side from the chamber whilst the others remained seated. When the Scottish votes, by order of the House, were being entered in the minutes there is no doubt that every care was taken to keep an accurate record. Too many interested parties were keeping their own count for slips, much less sharp practice, to be tolerated.

But confusion was possible and there is evidence enough that it occurred in good measure. Some disorder in taking votes probably explains the regulation of 26 May 1703. Confusion clearly did not creep into the minuted votes but it created difficulties on other occasions, an aspect which has to be taken into account when assessing privately compiled lists. In the Scottish Parliaments votes were not invariably formulated in terms of an affirmative and negative. The 'state of the vote' varied considerably according to the topic to be decided: 'Approve' or 'Noe'

---

[4] *Leven and Melville Papers: Letters and State Papers Chiefly Addressed to George, Earl of Melville* . . . (Bannatyne Club, LXXVII, Edinburgh, 1843), pp. 245–6.

[5] R.S. Rait, *The Parliaments of Scotland* (Glasgow, 1924), p. 414.

[6] *A.P.S.*, XI, 45.

in many instances, but also 'Proceed' or 'Delay',[7] 'Except' or 'Not'[8] and whether Parliament should be adjourned to '28 of January, or 1 February next: Carried 28 of January'.[9] on occasion it must have been difficult to know exactly what was being voted. It was also possible to vote *non liquet* or 'not clear', thereby formally abstaining. Inaudible Members were a trial to the clerks and to everybody else. And not infrequently there was clamour accompanied by procedural confusion. Sir Alexander Bruce reported on Crawford's management as President of Parliament in 1690 during a vote on an Act for the Visitation of Universities: the Earl of Crawford

> calls incessantly for the vote [to be called] even when an act is by order to be mended in some things yet will not have the patience to let it be read over again, and the clerks are prepared and fitted for the purpose, for they upon the first word of command start up to the reading of the roll. Then inmmediately is it interrupted and amendments sometimes made after it is begun to be voted . . .[10]

In the last session of the Scottish Parliament the calling of the roll on the second article of Union was interrupted by Hamilton and Fletcher of Saltoun, leading to a considerable commotion.[11] Inevitably there were mistakes in identity. On 29 June 1703 Parliament had to take cognisance of an alteration after Seton, Paymaster of the Army, had allegedly taken Sir Robert Dickson of Inveresk brusquely to task for being *non liquet* in a vote and thereby falling below expectation. 'Sir Robert answered he was not there, being unwell of a pain in his stomach . . .'[12] Human error in routine business was likely enough at all levels. Sir David Hume reported on 16 July 1703 the debate on adding Roxburghe's 'limitations' clause to the Act of Security. The House having been at length brought to a preliminary vote: 'Proceed to the consideration of the clause: and being put to the vote, carried (as I counted, by 17, the clerks marked only 7) Proceed.'[13] The clerks did not necessarily announce the numbers in a vote unless it was a particularly narrow one. Hume was often driven to an approximation of his own: by '25 votes, as I reckoned'.[14] But scrutiny

---

[7] Sir David Hume of Crossrig, *A Diary of the Proceedings in the Parliament and Privy Council of Scotland. May 21, 1700 – March 7 1707* (Bannatyne Club, XXVII, Edinburgh, 1828), p. 104.

[8] In the case of whether plain ribbon was to be exempted from a general prohibition on the importation of silk, 4 Jan. 1701 (*ibid.*, p. 43).

[9] *Ibid.*, p. 38 (30 Dec. 1700).

[10] National Library of Scotland, MS. 7012 (Yester MSS), fo. 98, [Sir A. Bruce] to [Tweeddale], 18 June 1690.

[11] *A Selection of the Papers of the Earls of Marchmont in the Possession of the Right Honourable Sir George Henry Rose* (3 vols., 1831), III, 427.

[12] Hume, *Diary*, p. 111.

[13] *Ibid.*, p. 118.

[14] *Ibid.*, p. 22 (27 Nov. 1700). See also *ibid.*, pp. 29, 44, 104, 106, 126 and *passim*.

was such as to ensure fair accuracy. Nor did the clerks always keep a record of names, as distinct from numbers, in a vote, so that the only way to check a division seems to have been to call the roll again. In August 1703 the fate of a clause in the Act of Security was decided by the Chancellor's casting vote whereupon 'some allege[d] the votes were not right marked, and moved that it might be voted over again, but that was let fall'.[15]

So in a privately compiled list mistakes would seem to be probable. The list of the seceders of 1702 (no. 30) contains the names of two members who remained in Parliament.[16] Two other privately recorded voting lists, that of 1702 on the Abjuration (no. 31) and that of 1704 on Hamilton's resolve (no. 36), disagree numerically with the weight of other evidence. The working list of 1703 (no. 33) is difficult to assess since the burgesses are missing and the vote it refers to is uncertain. Tarbat's list of peers (no. 21) is blatantly an attempt to prejudice Portland against the existing Scottish ministry and its supporters ('hott men') and in favour of Tarbat's own association ('moderate men').[17] His classification is nevertheless illuminating.

These lists are invaluable for the study of Scottish parliamentary groupings. Without the Club address of 1689 and the Country party address of 1700, combined with the voting and protest lists of 1701 (nos. 7, 23, 25–29), we should be ignorant of the opposition's membership at those times. The official votes of the Union Parliament should have made it possible before now to abandon preconceptions concerning that session and introduce into the discussion concerning it some element of precision. All in all there is probably enough evidence in the known lists to plot the main changes in party groupings between 1689 and the Union, thus permitting the formulation of firm conclusions of the nature of post-Revolution Scottish parliamentary politics.

---

[15] *Ibid.*, p. 126 (11 Aug. 1703).
[16] *Viz.* William Stewart of Ambrismore and Kenneth Mackenzie of Cromarty.
[17] Riley, *King William*, pp. 99–100.

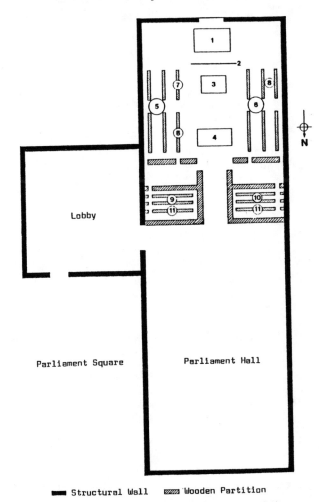

Structural Wall ▨ **Wooden Partition**

Fig. 4. The Parliament of Scotland, 1641–1707

Source: (seating arrangements) an engraving of the Parliament in session before 1690, printed in Nicolas Gueudeville, *Atlas Historique* (7 vols., Amsterdam, 1714–21), III, fig. 56, and corrected from information in C.S. Terry, *The Scottish Parliament* (Glasgow, 1905), pp. 80–1; (building) Scottish R.O., RHP 2685; 6525, items 11, 13, 33 (19th-century plans of building and precincts); inspection of the building itself.

1: Throne. 2: Bar. 3: Clerk Register and deputies. 4: Lords of Session. 5: Peers (Earls and above). 6: Peers (Viscounts and Barons). 7: Archbishops (to 1690). 8: Bishops (to 1690). 9: Shire Members. 10: Burgh Members. 11: 'Strangers' having business with the Parliament permitted to occupy rear forms

Note on Plan
The seating arrangements given here are correct, as is the layout of the building. However, we were unable to find a source which showed how the two were related. Our positioning of the seats is conjectural. It is possible that the benches, etc., did fill the whole of the space available and that there was no open area at the north end of the hall.

List of Lists

THE CONVENTION, 1678

1.   *2 July 1678*, marked list of the lords.
     (a)   B.L., Add. MS. 35125, f. 300.

THE CONVENTION, 1689

2.   *16 Mar. 1689*, those 'subscribing the Act declaring this to be a free and lawful meeting of the Estates'.
     (a)   *A.P.S.*, IX, 9–10.

3.   *23 Mar. 1689*, those 'subscribing the letter to William, King of England'.
     (a)   *A.P.S.*, IX, 20.

4.   *25 Mar. 1689*, those 'who absented themselves from this Convention'.
     (a)   *An Account of the Proceedings of the Estates in Scotland, 1689–90, Vol. I*, ed. E.W. Balfour-Melville (Scottish History Society, 3rd ser., XLVI, Edinburgh, 1954), pp. 16–17.

THE PARLIAMENT OF WILLIAM III, 1689–1702

5.   *10 July 1689*, those fined for continued absence.
     (a)   *A.P.S.*, IX, 102–3.

6.   *12 July 1689*, 'List of the Absents from the Parliament'.
     (a)   *Account of the Proceedings . . . Vol. I*, p. 165.

7.   *1689*, those subscribing the Club address.
     (a)   Scottish R.O., GD 26/1/4/156 (Leven and Melville MSS.).
     (b)   Sir W. Fraser, *The Melvilles, Earls of Melville and the Leslies, Earl of Leven* (3 vols., Edinburgh, 1890), III, 209–12.

8.   *1692*, 'A List of the Nobility who favour the addressing [i.e. episcopalian and 'conform'] Clergy', together with 'A List of the Nobility who favour the new [i.e. Presbyterian] Clergy'.
     (a)   Scottish R.O., GD 112/43/1/31 (Breadalbane MSS.).

9. *25 Apr. 1693*, those ordered to sign the Assurance on pain of expulsion.
    (a) A.P.S., IX, 249.

10. *25 Apr. 1693*, those expelled for not having taken the Oath of Allegiance.
    (a) A.P.S., IX, 249–50.

11. *28 Apr. 1693*, those shire and burgh Members fined and expelled for absence
    (some subsequently excused on account of extenuating circumstances: A.P.S.,
    IX, 261).
    (a) A.P.S., IX, 250–1.

12. *28 Apr. 1693*, those lords fined for absence.
    (a) A.P.S., IX, 251.

13. *1695*, roll of Parliament variously marked to indicate the dispositions of
    Members towards the Earl of Breadalbane, probably as shown by the votes
    of 10 June 1695 over his committal on a charge of treason: seems to provide
    the basis for lists 14–20 below.
    (a) Scottish R.O., GD 112/43/1/2/35X.

14. *1695*, list of 32 peers, barons and burgesses, supporters of Breadalbane.
    (a) Scottish R.O., GD 112/43/1/2/33.

15. *1695*, list of Members for and against Breadalbane.
    (a) Scottish R.O., GD 112/43/1/2/36X.

16. *1695*, list of Members opposed to Breadalbane but with indications of which
    were to be solicited and by whom.
    (a) Scottish R.O., GD 112/43/1/2/39X.

17. *1695*, list of what appear to be Members opposed to Breadalbane, with some
    names marked, probably as persons to be solicited.
    (a) Scottish R.O., GD 112/43/1/2/38X.

18. *1695*, Members divided into categories: 'those who voted against the Earl of
    B[readalbane] but are to be solicited'; 'those who are to [be] written [to] for
    express'; 'those who were out of the town and out of the parliament since
    the time of the vote who are for the Earl of B[readalbane]'; and 'those whose
    votes were dubious one vote for the Earl of B[readalbane] and the other
    against him and concerning whom they clearly differed'.
    (a) Scottish R.O., GD 112/43/1/2/37X.

19. *1695*, 'those who voted against the Earl of Breadalbane'.
    (a) Scottish R.O., 112/43/1/2/40X.

20. *1695*, Members 'as were to be solicited and by whom' in Breadalbane's
    case.
    (a) Scottish R.O., GD 112/43/1/2/50.

21. *25 June 1695*, Lord Tarbat's list, sent to the Earl of Portland, of the Scots nobility, classified into 'Recusants', 'Absents and minors', 'Moderate men' and 'Hot men'.
    (a) Nottingham Univ. Lib., PwA 842 (Portland [Bentinck] MSS.).

22. *10 Sept. 1696*, those who signed the Association.
    (a) *A.P.S.*, X, 10–11.

23. *1700*, signatories of the Country party address requesting the summoning of Parliament.
    (a) Buccleuch (Drumlanrig) MSS. (the Duke of Buccleuch, Drumlanrig, Thornhill, Dumfriesshire), 'Colnaghi MSS.' (unnumbered).
    (b) P.W.J. Riley, *King William and the Scottish Politicians* (Edinburgh, 1979), Appendix A.

24. *1700/1*, list of burgh commissioners divided into 'Court' and 'Country'.
    (a) Sandeman Lib., Perth, Perth burgh records B59/34/13.

25. *14 Jan 1701*, those who voted for an act and dissented from an address concerning Caledonia.
    (a) *A.P.S.*, X, 246; Scottish R.O., GD 406/M1/2/238 (Hamilton MSS.).
    (b) Riley, *King William*, appendix A.

26. *16 Jan. 1701*, those who voted there should be an address concerning Caledonia.
    (a) *A.P.S.*, X, 247–8.
    (b) Riley, *King William*, appendix A.

27. *17 Jan. 1701*, those who dissented from the address on Caledonia.
    (a) *A.P.S.*, X, 251.
    (b) Riley, *King William*, appendix A.

28. *27 Jan. 1701*. those who 'desired their dissent from continuing the forces till December 1702 to be marked'.
    (a) *A.P.S.*, X, 269.
    (b) Riley, *King William*, appendix A.

29. *31 Jan. 1701*, those who 'desired their dissent from continuing for four months the 1100 men over and above the 3000 to be marked'.
    (a) *A.P.S.*, X, 294.
    (b) Riley, *King William*, appendix A.

FIRST PARLIAMENT OF ANNE, 1702

30. *9 June 1702*, the seceders.
    (a) Blair Atholl MSS. (the Duke of Atholl, Blair Castle, Blair Atholl, Perthshire), 43/vi/33. Two Members listed who did not secede.

31. *27 June 1702*, division over the proposed Act of Abjuration.
    (a) Blair Atholl MSS., 43/vi/32.
    (b) P.W.J. Riley, 'The Abjuration Vote of 27 June 1702 in the Scottish Parliament', *Parliamentary History*, II (1983), 176–90.

SECOND PARLIAMENT OF ANNE, 1703–7

32. *1702/3*, MS. analysis of election results with annotations appearing to indicate likely support for the Court or opposition.
    (a) Nat. Lib. Scotland, MS. 14498, ff. 82–3.

33. *July–Aug. 1703*, a list of peers and barons divided into 'for us', 'against us' and 'without assistance'. Probably a working list relating to a clause of the Act of Security.
    (a) Buccleuch (Drumlanrig) MSS., 1224.

34. *10 Sept. 1703*, those for and those against addressing the Queen to give her assent to the Act for Security, marked in MS. on a copy of a printed list of the Parliament, 6 May 1703.
    (a) Bodl. Lib., MS. Carte 180, f. 133.

35. *13 Sept. 1703*, 'Protestation of the Marquess of Tweeddale and others', against the Act for Allowing the Importation of all Wines and Foreign Liquors.
    (a) *A.P.S.*, XI, 102.

36. *17 July 1704*, the division on 'the Duke of Hamilton's Resolve, Not to name the Successor till we have a previous treaty with England for regulating our Commerce, and other Concerns with that nation', most probably the vote joining the separate motions of Hamilton and Rothes.
    (a) A. Boyer, *The History of the Reign of Queen Anne Digested into Annals* (3 vols., 1703–13), III, appendix, pp. 41–4. Another version, differing only in one particular, is Scottish R.O., GD 112/43/1/27.
    (c) P.W.J. Riley, *The Union of England and Scotland* (Manchester, 1979), p. 111 n. 173.

37. *1 Sept. 1705,,* 'Protestation of the Duke of Atholl and others concerning the Act for a Treaty with England'.
    (a) *A.P.S.*, XI, 236–7.

38. *1 Sept. 1705*, 'Protestation of the Duke of Atholl and others against approving the Act for a Treaty with England'.
    (a) *A.P.S.*, XI, 237.

39. *25 Oct. 1706*, 'Protestation of the Earl of Erroll and others against continuing standing forces within the Town of Edinburgh'.
    (a) *A.P.S.*, XI, 309.

40. *4 Nov. 1706*, those for and those against the first article of Union.
     (a) *A.P.S.*, XI, 313–5; *A List of the Nobility and Gentry now Sitting in the Scots Parliament who were For and Against the* [first article of the] *Union of the Two Kingdoms*: copy in Nat. Library of Scotland, Hall MSS., 195, f. 6. The latter has one omission from the pro-Union list.
     (b) Riley, *Union*, appendix A.
     (c) *Ibid.*, pp. 276–81 and appendix A.

41. *4 Nov. 1706*, 'Protestation of the Duke of Atholl' and others, against the first article of Union.
     (a) *A.P.S.*, XI, 313.

42. *12 Nov. 1706*, those for and those against the Act for Security of the True Protestant Religion and Government of the Church of Scotland.
     (a) *A.P.S.*, XI, 312–2; '. . . *The Act for Security of the True Protestant Religion and Government of the Church, as by Law Established within this Kingdom . . . the List of Members as they Voted Pro or Con . . .*: copy in Nat. Lib. Scotland, MS. 6. 365 (30).

43. *14 Nov. 1706*, those for proceeding to the second article of Union and those for proceeding to the articles relating to trade and taxes.
     (a) *A.P.S.*, XI, 323–4.

44. *15 Nov. 1706*, those for and those against the second article of Union.
     (a) *A.P.S.*, XI, 326–7.

45. *15 Nov. 1706*, protestation of the Earl Marischal and others, against the second article of Union.
     (a) *A.P.S.*, XI, 325–6.

46. *18 Nov. 1706*, protestation of the Marquess of Annandale and others against the proposed Union.
     (a) *A.P.S.*, XI, 328–9.

47. *18 Nov. 1706*, those for and those against the third article of Union.
     (a) *A.P.S.*, XI, 329–30.

48. *21 Nov. 1706*, those for and those against the fourth article of Union, 'Reserving the consideration of the several branches of trade till the parliament comes to the subsequent articles'.
     (a) *A.P.S.*, XI, 332–4.

49. *27 Nov. 1706*, those for and those against the seventh article of Union, without opposition amendment.
     (a) *A.P.S.*, XI, 339–40.

50. *29 Nov. 1706*, those for and those against the proclamation against unlawful convocations.
     (a) *A.P.S.*, XI, 341–2.

51. *6 Dec. 1706*, division on the state of the vote on the 14th article of Union; two options voted on in a single vote: to approve the article as amended or not, or approve or amend.
(a) *A.P.S.*, XI, 346–8.

52. *6 Dec. 1706*, those for and those against the 14th article of Union.
(a) *A.P.S.*, XI, 348–50.

53. *7 Dec. 1706*, division on the state of the vote on the 15th article of Union: approve of the first paragraph or 'whether we shall engage in the payment of the debts of England'.
(a) *A.P.S.*, XI, 351–2.

54. *7 Dec. 1706*, those for and those against the first clause of the 15th article of Union.
(a) *A.P.S.*, XI, 354–5.

55. *20 Dec. 1706*, those for and against the report of the committee on the eighth article of Union, concerning beef and pork drawbacks.
(a) *A.P.S.*, XI, 360–2.

56. *23 Dec. 1706*, division on the state of the vote on the eighth article of Union: drawbacks to be alterable by the Parliament of Great Britain or drawbacks to remain for the duration of the imposition on salt.
(a) *A.P.S.*, XI, 362–4.

57. *23 Dec. 1706*, those for and those against the clause of the eighth article of Union permitting drawbacks to be alterable by the Parliament of Great Britain.
(a) *A.P.S.*, XI, 364–5.

58. *24 Dec. 1706*, divisions on alternative clauses of the eighth article of Union: exemption from salt duty for seven years or exemption from duties on home produced salt for all time.
(a) *A.P.S.*, XI, 366–8.

59. *27 Dec. 1706*, those for and those against the proclamation discharging unwarrantable and seditious convocations and meetings.
(a) *A.P.S.*, XI, 370–1.

60. *27 Dec. 1706*, protestation of George Lockhart of Carnwath and others, that the rights of barons, freeholders and heritors should not be prejudged by the proclamation against assemblies.
(a) *A.P.S.*, XI, 369, 371.

61. *30 Dec. 1706*, division on the state of the vote on the 15th article of Union: approve as amended or whether the Company of Scotland trading to Africa and the Indies should be dissolved without consent of the proprietors.
(a) *A.P.S.*, XI, 373–4.

62. *30 Dec. 1706*, those for and those against the 15th article of Union as amended.
    (a) *A.P.S.*, XI, 375–6.

63. *31 Dec. 1706*, those for and those against amending the 18th article of Union, to exempt Scotsmen from the English sacramental test.
    (a) *A.P.S.*, XI, 377–8.

64. *31 Dec. 1706*, those for and those against the 18th article of Union.
    (a) *A.P.S.*, XI, 378–80.

65. *6 Jan. 1707*, division on the state of the vote on the 21st article of Union: approve or add the clause.
    (a) *A.P.S.*, XI, 383–4.

66. *6 Jan. 1707*, those for and those against the 21st article of Union.
    (a) *A.P.S.*, XI, 385–6.

67. *7 Jan. 1707*, those for and those against the first paragraph of the 22nd article of Union.
    (a) *A.P.S.*, XI, 388–90.

68. *8 Jan 1707*, protestation of the Earl of Marchmont and others, against protests against the 22nd article of Union.
    (a) *A.P.S.*, XI, 390–1.

69. *9 Jan. 1707*, protestation of Lord Balmerino and others, against the protests of the Earl of Marchmont and others the previous day (see above, no. 68).
    (a) *A.P.S.*, XI, 391.

70. *9 Jan. 1707*, division on the state of the vote on the 22nd article of Union: approve or add the clause 'the said parliament of Great Britain shall meet and sit once in three years at least, in that part of Great Britain called Scotland'.
    (a) *A.P.S.*, XI, 392–3.

71. *9 Jan. 1707*, those for and those against the third paragraph of the 22nd article.
    (a) *A.P.S.*, XI, 393–5.

72. *9 Jan. 1707*, those for and against the 22nd article of Union 'as explained'.
    (a) *A.P.S.*, XI, 395–6.

73. *10 Jan. 1707*, those for and those against adding to the 22nd article of Union a clause imposing a Presbyterian test.
    (a) *A.P.S.*, XI, 397–8.

74. *13 Jan. 1707*, those for and those against adding to the 23rd article of Union a clause 'in relation to all the peers of Scotland their sitting covered in the House of Peers of Great Britain'.
    (a) *A.P.S.*, XI, 400–1.

75. *16 Jan. 1707*, 'Approve the Act Ratifying and Approving the Treaty of Union . . . Yea or Not'.
   (a) *A.P.S.*, XI, 404–6.
   (b) Riley, *Union*, appendix A.
   (c) *Ibid.*, pp. 276–81 and appendix A.

76. *21 Jan. 1707*, division on whether the resolve to print the lists of voters and protesters against the election of representative peers and 45 Members from the Scottish Parliament should be inserted in the previous day's minutes or not.
   (a) *A.P.S.*, XI, 416–17.

77. *24 Jan. 1707*, vote on the alternative clauses concerning Scottish representation in the Parliament of Great Britain: that no peer or eldest son of a peer should represent a shire or burgh or that none were to elect or be elected except those allowed by Scots law to represent a shire or burgh.
   (a) *A.P.S.*, XI, 418–20.

78. *31 Jan. 1707*, vote on allowances to Union commissioners.
   (a) *A.P.S.*, XI, 422–3.

79. *10 Mar. 1707*, division on whether the compensation to the Company of Scotland's shareholders was to be paid to the proprietors or to persons to be appointed by the general council.
   (a) *A.P.S.*, XI, 439–40.